# FOYLE MARITIME MEMORIES

## Photographs from the Bigger and McDonald Collection 1927–1939

**Brian Mitchell**
**and Libraries NI**

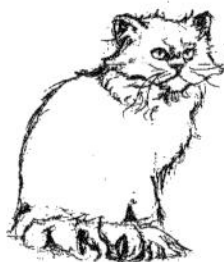

Published 2018 by Colourpoint Books
An imprint of Colourpoint Creative Ltd
Colourpoint House, Jubilee Business Park
Jubilee Road, Newtownards, BT23 4YH
Tel: 028 9182 6339
Fax: 028 9182 1900
E-mail: sales@colourpoint.co.uk
Web: www.colourpoint.co.uk

First Edition
First Impression



A catalogue record for this book is available from the British Library.

Designed by April Sky Design, Newtownards
Tel: 028 9182 7195 • Web: www.aprilsky.co.uk

Printed by W&G Baird Ltd, Antrim

ISBN 978-1-78073-175-9

# INTRODUCTION

On Friday 15 April 1927, the *Derry Standard* began to publish local photographs in the pages of its newspaper. The editorial of that day proclaimed:

> A newspaper, if it is to be a faithful mirror of life, must always be progressive… And to-day, following our rule of considering our readers' interests and wishes as paramount, we introduce a feature which we hope will meet with their appreciation. It has been suggested to us that at a time when the British public are protesting against the harm which is done to home interests by foreign propaganda on the films, there is a similar danger of Derry and the North-West suffering through the lack of a newspaper which can show, through pictures, something of the life and progress of the district. We have, accordingly, made arrangements at much expense to ourselves to meet that want. A thoroughly up-to-date process engraving plant has been installed in the office, the services of an experienced photographer and process engineer have been secured, and we hope to present in the *Derry Standard* pictures of local doings which can bear comparison with those of any other newspaper in the land.

In 1968, David Bigger and Terence McDonald rescued from destruction 14,000 original plate glass negatives belonging to the *Derry Standard* newspaper, which had closed in 1966. They then carried out extensive work in conserving, cataloguing and researching the photos. This unique collection of photographs, of high quality, gives unrivalled insight into Derry and the North-West before the Second World War. This was beautifully demonstrated in a book *In Sunshine or In Shadow: Photographs from the Derry Standard, 1928–39* by David Bigger and Terence McDonald, published by Friar's Bush Press, Belfast, in 1990.

Today this collection of photographs, known as the Bigger and McDonald Collection, are in the care of Libraries NI. The value of this collection is further enhanced by the fact that microfilm copy of the *Derry Standard* from 1927 through to 1939, except 1928, is held by Libraries NI at Derry Central Library. This means that many of the photographs in this collection can be dated and further detail gleaned from captions and, in some cases, reports that accompanied each photograph in the *Derry Standard*. In this period the *Standard* was published every Monday, Wednesday and Friday!

I have always had a great interest in the maritime history of this city as it developed as a gateway to North-West Ireland and as a corridor across the Atlantic between Western Europe and North America.

The Bigger and McDonald Collection includes over 300 photographs relating to this maritime activity. It covers all port activity with photographs of the quays, loading and unloading of ships, tug-tenders plying between Derry and Moville, transatlantic liners, the Scotch Boat, and of emigrants and passengers on board the tenders, liners and cross-channel steamers.

Indeed, the first photograph published in the *Derry*

*Standard* on 15 April 1927 was of 'Emigrants leaving Derry to join the *Transylvania* at Moville for Halifax and New York, boarding the tender at the Quay.' This seems very appropriate, as Derry, and its deep-water harbour at Moville, continued through the inter-war years to be an important departure point for Irish emigrants to both Canada and United States.

This photographic archive also documents the crowds that attended big occasions such as visits by Royal Navy destroyers and the City of Derry Rowing Club's annual regatta.

The *Standard* photographed and recorded the arrival of military flying boats on the Foyle. You can almost sense the awe at the first appearance of the RAF's Supermarine Southampton Flying Boats on the Foyle in September 1931 and the arrival of an Italian seaplane, to refuel, on Rosses Bay in June 1932. The *Standard*'s headline of 17 June 1932 read 'The Arctic Survey. Arrival of Italian Seaplane in Derry. Exciting Scenes at the Quay.' It reported that on Wednesday evening, 15 June 1932, the seaplane *I. Slan*, which is to take part in an international Arctic survey on behalf of the Italian Air Ministry, arrived from Amsterdam, where it made a stop on the journey from Rome, encircled the city, and dropped gracefully on the waters of the River Foyle at Rosses Bay. The newspaper also reported that 'in an incredibly short time thousands of people gathered' on the quayside.

It is clear, from following reports in the *Derry Standard*, that all through June 1933 there was a great air of anticipation in Derry concerning the arrival of the Italian squadron of 24 seaplanes intending to cross the Atlantic to Chicago's World Fair.

*Standard* of Wednesday 14 June 1933 reported details of the proposed flight from Rome to Chicago's World Fair:

> …twenty-four machines will take off from the aviation base at Orbetello on the first stage of the venture, to Amsterdam. General Balbo will lead his squadron over the North Sea and the Firth of Forth to Derry, where a brief halt will be made for refuelling and reconditioning. Thereafter the flight will be by way of Reykjavik (Iceland), Cartright (Labrador), Montreal, Lake Ontario and Lake Erie to Lake Michigan and Chicago… The Moville fishermen and their boats will, it is understood, be engaged in refuelling the airships at Culmore.

*Standard* of Friday 23 June 1933 produced a cartoon with the caption: 'The Arrival of the Italian Airmen is still anxiously awaited in Derry.' Set in a maternity ward, the cartoon depicts two men. One asks; 'Have you any idea, Professor, when I may expect the arrival?' The other man responds: 'Patience, Mr Derry, Patience! I am expecting the arrival almost any hour!'

Finally, *Standard* of Monday 3 July 1933 proclaims 'Italian Airmen arrive in Londonderry' and reports that the:

> … Italian Transatlantic Air Armada left its base at Orbetello, near Rome, at 5.35 a.m. on Saturday morning [1 July], and, flying via Amsterdam, arrived in Derry at fifteen minutes after noon yesterday [Sunday 2 July]. Thus the patience of the people of Derry was rewarded at last, and they saw the fleet of twenty-four huge flying-boats which has undertaken one of the most romantic and courageous feats in the history of aviation… The city was agog with excitement when first there was seen

three squadrons which appeared to be nothing more than so many black specks against the background of an azure sky. The airboats were first seen rising from behind the trees on the Culmore side of Browning Drive and Ebrington Military Barracks… The airmen were given a rousing reception… The banks of the river and the lough at Culmore were crowded, as were also the quays and the Guildhall Square.

The year before, Derry had been the centre of another big trans-Atlantic news story that had captured the world's imagination: the arrival of Amelia Earhart on Saturday 21 May 1932, the first woman to fly the Atlantic solo, at Robert Gallagher's farm at Ballyarnet, just to the north of Derry. She had taken off from Newfoundland, hoping to land in Paris, but owing to bad weather and technical problems she altered her course and, after a flight lasting almost 15 hours, landed near Derry.

Six photographs of this momentous event are held in Bigger and McDonald Collection. They include Amelia's plane *Friendship* – a Lockheed Vega aircraft – which had flown over 2,000 miles across the Atlantic; Amelia standing in the doorway of Robert Gallagher's house, Springfield; and four photographs showing the 'dismantling' of 'Miss Earhart's aeroplane'. These were published in the *Derry Standard* of 30 May 1932.

A few days later, on Monday 23 May, in London, Amelia declared to journalists:

I had made up my mind to fly alone, because if there is a man in the machine you can bet your life he wants to take control. Well, I had already flown the Atlantic with men in control, and I was determined that if I did it again I was the one who was going to control the machine.

I hope you will agree that this collection of photographs is truly unique, and that we owe a great debt of gratitude to David Bigger and Terence McDonald for salvaging them, and, of course, to the *Derry Standard* who, in 1927, invested in the technology to produce and process such high-quality photographs. It is clear that some of the images have deteriorated which is perhaps not surprising as the large collection of fragile glass negatives were rescued by David and Terry from almost certain destruction as they had been 'abandoned' without any care and attention.

I have identified against each photograph a catalogue number that identifies the photograph within the Bigger and McDonald Collection. I have also recorded, when found, the date of insertion of that photograph in the *Derry Standard*.

The complete Bigger and McDonald photographic archive, together with microfilm copy of the *Derry Standard*, can be examined in Derry Central Library (35 Foyle Street, Derry/Londonderry, BT48 6AL, email derrycentral.library@librariesni.org.uk).

# SETTING THE SCENE

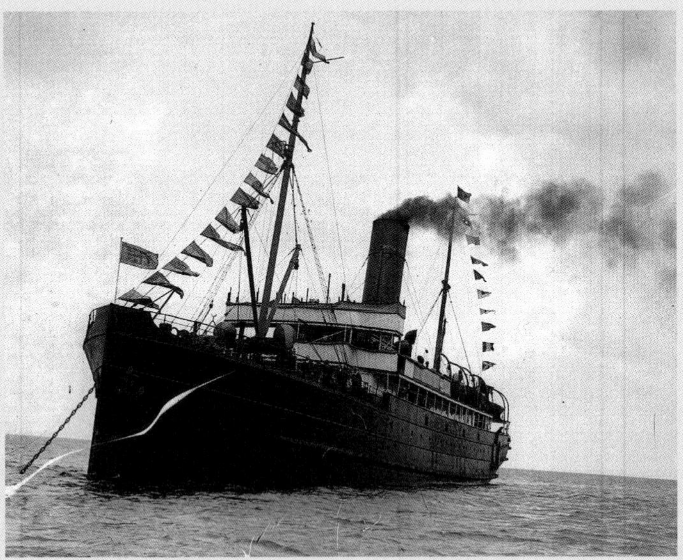

'The S.S. *Lairdsrose*, with members of the Irish Society, at anchor off Inishowen Head.' *(POR 15-1, 21 July 1933)*

The *Derry Standard* of Friday 21 July 1933 reported that members of The Honourable The Irish Society and Commissioners of Derry Port and Harbour Board on Thursday 20 July 1933:

> ...made their annual inspection of the harbour and the River Foyle, and incidentally had the opportunity of seeing some of the most delightful scenery in Ireland. Derry has gained a fine reputation as a safe and commodious port, and the Society, as they viewed the equipment, fully endorsed this general verdict. Those who were making the trip for the first time took a keen interest in Moville, where the trans-Atlantic liners embark and disembark passengers. From this prettily situated little Donegal town the waterway to Derry, a distance of about 20 miles, is well marked and lighted and there is a minimum depth in the shallowest parts of 18 feet at low water. The rise of the tide is from six feet to eight feet, and vessels of over 400 feet in length and drawing upwards of 22 feet of water use the port regularly.
>
> Another place of much interest was the pilot station at Inishowen Head. The Head marks the entrance to the port, and at low water, ordinary spring tides, there is a depth of over fifty feet from there to Moville, at which place there is safe anchorage for all classes of vessels. Derry geographically is the natural distributing port for a large area, and in addition to the regular cross-Channel and trans-Atlantic services, it enjoys a big Continental and foreign trade.
>
> The equipment at the harbour is of the most up-to-date character. There are two-miles of quays fitted with stationary and travelling cranes capable of dealing with weights up to 60 tons, commodious transit sheds, and extensive warehouse accommodation.
>
> The trip was made on one of the Burns-Laird steamers and proved to be thoroughly enjoyable.

# HISTORICAL BACKGROUND

## Londonderry Port and Harbour Commissioners

The Londonderry Port and Harbour Commissioners were constituted in 1854 to manage all matters relating to shipping navigation and quays downstream from the then wooden bridge, at the bottom of Bridge Street, to the mouth of Lough Foyle.

Within seven years the Harbour Commissioners had spent nearly £150,000 on improving harbour facilities. A line of quays, from the bridge to the new graving dock at the Rock, were completed together with construction of quays at Waterside from the bridge to the Londonderry and Coleraine railway station.

The Harbour Commissioners developed tramways to facilitate the delivery of goods and produce between the railways, ships and warehouses. *The Irish Builder* of 1 January 1868 reported that the Harbour Commissioners had almost completed, at a cost of £3,000, the laying down of a tramway, two and a half miles in length, along their line of quays on both sides of the River Foyle between the Londonderry and Coleraine Railway Terminus at Waterside and the Lough Swilly Railway Terminus at the Rock Mill, with sidings alongside the principal warehouses. By 1924, traffic hauled on this tramway amounted to 179,097 tons annually.

## Development of Transatlantic Passenger Trade

The Harbour Commissioners soon demonstrated a willingness to develop new opportunities, especially in their efforts to attract transatlantic mail and passenger steamers to Derry. The Allan Line, in 1856, was contracted by the Canadian Government to provide a mail service between Quebec and Liverpool. In November 1859, the Canadian Post Master General agreed to establish a weekly mail service that also included Ireland.

Sidney Smith, the Canadian Postmaster General and Hugh Allan, owner of the shipping line, were hosted to a reception by the mayor and Harbour Commissioners in Derry on 5 May 1860. Sidney Smith declared that 'the Canadians had been the first to discover the plain geographical truth that Londonderry was the nearest port to the Canadian continent.' The Harbour Commissioners facilitated the establishment of this Canadian mail and passenger service.

In 1861, the Allan Line introduced weekly steamship sailings from Liverpool, calling at Moville, to Quebec and Montreal during the summer and to Halifax, Nova Scotia and Portland, Maine during the winter. This service, from Liverpool via Moville to Canada continued until the First World War.

This was followed, in 1866, by the Anchor Line's Glasgow to New York steamships calling at Moville. This service to New York, except during the First World War, continued until 1939. In 1916 the Anchor Line and another Glasgow company, the Donaldson Line, merged their services and formed a joint company, Anchor-Donaldson, to operate the route, via Moville, to Canada.

From 1861 right through to 1939 ocean-going liners called at Moville, in the deeper waters of Lough Foyle, some 18 miles downstream from Derry, to pick up emigrants who were ferried from Derry in paddle tenders.

By making Derry a 'port of call', where steamers took but a few hours to embark and disembark passengers and mail at Moville, on voyages from Liverpool and Glasgow to North America, the city's position as a premier emigrant port in Ireland was confirmed and reinforced. By 1900, the railway companies in Ireland were offering cheap rail tickets to those intending emigrants, embarking at Derry, who boarded trains at railway stations north of a line that stretched from Sligo on the west coast to Dublin on the east coast. In effect, it was assumed that if you lived north of this line you emigrated from Derry, and if you lived in the southern half of Ireland you embarked at Queenstown (now Cobh), in Cork.

Emigration from Ireland fell dramatically from 1931 as legislation ending uncontrolled immigration to the US became fully operational. The outbreak of war in 1939 meant the end of this emigrant trade. With the return of peace, the transatlantic liners didn't come back to Derry.

**Tourism: 'Come Back to Erin'**

From the early 1900s, the links forged by mass emigration together with Derry's position as an Irish transatlantic hub became a tourist asset. In *Derry Almanac* of 1910 the Anchor Line, with weekly sailings to and from Derry and New York, was promoting 'Holiday Trips – First and Second Class Return Tickets'.

The overall reduction in European emigration led shipping companies to turn to tourism to fill their vessels. The shipping companies, in their colourful posters, emphasised the style and romance of the ocean liners to encourage holidays abroad. 'Tourist third cabin' took over from 2nd class accommodation in the mid-1920s as liners were adapted to meet the new requirements of passengers as tourists as opposed to emigrants. Many of the tourists were former emigrants, revisiting their homeland and making contact with friends and relatives.

In the inter-war years Derry, Belfast and Cobh were the entry points for transatlantic tourists who arrived by sea. Today international entry to Ireland is by air through Dublin, Cork, Shannon and Belfast International airports.

In the inter-war period the Anchor Line ran at least two poster campaigns:

COME to ULSTER
Travel by ANCHOR LINE
To Londonderry or Belfast

Ireland
Come Back to Erin
ANCHOR LINE
New York and Londonderry

**Cross-Channel Trade: Passengers and Livestock**

Derry's cross-channel trade was the port's core business. The export of livestock was crucial to the growth and prosperity of cross-channel trade. Livestock exports to Glasgow, Heysham and Liverpool continued to prosper through the inter-war years.

*Londonderry Sentinel* of 1 January 1925 reported: 'There was great buoyancy in the livestock shipping trade during the year [1924]. The total shipments of livestock – cattle, pigs, sheep, and horses – amounted to no fewer than 120,196 head. Taking cattle, the shipments reached 90,988… Glasgow continues to be easily the best customer of the port in the matter of livestock shipments'.

In 1924, 66,877 cattle were shipped to Glasgow alone, with 17,027 destined for Heysham and 7,084 for Liverpool. In the same year 25,744 sheep, 3,204 pigs and 260 horses were shipped to Glasgow, Heysham and Liverpool.

The cross-channel passenger trade from Derry was at its peak in 1910. In 1910 a passenger steamer left for England, from Derry, six times a week with sailings to Heysham, with Laird Line, every Monday and Thursday, to Fleetwood every Tuesday and Friday, and to Liverpool, with Belfast Steamship Company, every Wednesday and Saturday; and there were six passenger sailings, on the Scotch Boat, each week to Greenock and Glasgow, with G&J Burns Ltd steamers departing every Monday and Thursday and Laird Line sailings every Tuesday, Wednesday, Friday and Saturday.

The decline in passenger services to England began in 1912 when the service to Fleetwood ended. Ten years later, in 1922, the steamers to Liverpool ceased carrying passengers but continued as cargo and livestock boats until 27 September 1965. The Heysham steamers stopped carrying passengers in the early 1930s but remained in operation for cargo until 11 October 1963.

Passenger sailings from Derry to Glasgow, however, thrived in the inter-war years.

In 1922, the two old-established Glasgow companies, G&J Burns and Laird Line, who had pioneered passenger, goods and livestock routes between Scotland and Ireland, amalgamated to form Burns & Laird Lines Ltd.

## Scotch Boat

The Scotch Boat carried passengers, emigrants, seasonal migrants, holidaymakers and livestock from Derry to Glasgow. It was an important part of Derry's maritime history; indeed for 137 years, running from 1829 until the autumn of 1966, there was a timetabled passenger service between Derry and Glasgow.

The Derry–Glasgow steerage passenger trade was initially dominated by the emigrant and the seasonal harvest worker. In the inter-war years, during July and August, and in particular during the Paisley and Glasgow Fairs, the Scotch Boats were loaded to capacity with Scottish holidaymakers destined for the holiday resorts of north west Ireland.

Burns & Laird Ships, such as the *Rose* (renamed, in 1929, *Lairdsrose), Maple* (renamed *Lairdsglen), Olive* (renamed *Lairdsbank)* and *Thistle* were all associated with the Derry–Glasgow crossing in the inter-war years. The *Rose* (1,100 tons, 251 feet in length), for example, had a speed of 15 knots with berths for 100 saloon passengers and large steerage accommodation. At the general renaming of Burns & Laird ships in 1929 the *Rose* merely added the prefix Lairds to her name, which gave her the distinction of being the only Laird Line steamer permitted to retain her old name.

In 1930 Burns & Laird ships sailed from their Prince's Quay berth, every weekday at 6.30pm, for Glasgow. Indeed, a Derry–Glasgow passenger service continued until September 1966 when Burns & Laird transferred their last remaining passenger steamer on this route, the *Lairdsloch*, to the Dublin–Glasgow service.

## Foreign Trade and Dredging the Foyle

With the increasing size of grain carriers from the USA and of transatlantic liners, it was vital to keep deep-water channels to Moville and Derry quays free of silt.

The grain trade was the backbone of Derry's foreign trade and as a consequence, the Harbour Commissioners deepened the harbour channel whereby vessels of heaviest tonnage could discharge their cargoes. The grain came to Liverpool in large ships from America and was then transferred to smaller ships, carrying some 6,000 tons of grain, which could berth at Queen's Quay.

In February 1887, the *Hercules* bucket dredger, built by Harland and Wolff, was delivered to the Harbour Commissioners. It was one of the largest and most powerful dredging machines in the United Kingdom at the time, and it was immediately set to work to cut a deep-water channel through Lough Foyle and Rosses Bay. A crew of 13 were required to operate the port's dredger.

Owing to the work of this dredger, vessels drawing up to 25 feet could come right up to Queen's Quay. Grain for William McCorkell & Co Ltd was discharged here and stored in their mill. McCorkell's Mill remained the most distinctive landmark along the quay until it was demolished in January 1991.

At the annual meeting of the Harbour Commissioners on Monday 16 January 1911 it was reported that the *Hercules,* during 1910, had been at work at 'the Abercorn Quay, the Rock Jetty, and the channel through Rosses Bay, at a total expenditure of £3,053. The depth of water in the channel was satisfactory, and they had at the quay at present a vessel with about 6,000 tons of Indian corn', which was the largest cargo of Indian corn ever discharged in Derry.

Twenty years later, in 1930, the Queen's Quay berth was still being dredged by the *Hercules* to 25 feet LWOST (Low Water of Ordinary Spring Tides) to enable discharge of large vessels. The backbone of foreign trade in the inter-war years continued to be large shipments of maize from north and south America, initially destined for Watts distillery but increasingly as a cheap source of animal feed, and William McCorkell & Co became one of its chief suppliers. In 1924, 68,398 tons of maize were imported. The other major foreign import was timber, now coming as often from Norway and Sweden as from Canada.

An overview of the trade of Derry port, in terms of numbers and tonnages of vessels entering the port, in the inter-war years is summed up in the table below:

| | 1928 | | 1929 | |
|---|---|---|---|---|
| **Trade** | **Vessels** | **Tons** | **Vessels** | **Tons** |
| Home Trade | 1,230 | 319,000 | 1,141 | 307,773 |
| Foreign Trade | 64 | 89,667 | 59 | 87,517 |
| Transatlantic Mail and Passenger Steamers | 72 | 713,551 | 64 | 632,241 |
| **Total** | **1,366** | **1,122,278** | **1,264** | **1,027,531** |

**Further Reading**

Gavin, Robert, Kelly, William P and O'Reilly, Dolores; *Atlantic Gateway: The port and city of Londonderry since 1700;* Four Courts Press, Dublin, 2009

Mitchell, Brian; *Derry~Londonderry: Gateway to a New World – The story of emigration from the Foyle by sail and steam;* Eglinton, 2014

Bigger, David and McDonald, Terence; *In Sunshine or In Shadow: Photographs from the Derry Standard, 1928–39;* Friar's Bush Press, Belfast, 1990

Brian Mitchell
June 2018

# QUAYS

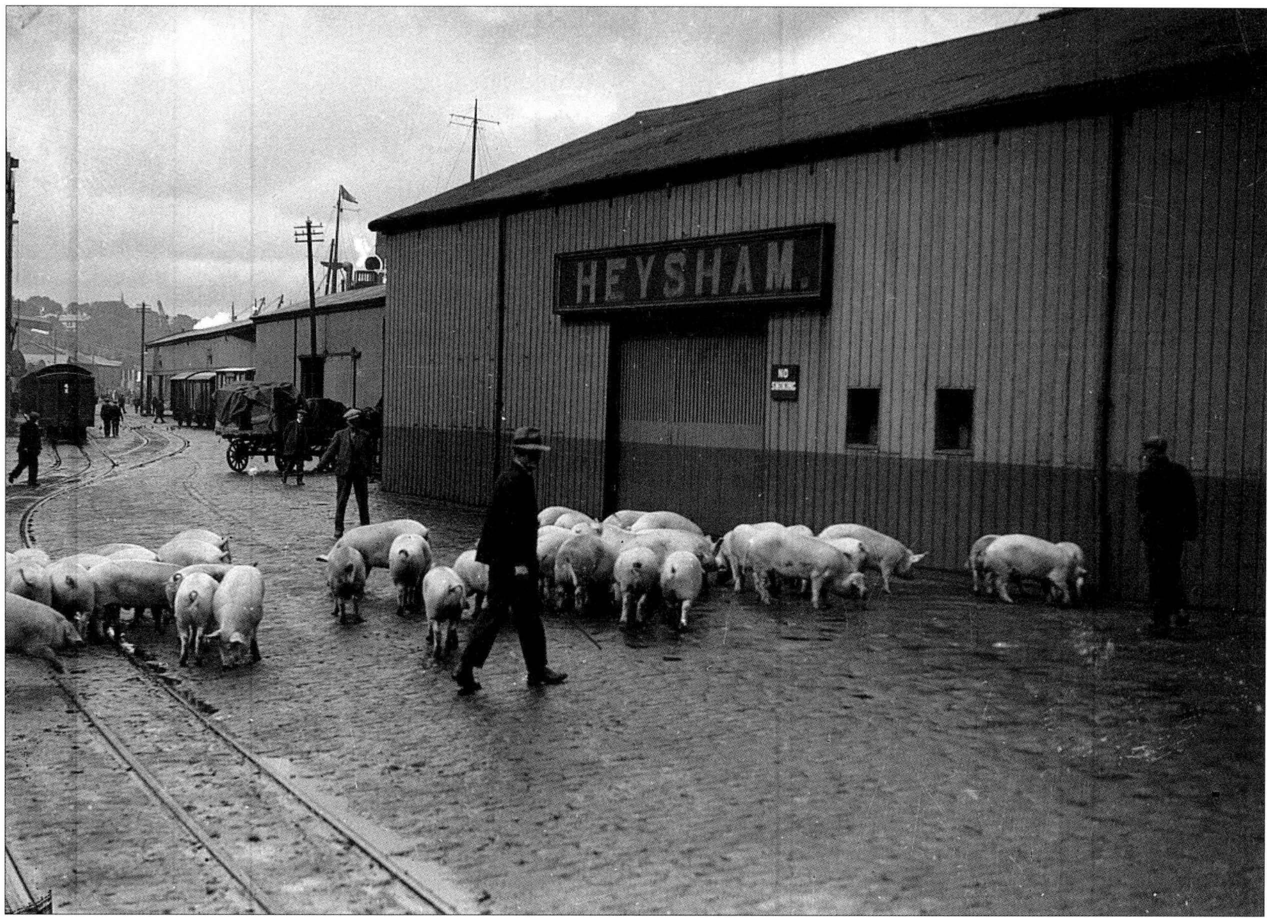


Pigs on their way to the Heysham steamer in August 1929. Livestock exports to Glasgow, Heysham and Liverpool remained buoyant through the inter-war years. In 1924, 120,196 head of livestock – cattle, sheep, pigs and horses – were shipped from Derry to Glasgow, Heysham and Liverpool. Cattle shipments totalled 90,988; sheep 25,744; pigs 3,204; and horses 260. The Heysham steamer stopped carrying passengers in 1930 but remained in operation for cargo until October 1963. *(POR 3-10, 9 August 1929)*

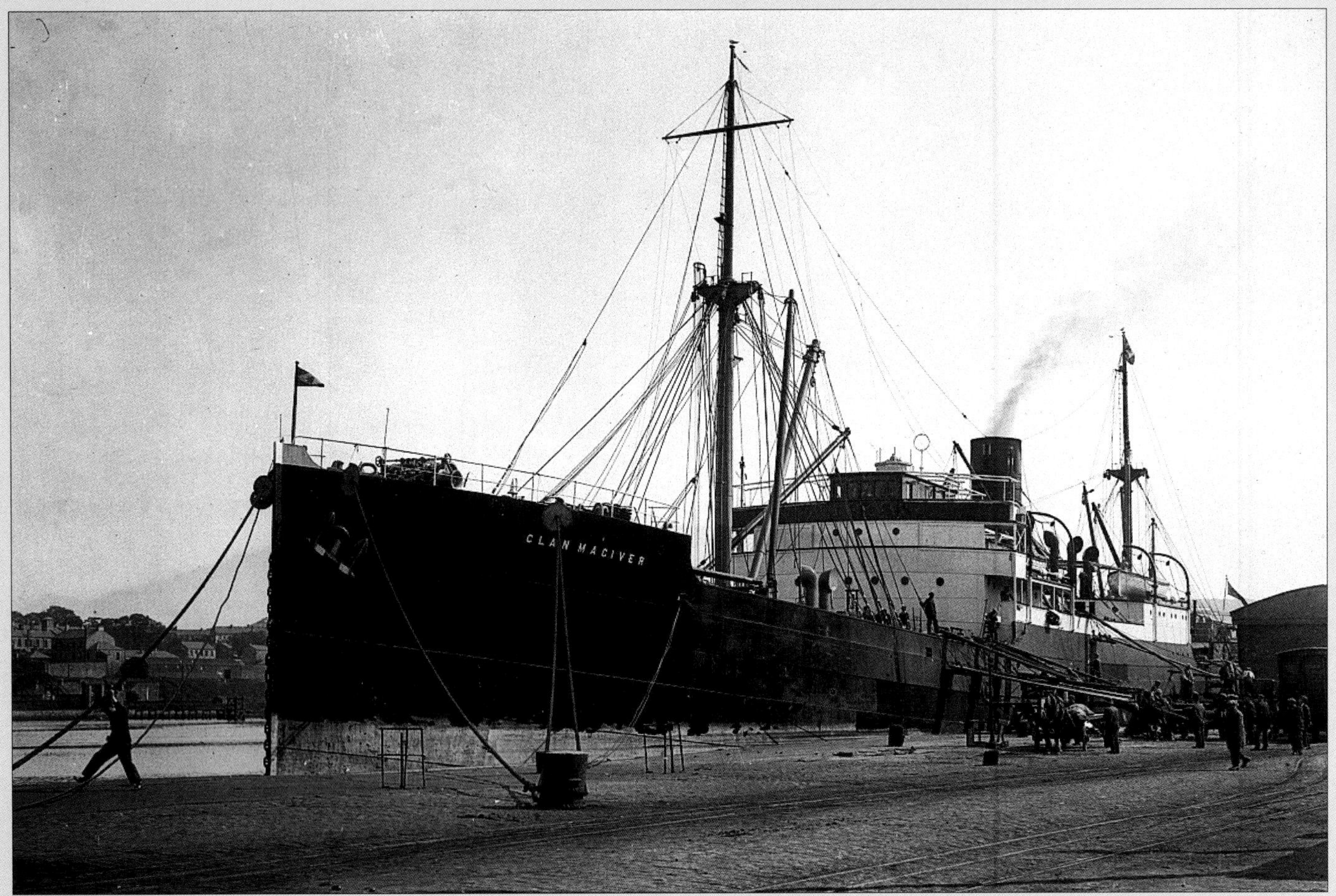


The SS *Clan Maciver* (4,606 tons), the first Clan Line vessel to arrive at Derry in September 1930. In the 1930s Clan Line, with headquarters in Glasgow, was the largest cargo carrying concern in the world. Founded 1877, Clan Line ceased trading in 1981. The ships of the Clan Line were often distinguishable by their name, with prefix 'Clan'. *(POR 2-8, 3 September 1930)*

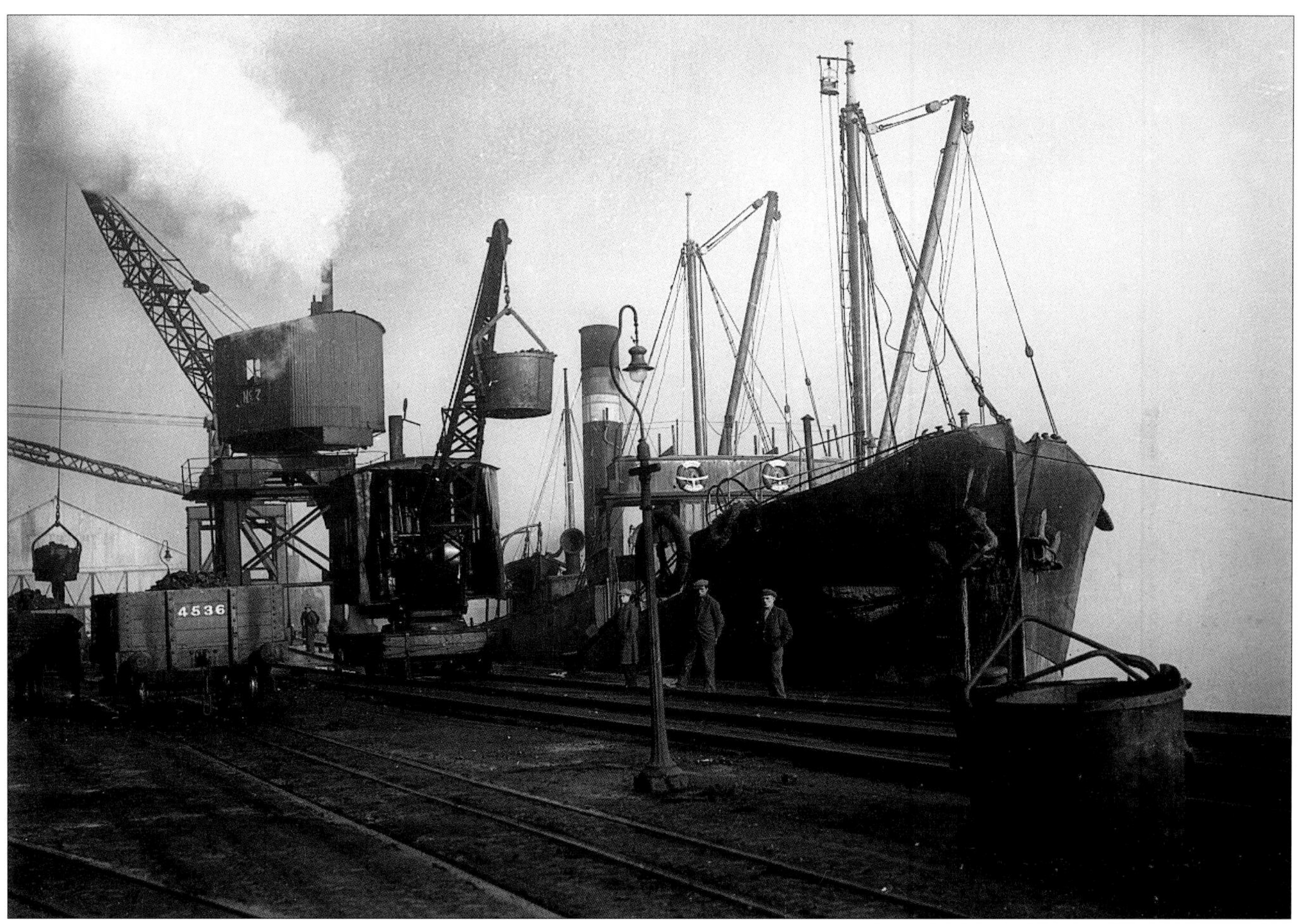


'The S.S. *Wythburn* discharging a cargo of Brytehouse Coal at Derry Quay for Messrs. Frederick Wolseley & Co., Queen's Quay, who are the Sole Importers' in February 1931. *(POR 5-11, 6 February 1931)*

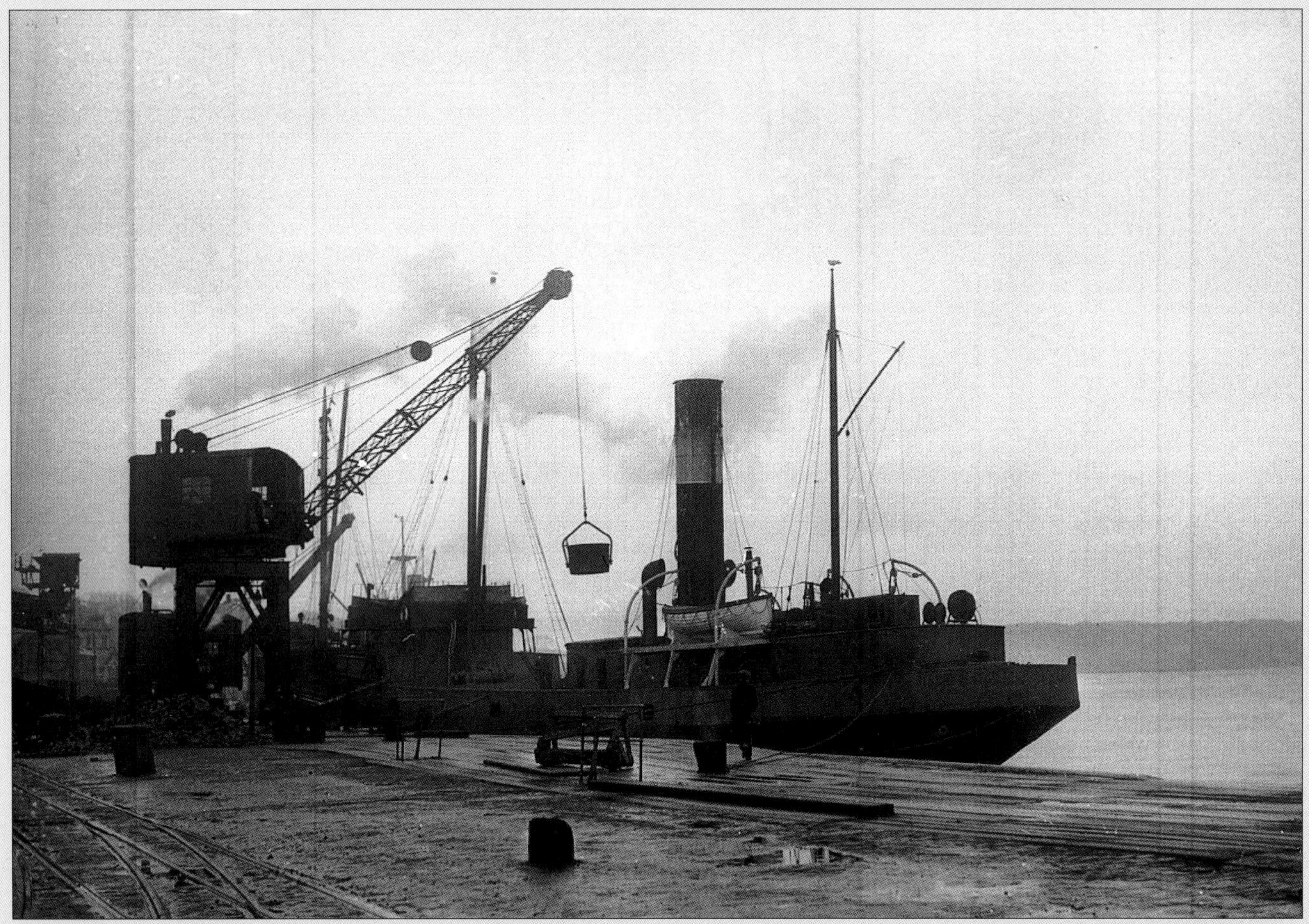

'S.S. *Yewtree* discharging at Queen's Quay 1,000 tons Sunbeam Silkstone Best House Coal for Messrs. Samuel Morrison & Co.' in February 1931. *(POR 3-5, 13 February 1931)*

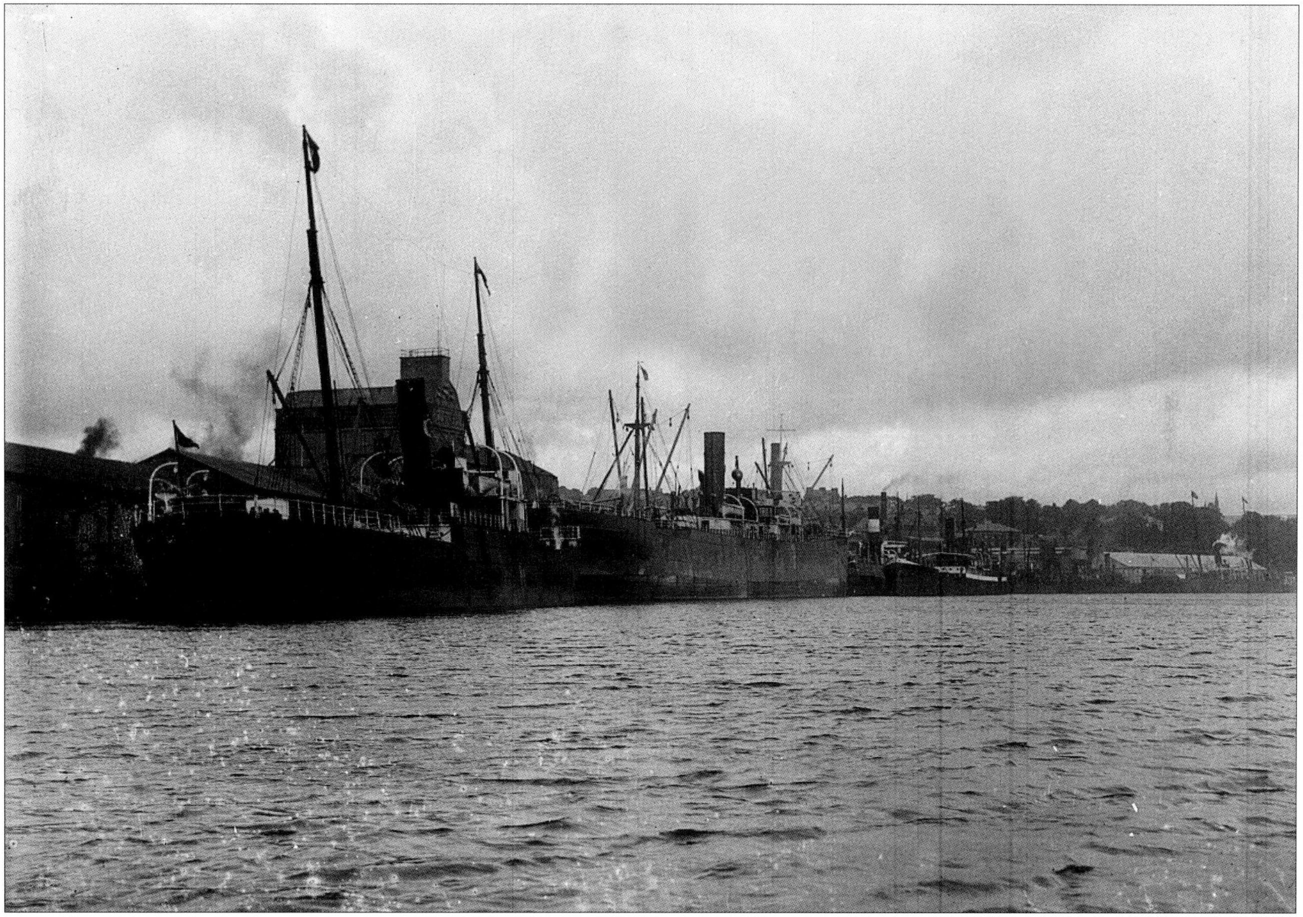

'Shipping boom at Derry Quay, where almost a record number of vessels are berthed at present' in July 1931. This was a common scene along Derry's quays in inter-war years. *Derry Standard* of 17 July 1929 published a photograph of 'Four foreign trading vessels which have arrived at Derry Quay. Two have cargoes of Maize, one of Timber and one General.' *(POR 1-6, 29 July 1931)*

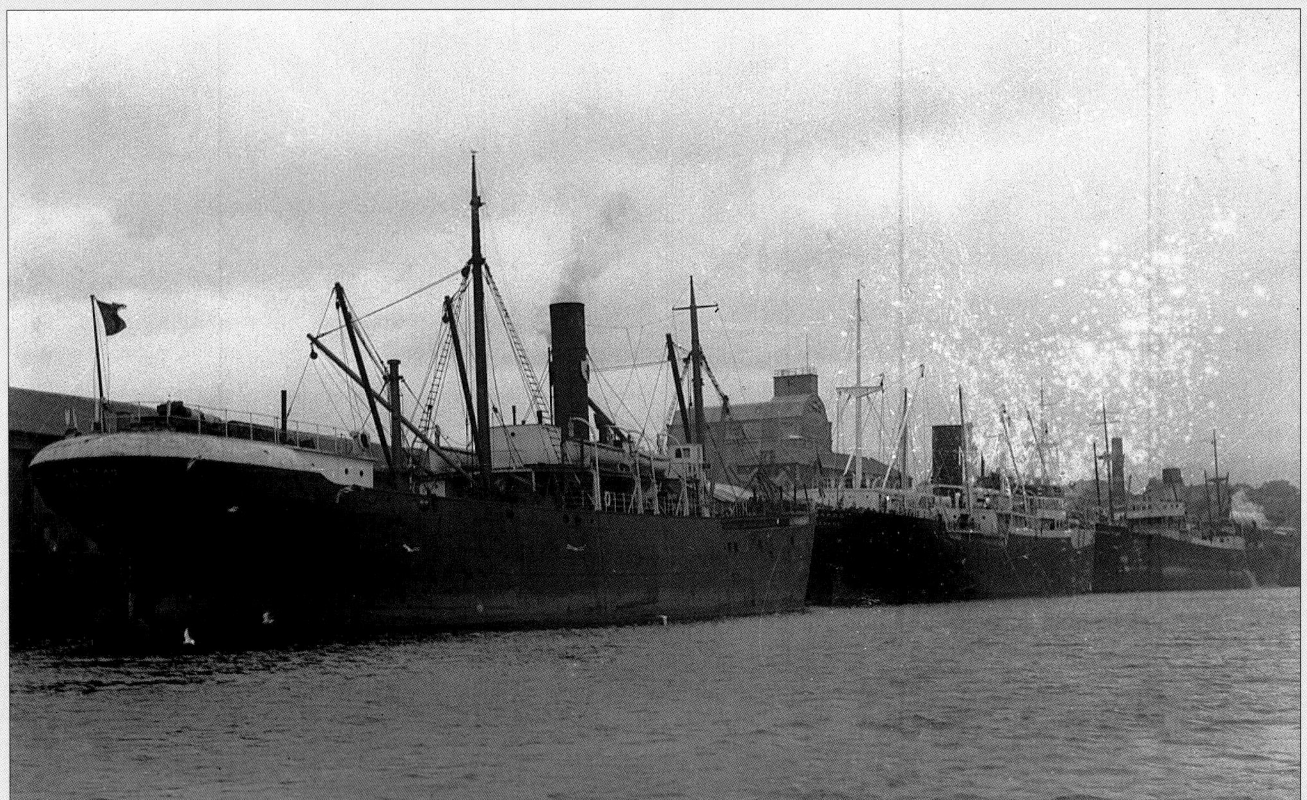

'Three large cargo steamers discharging at Derry Quay' in August 1934. This extended view of large cargo ships berthed along Queen's Quay is dominated by the distinctive outline of the concrete grain silo (built 1916) attached to McCorkell's Mill which was one of Derry's great 19th century warehouses. Grain for William McCorkell & Co Ltd was discharged here. Six storeys high, of stone and brick construction, McCorkell's Mill (on site of Quayside Centre) fronted onto the quayside. In the 1860s McCorkells built a balcony at the top of this warehouse to enable friends and relatives to watch the final departure of their loved ones in sailing ships bound for North America. The silo and mill were demolished on 14 January 1991. *(POR 1-10, 29 August 1934)*

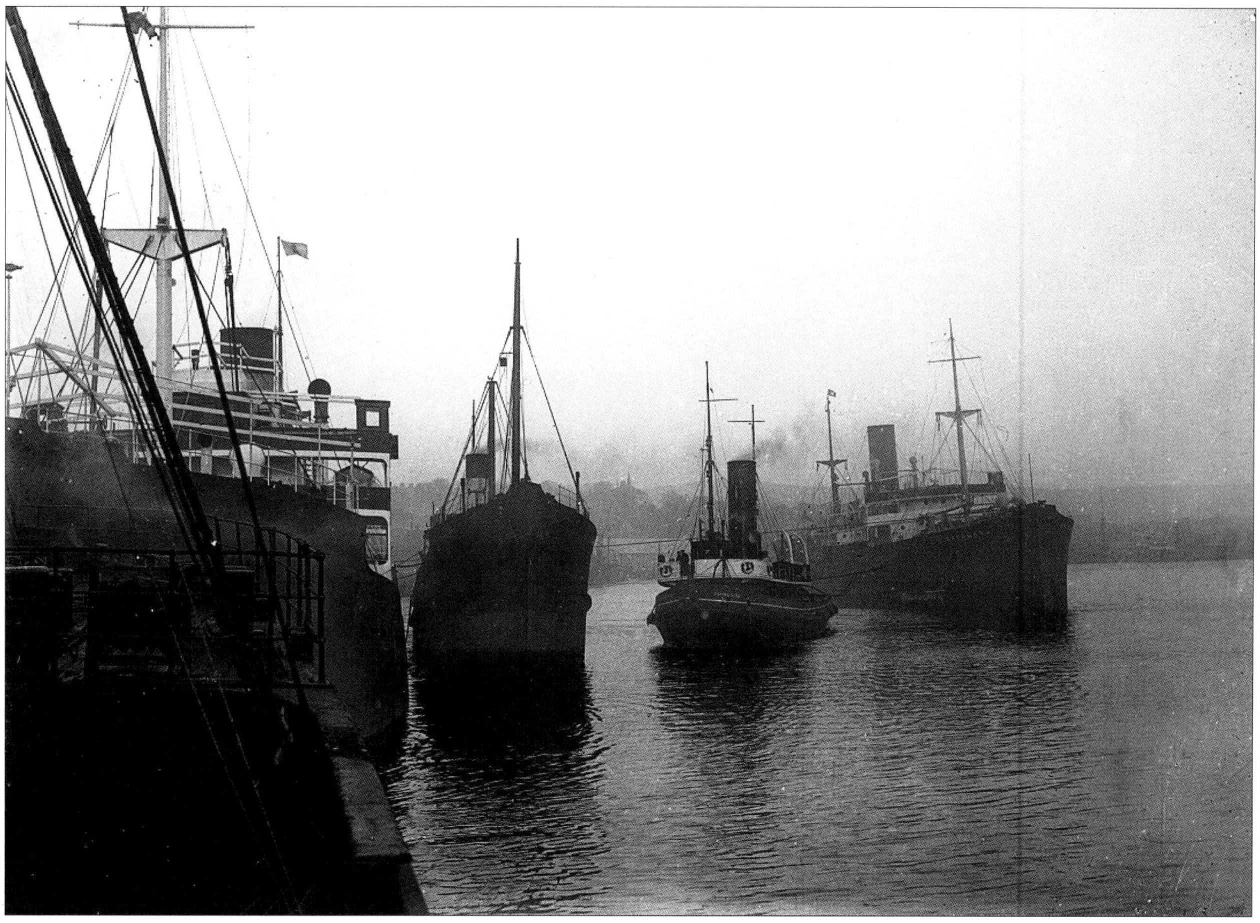

A bustling Derry Quay. During 1927 the total shipping tonnage arriving at the port of Londonderry was 1,078,462; consisting of tonnage of 709,758 of 'Transatlantic steamers' calling at Moville, and of 277,383 in 'Home trade' and 91,321 in 'Foreign trade' calling at the quays in the heart of the city. In 1927, 185,671 tons of coal and 60,261 tons of maize were imported, and 84,637 head of livestock, of cattle, sheep and pigs, were shipped to Glasgow, Heysham and Liverpool. *(POR 2-9)*

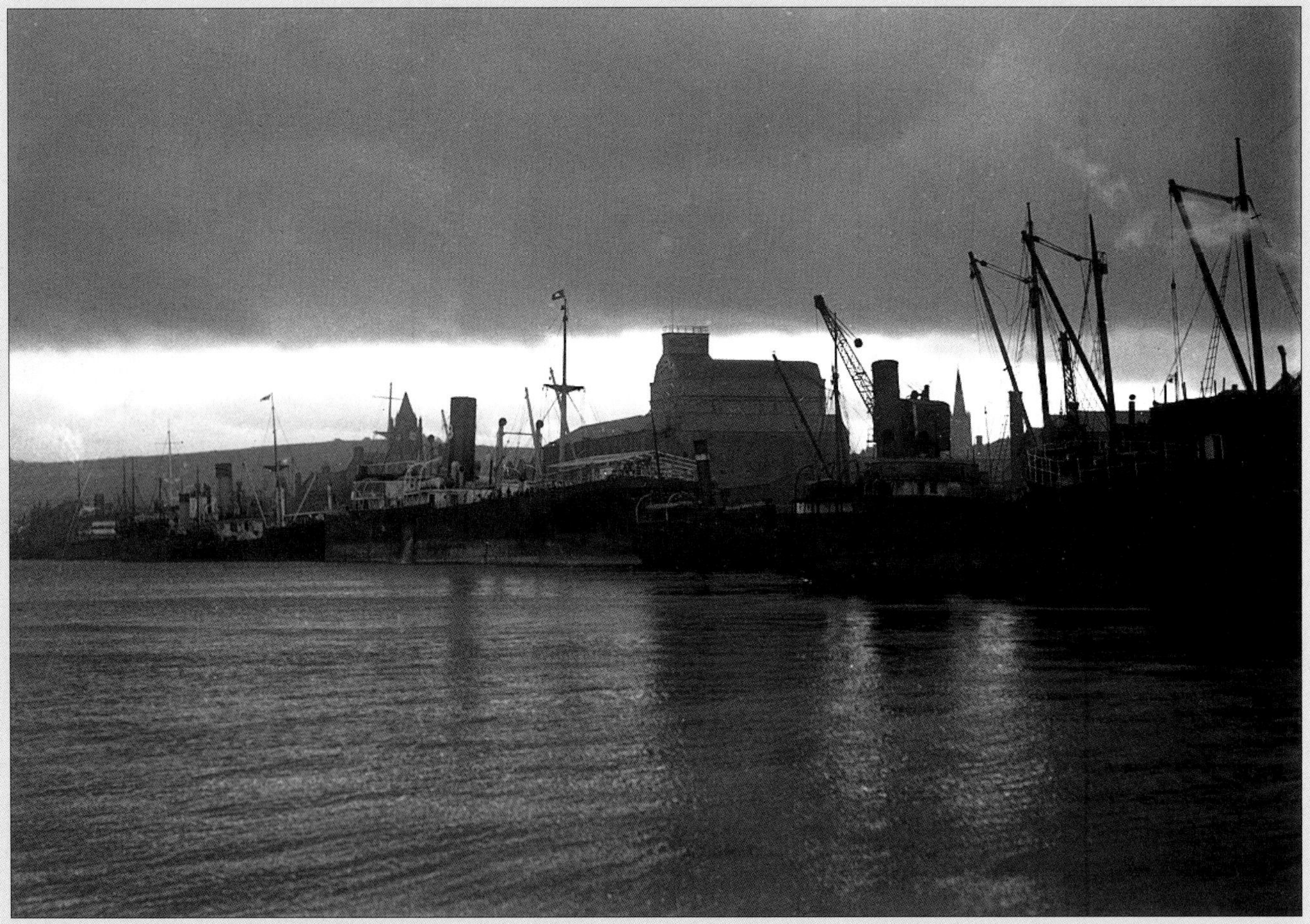

Ships in a line occupying the full length of Queen's Quay. The boat in the centre of the photograph is most likely a large grain vessel like that seen on page 14. Again, the outline of the silo at McCorkell's Mill forms a distinctive backdrop to the quayside. *(POR 2-12)*

The Warehouses of grain merchants William Thompson & Co and William McCorkell & Co on Queen's Quay. The outside balcony, built in the 1860s, which ran the entire length of McCorkell's Mill on the top floor (5th floor, below roof), has now been removed and the distinctive outline of silo attached to McCorkell's Mill is clearly visible. *(POR 5-12)*

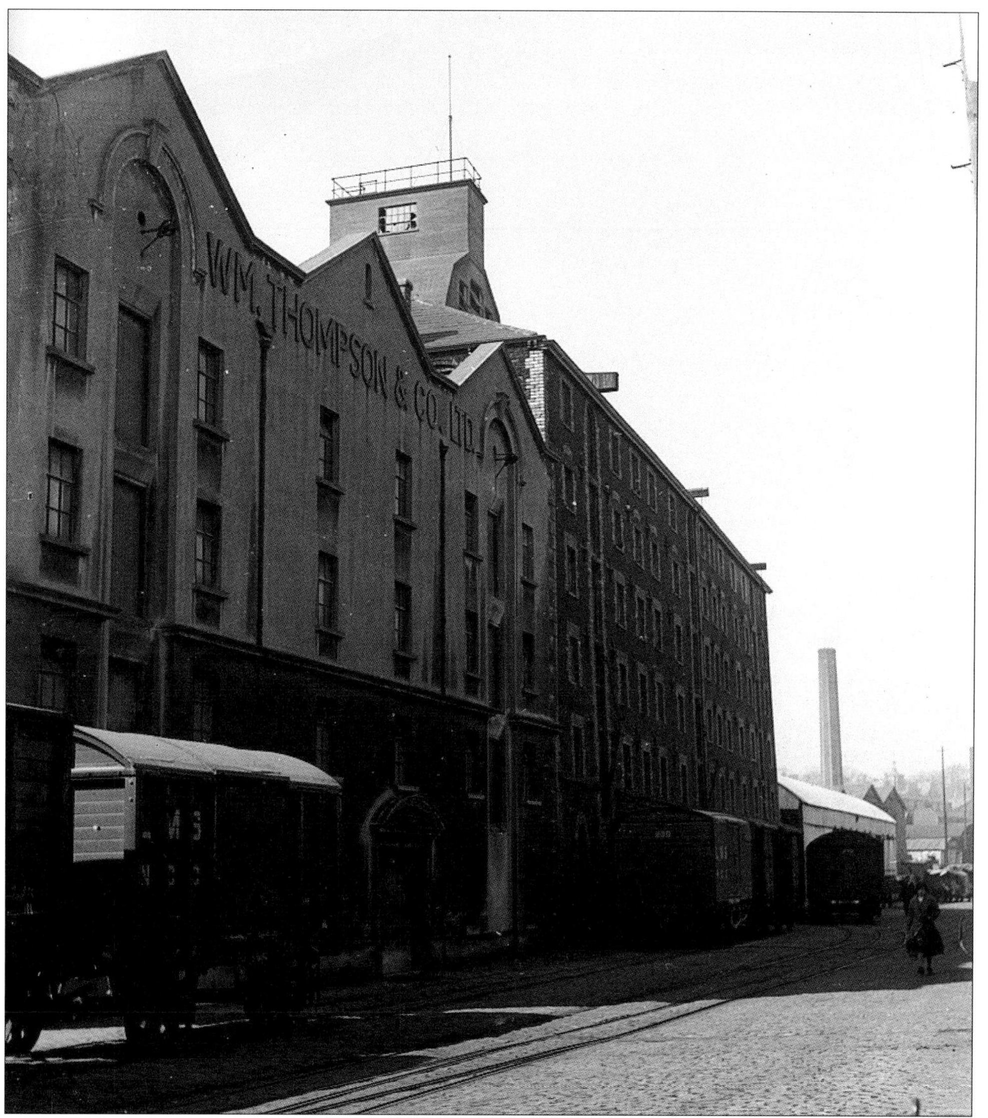

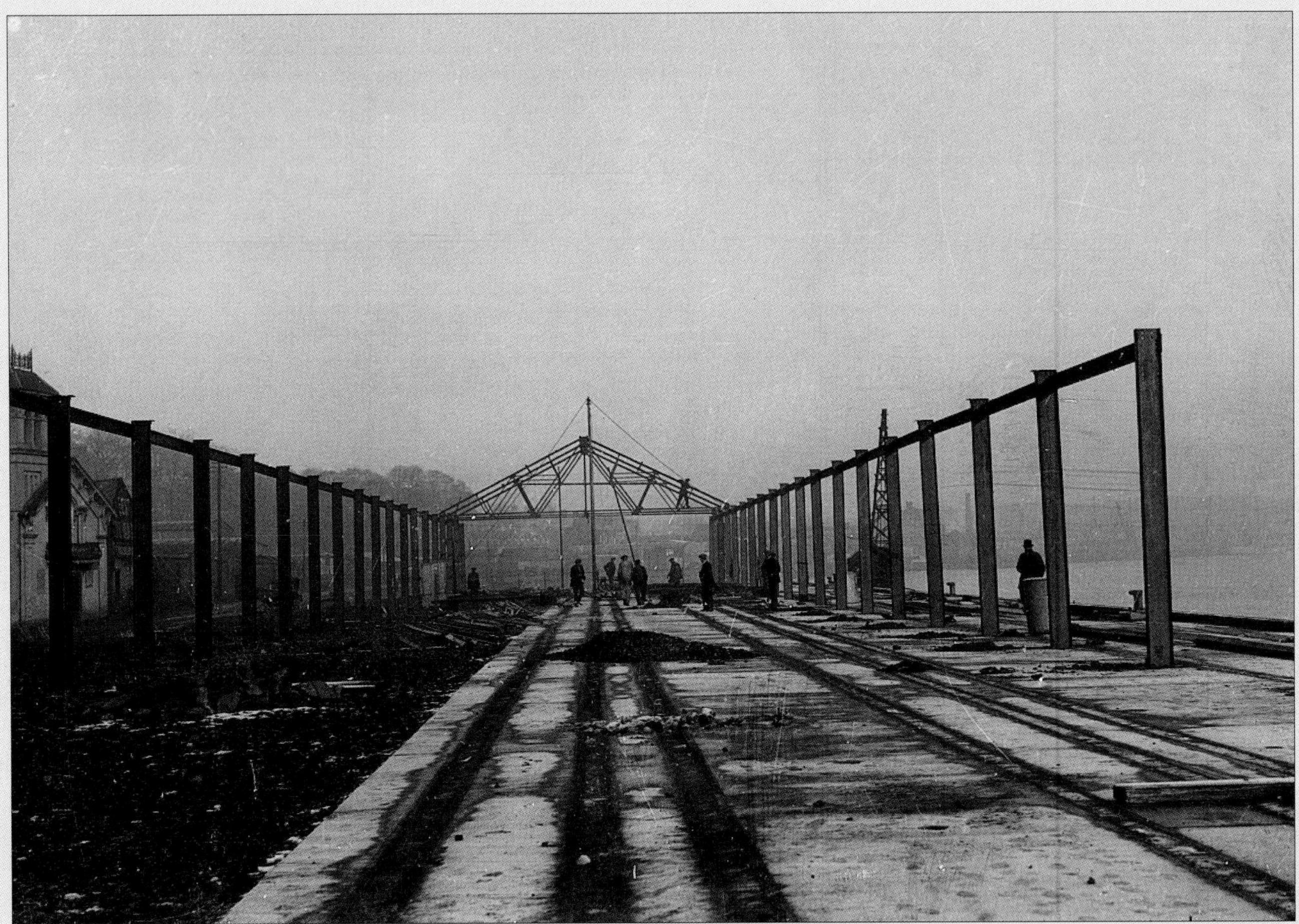

'A new shed in the course of erection' in January 1930 on the extension to Queen's Quay. It is being constructed in front of the Boating Club House of City of Derry Rowing Club on Boating Club Lane. This quaint building, built 1869, still stands and is occupied today by Quaywest Wine Bar and Restaurant. *(POR 6-13, 17 January 1930)*

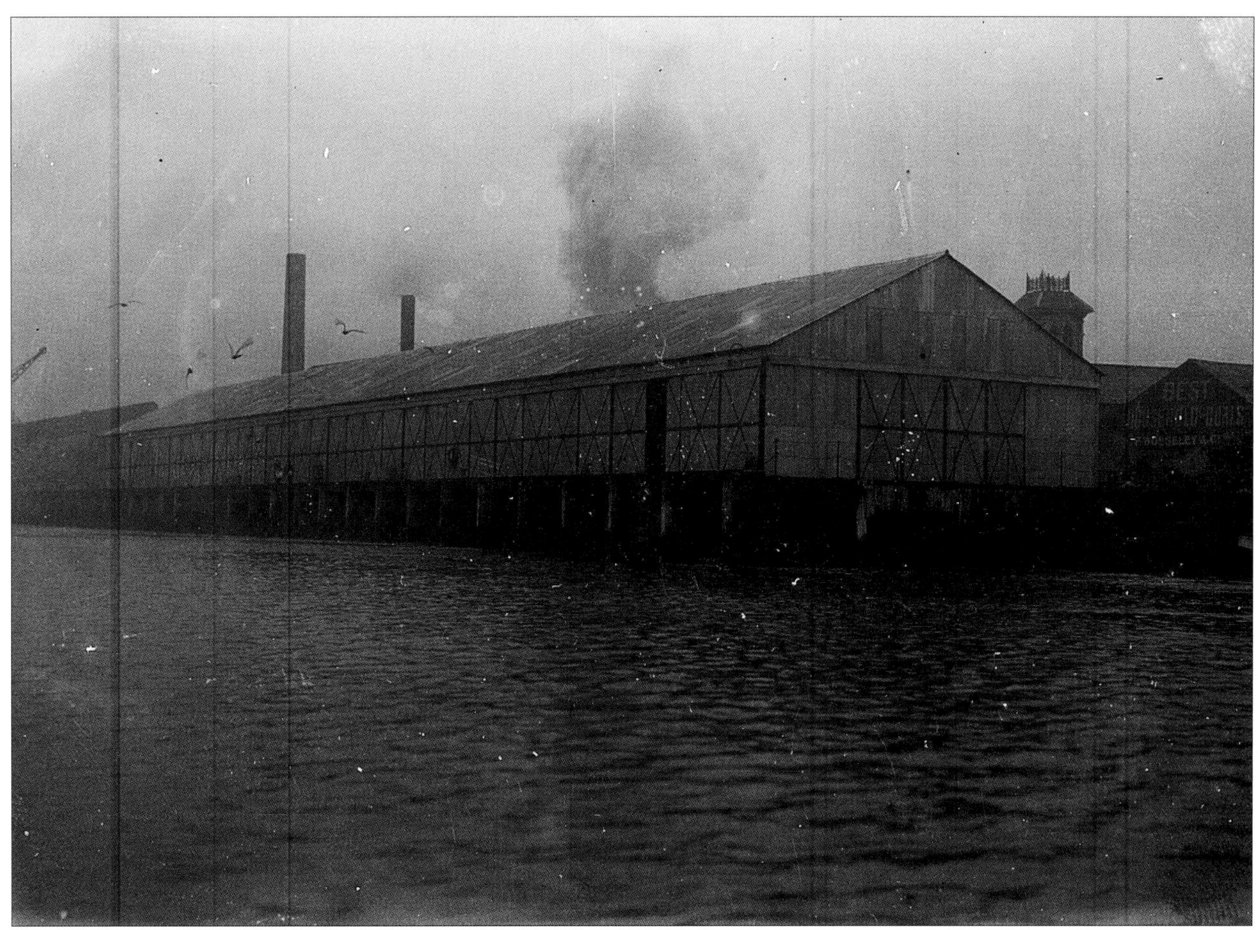

The completed shed in front of the Boating Club House on Queen's Quay. *(POR 11-12)*

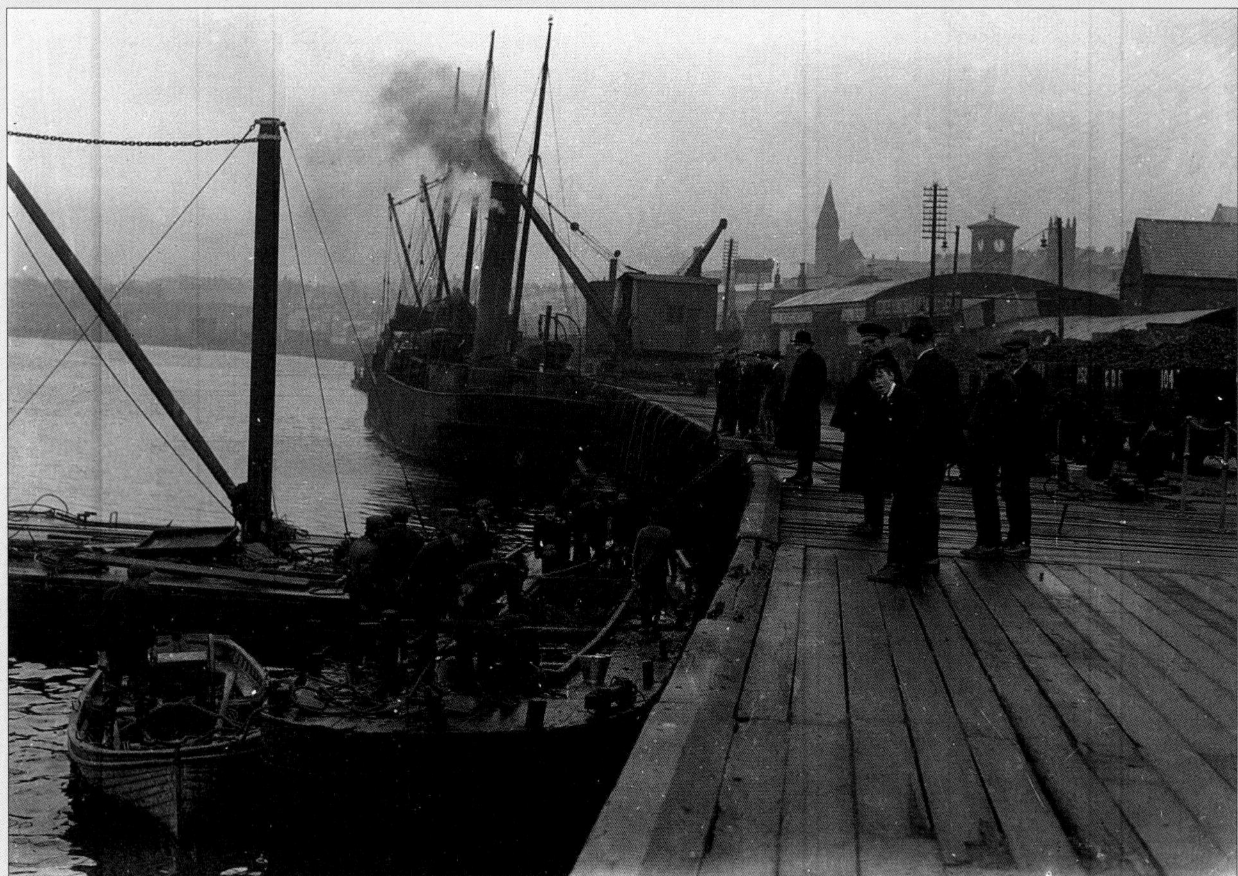

'The Strabane lighter which sank at the Waterside Wharf with a cargo of coal' was re-floated in January 1930. A tug was used to tow lighters up the River Foyle to the Strabane canal, where horses on a path took over to tow the barges into Strabane. The Strabane Canal, four miles long to connect Strabane to the navigable River Foyle and thence to the port of Derry, was opened in 1796. The locks were designed to accommodate sea-going schooners, capable of carrying 300 tons of cargo. Owing to poor income generation, arising from competition with the Derry to Strabane Railway (opened 1847), the canal fell into disrepair and by 1910 there was less than 2 feet of water in parts. In 1921 the canal was taken over by the Strabane and Foyle Navigation Company. The 1930s and 1940s saw the total neglect of the canal and as the water dried up traffic on the canal ceased. The canal was officially closed in 1962. *(POR 4-15, 29 January 1930)*

‘A three-masted schooner at Derry Quay with a cargo of ice’ in April 1932. Although occasional sailing ships still entered the port in the inter-war years the *Derry Standard* of 11 April 1932 did note: ‘This type of vessel is rapidly disappearing.’ *(POR 7-2, 11 April 1932)*

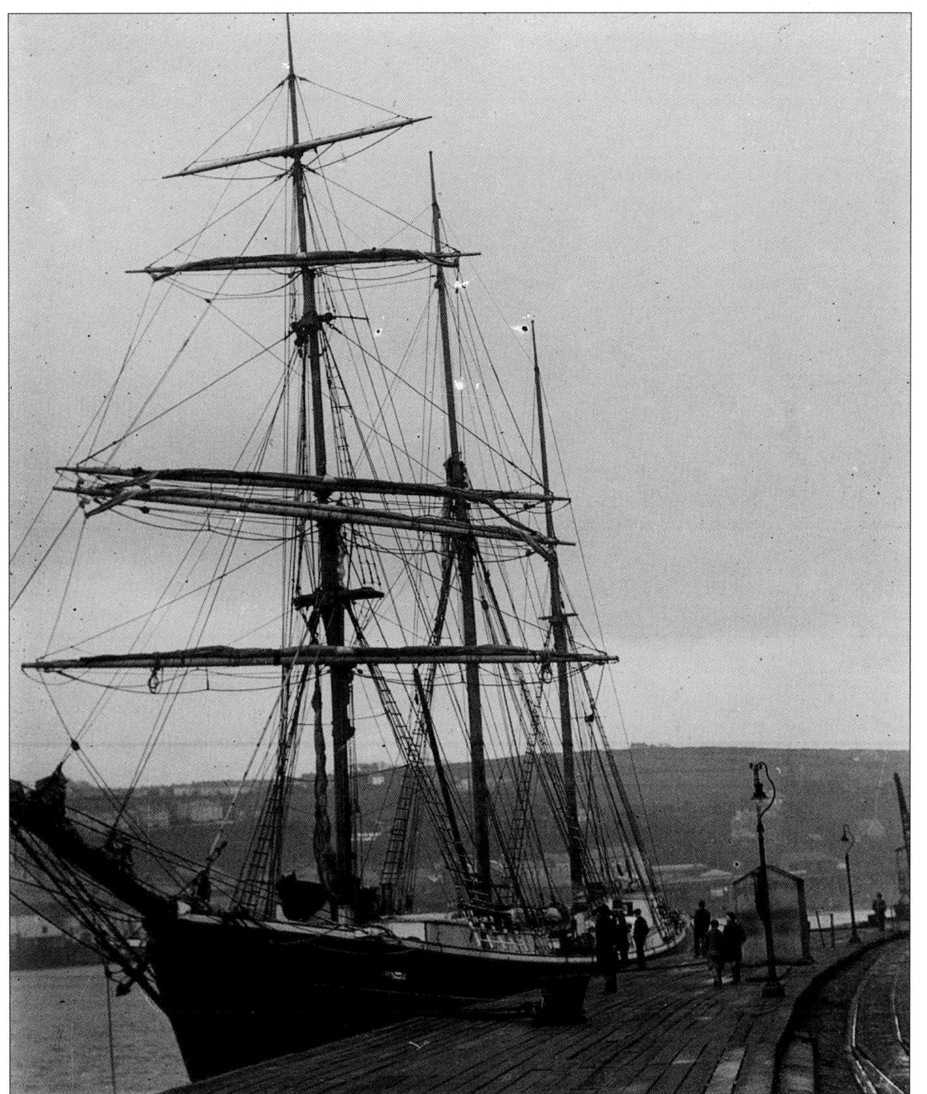

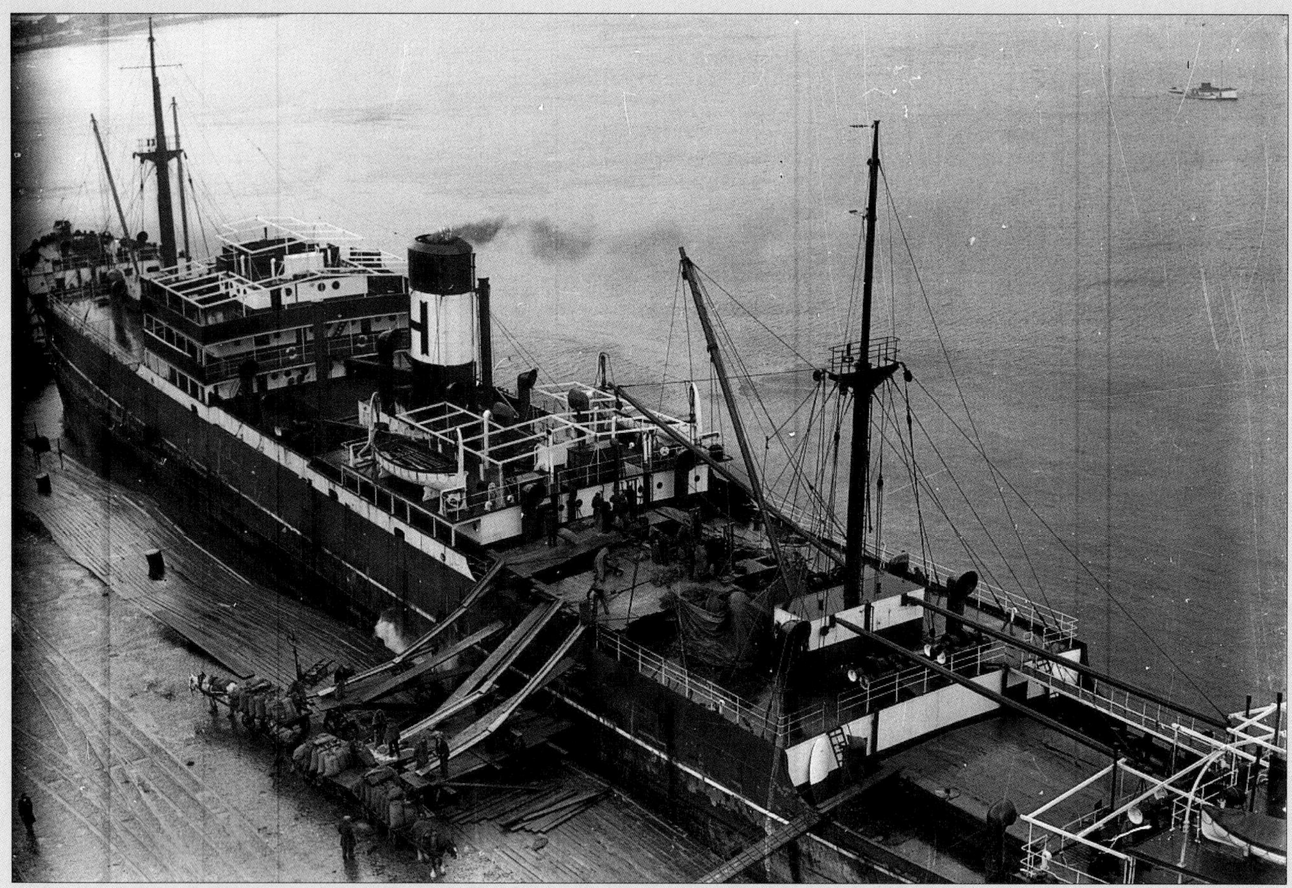

Photographed in October 1935, from the top floor of McCorkell's Mill, SS *Harbury* (5,081 tons, 418 feet long), 'the largest vessel that has ever discharged at Derry Quay', is unloading its cargo of 'Barley for Messrs. Wm. McCorkell & Co., Ltd., and Messrs. Wm. Thompson & Co., Ltd'. It had sailed from 'the port of Nicolaieff'. Nicolaieff, known as Mykolaiv today, is located in Ukraine's steppe region, 40 miles from the Black Sea along the estuary of the River Bug.

Boats such as this were filled to the brim with grain and it took three to four days to empty the hold. Men inside the boat, standing knee-high in grain, bagged the grain while dockers on the quay either loaded the sixteen-stone bags on to horse-drawn carts or carried them on their shoulders to be emptied into a grill at McCorkell's Mill, bringing the bag back to the boat to get filled again. *(POR 11-5, 30 October 1935)*

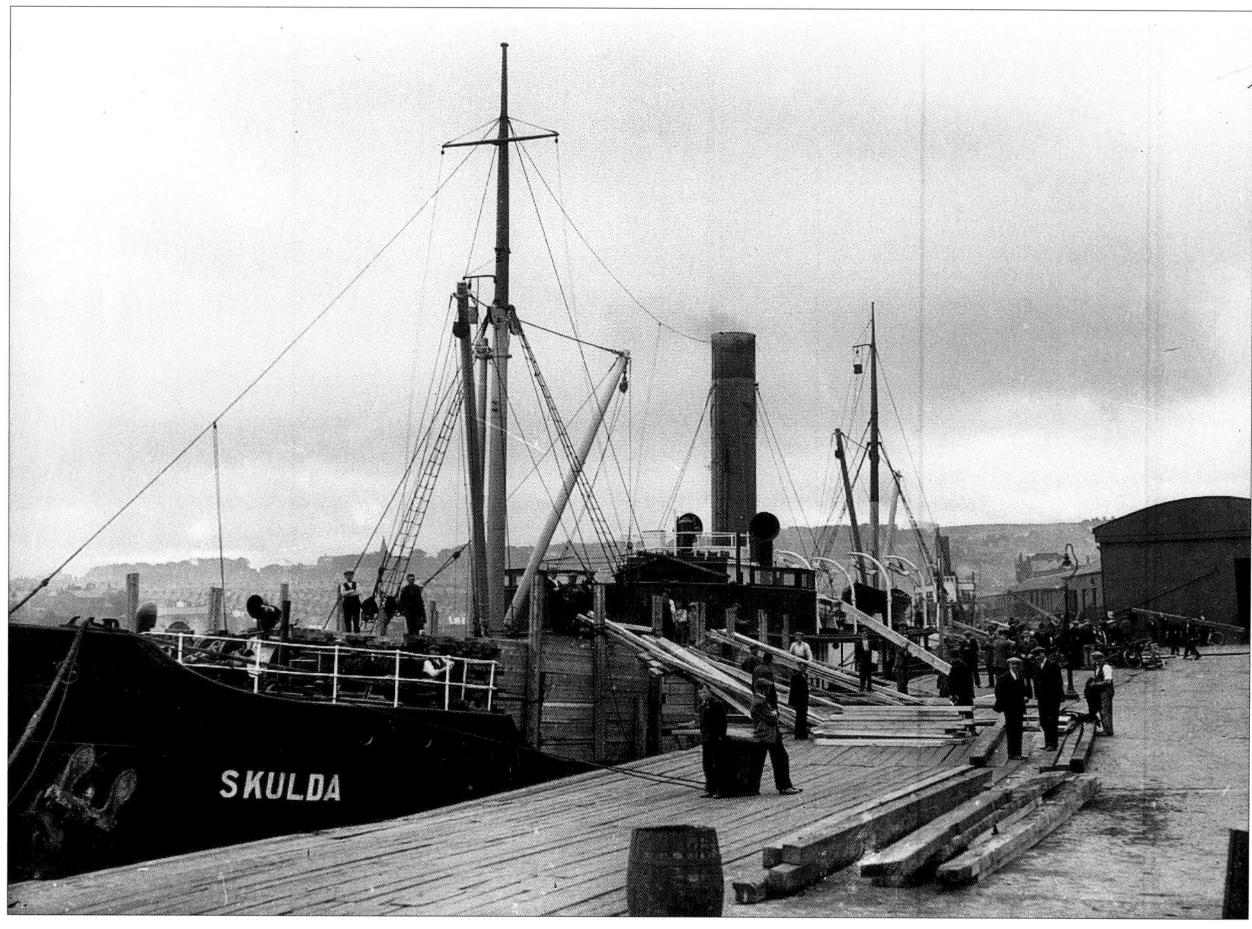


A cargo of Canadian deals (a softwood) for Robert Keys & Co being unloaded from the SS *Skulda* at Queen's Quay in July 1937. The labour-intensive nature of the work is very clear from the presence of a large number of dockers. Timber from Canada as well as Norway and Sweden was a major foreign import in this period. The backbone of foreign trade in the inter-war years continued to be large shipments of maize from north and south America, initially destined for Watts distillery but increasingly as a cheap source of animal feed, and William McCorkell & Co became one of its chief suppliers. *(POR 2-5, 19 July 1937)*

# DOCKERS

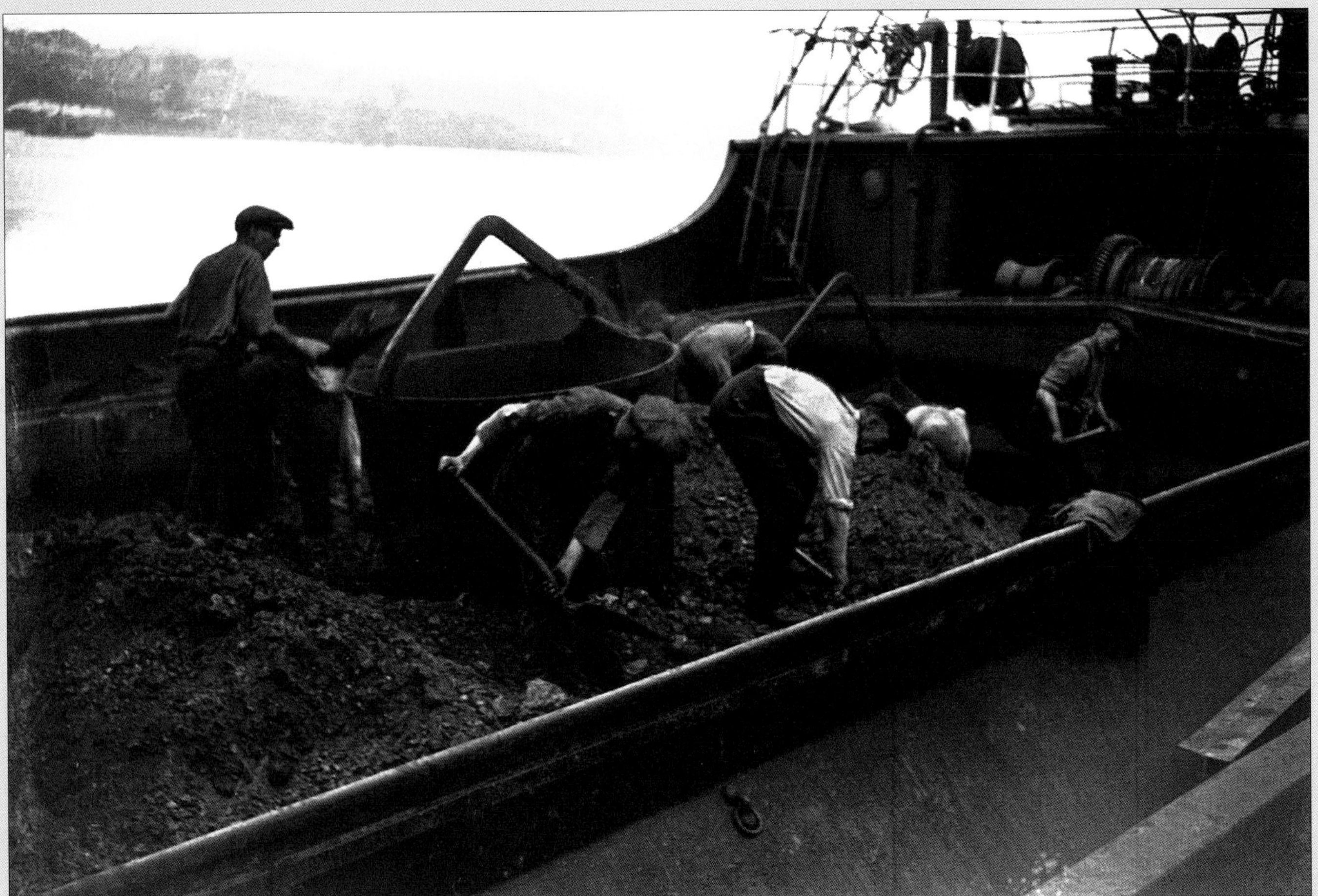

Unloading coal. Coal was imported in large quantities to Derry; in 1924, it amounted to 187,094 tons. It was imported in small ships, carrying between 500 and 900 tons of coal, which was discharged by steam crane. Right up to the 1960s the work of a docker was very physical as he had to shovel a ton of coal into a bucket which was then lifted from the hold by steam crane. Today it is done by a grab which can lift 12 tons in one go. *(POR 1-14)*

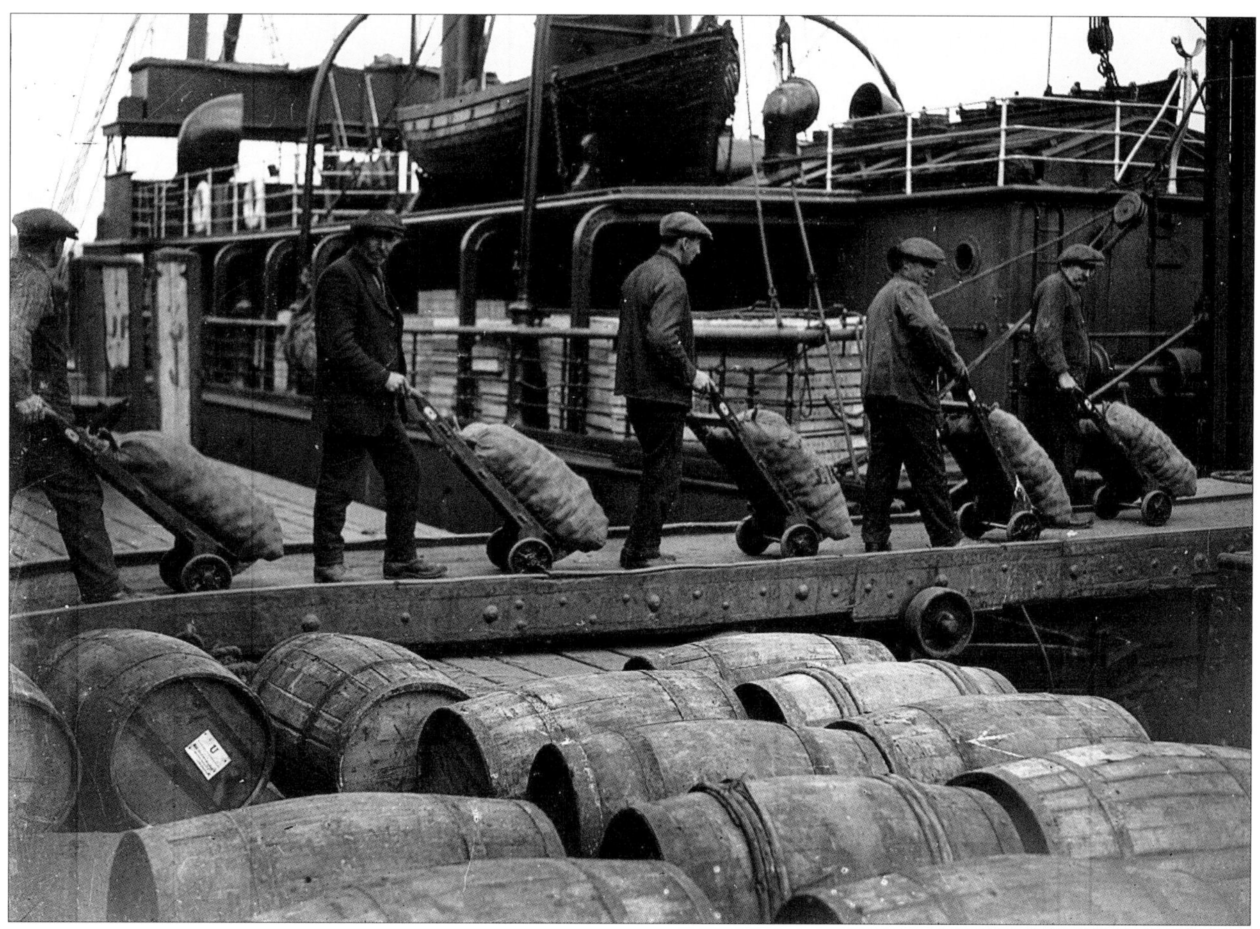

Loading a 'Spud Boat'. Five dockers loading a cargo of potatoes – they would have spent all day carrying one bag at a time from the warehouse shed to the boat. *(POR 11-3)*

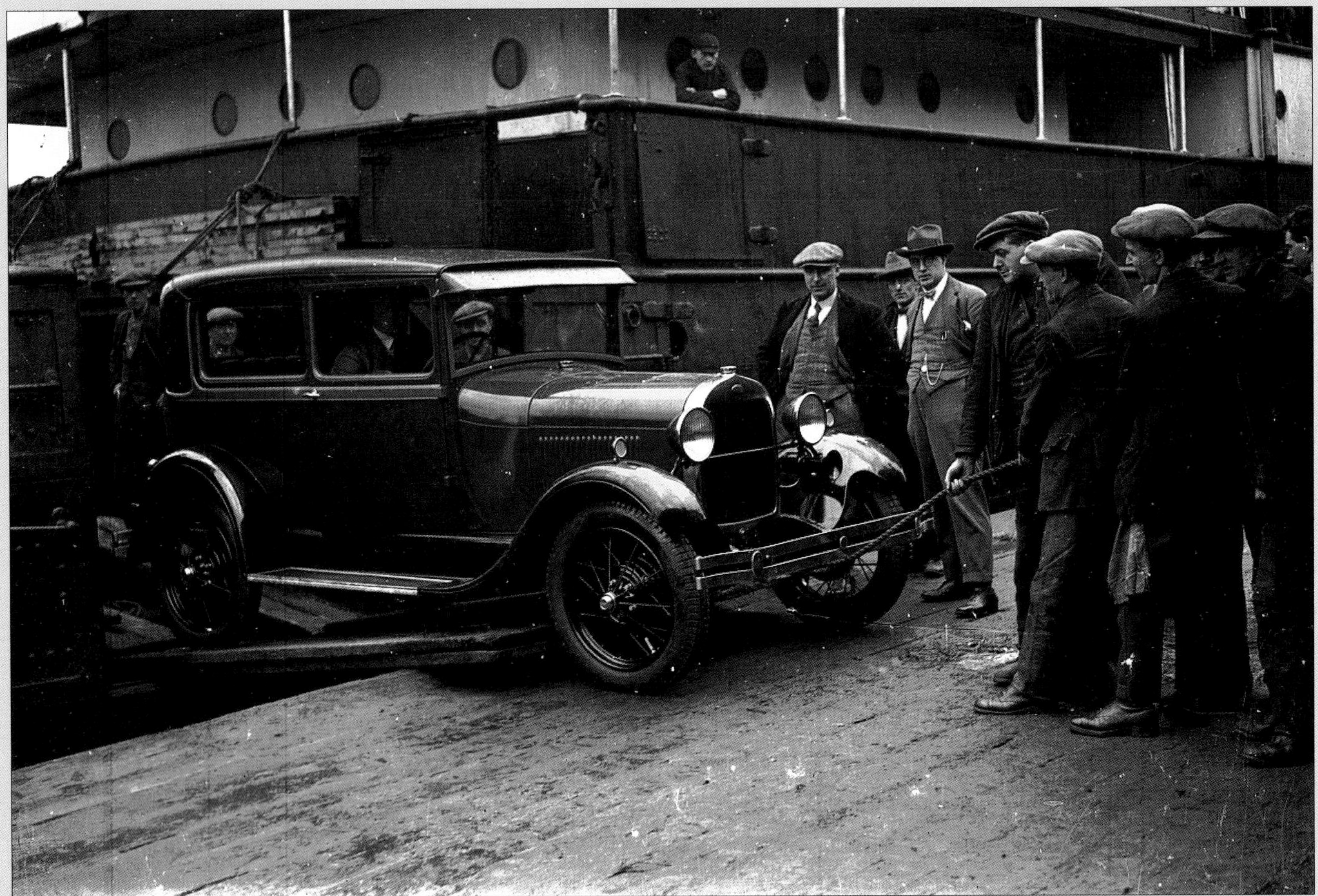

Possibly pulled by the men holding the rope fixed to the front bumper, this car is carefully unloaded from ship to quay. As can also be seen in the photograph on page 41, cars were occasionally transported and may either belong to a passenger or it could be a new import. It is possible the man with the trilby hat and watch chain looking at the photographer could be the owner. *(POR 11-6)*

# SCOTCH BOAT

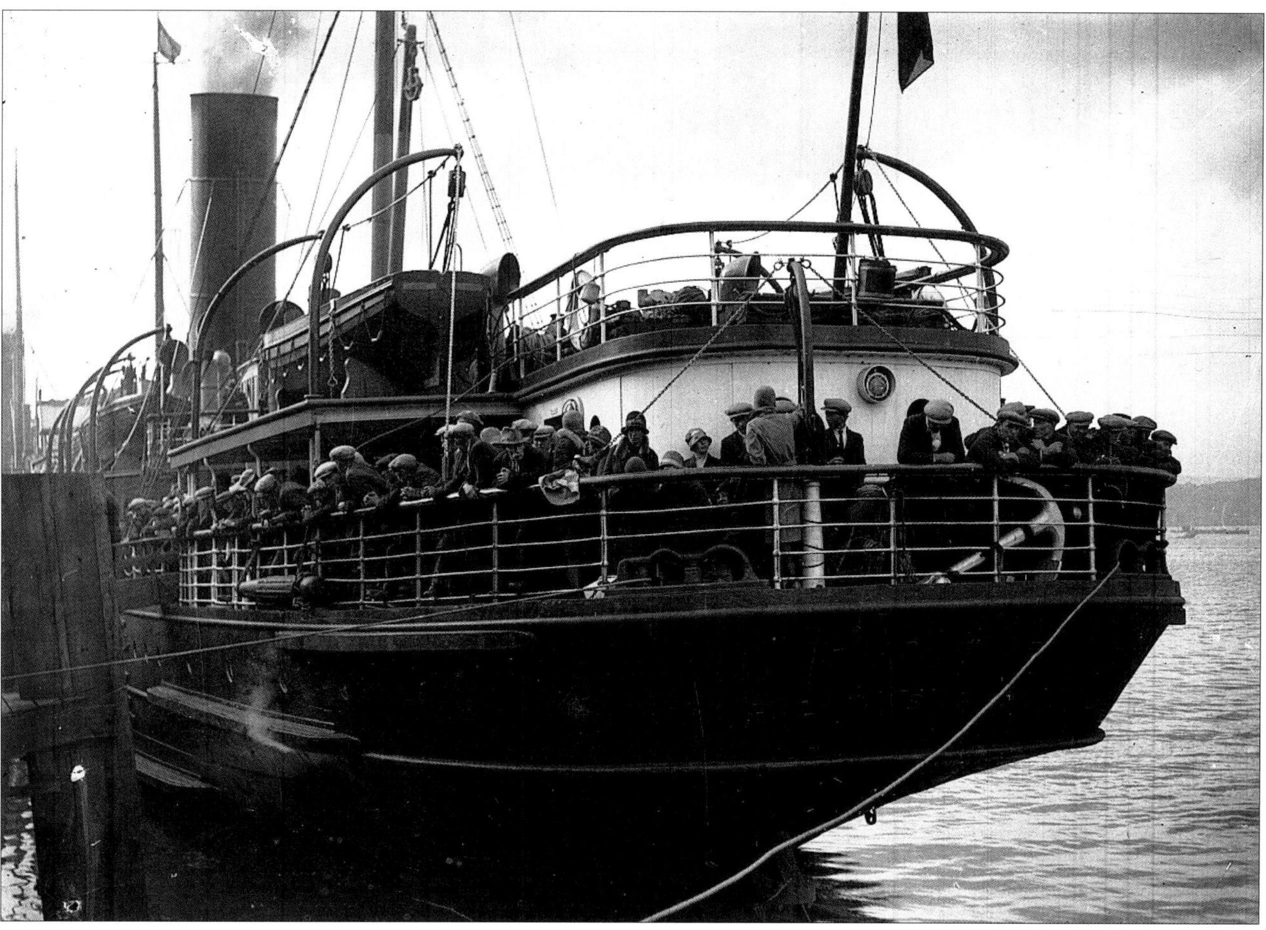

Every summer Scottish holidaymakers arrived in Derry on the Scotch Boat from Glasgow. This stern view of Burns & Laird Steamer *Rose*, showing a packed deck, mostly of men wearing cloth caps, was published in the *Derry Standard* of 18 July 1927 with caption: 'The Scotch Fair – Hundreds of visitors from Scotland have arrived in Derry during the last few days: A contingent of holiday makers on the Glasgow boat.' During July and August, and in particular during the Paisley and Glasgow Fairs, the Scotch Boats were loaded to capacity with Scottish holiday makers destined for the holiday resorts of north-west Ireland. *Rose* was renamed *Lairdsrose* in 1929. *(POR 16-9, 18 July 1927)*

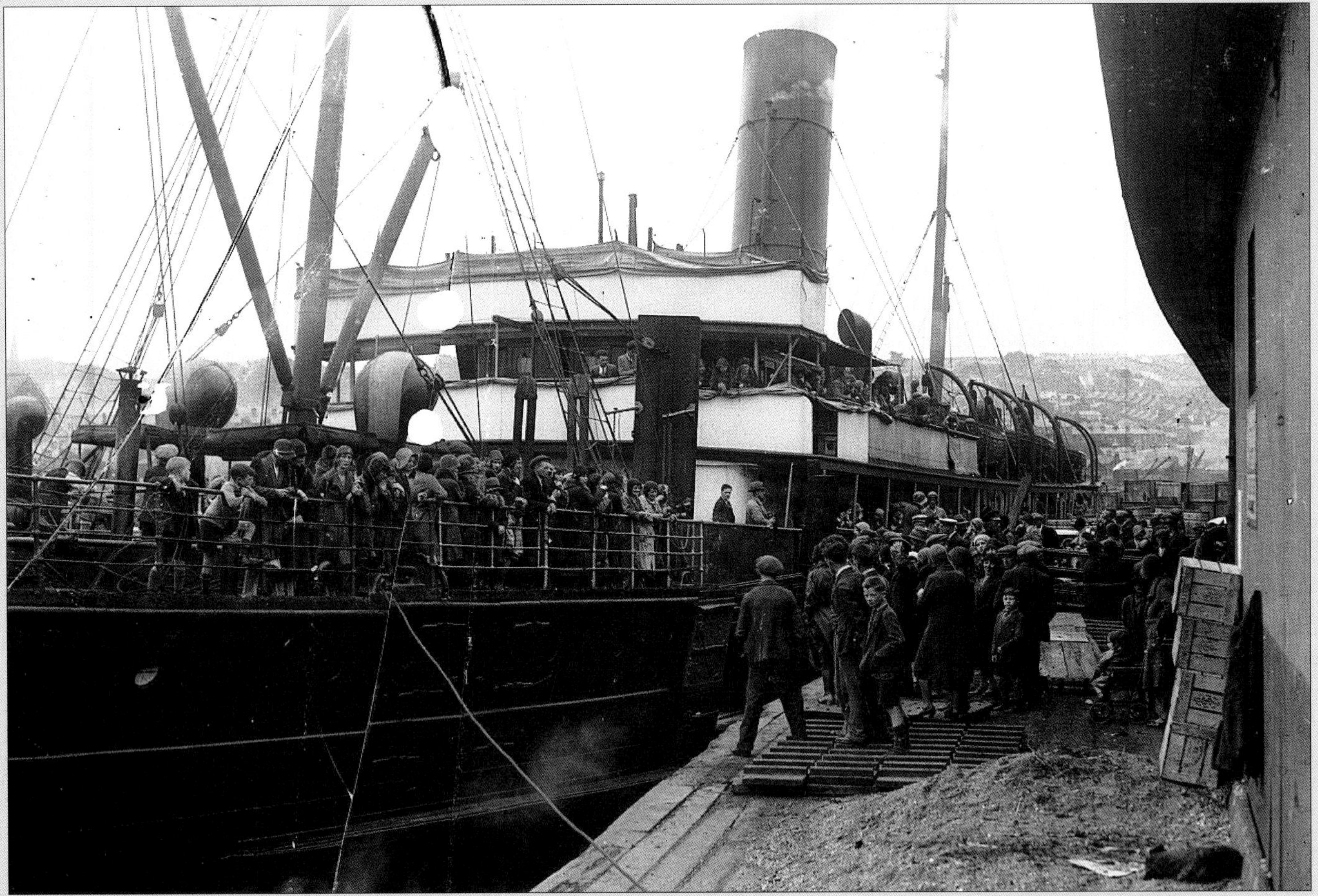

This photograph shows Burns & Laird steamer *Lairdsrose*, with full complement of 'Scotch holidaymakers', returning to Glasgow, just prior to its departure from Derry in August 1931. Passenger service between Derry and Glasgow ended in the autumn of 1966 when the *Lairdsloch* was transferred to the Dublin–Glasgow route. *(POR 16-2, 3 August 1931)*

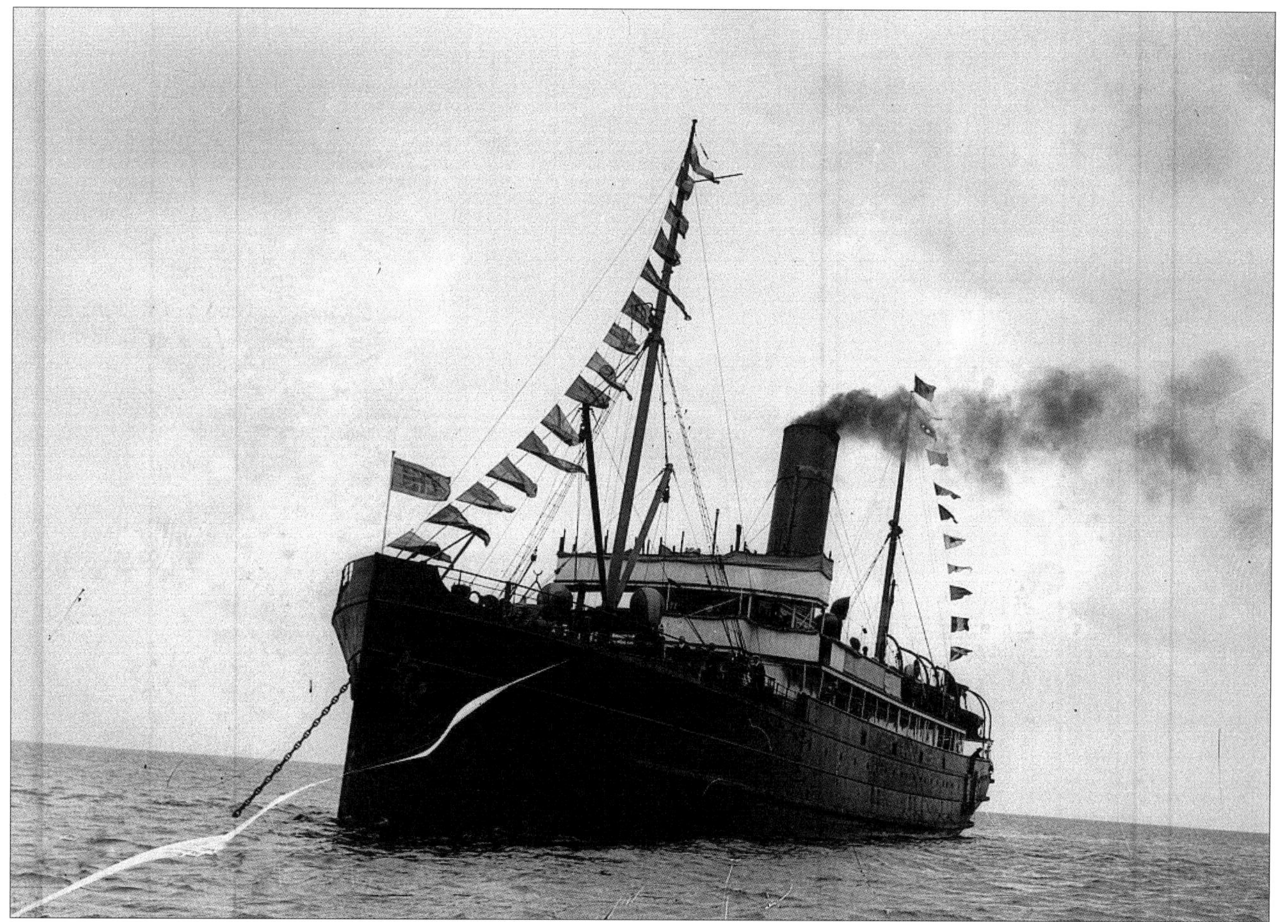

*Lairdsrose* at anchor off the pilot station at Inishowen Head on Thursday 20 July 1933. Members of The Honourable The Irish Society and Commissioners of Derry Port and Harbour Board were making 'their annual inspection of the harbour and the River Foyle' on board Burns & Laird steamer *Lairdsrose*. They anchored off the pilot station at Inishowen Head, which 'marks the entrance to the port, and at low water, ordinary spring tides, there is a depth of over fifty feet from there to Moville, at which place there is safe anchorage for all classes of vessels.' *(POR 15-1, 21 July 1933)*

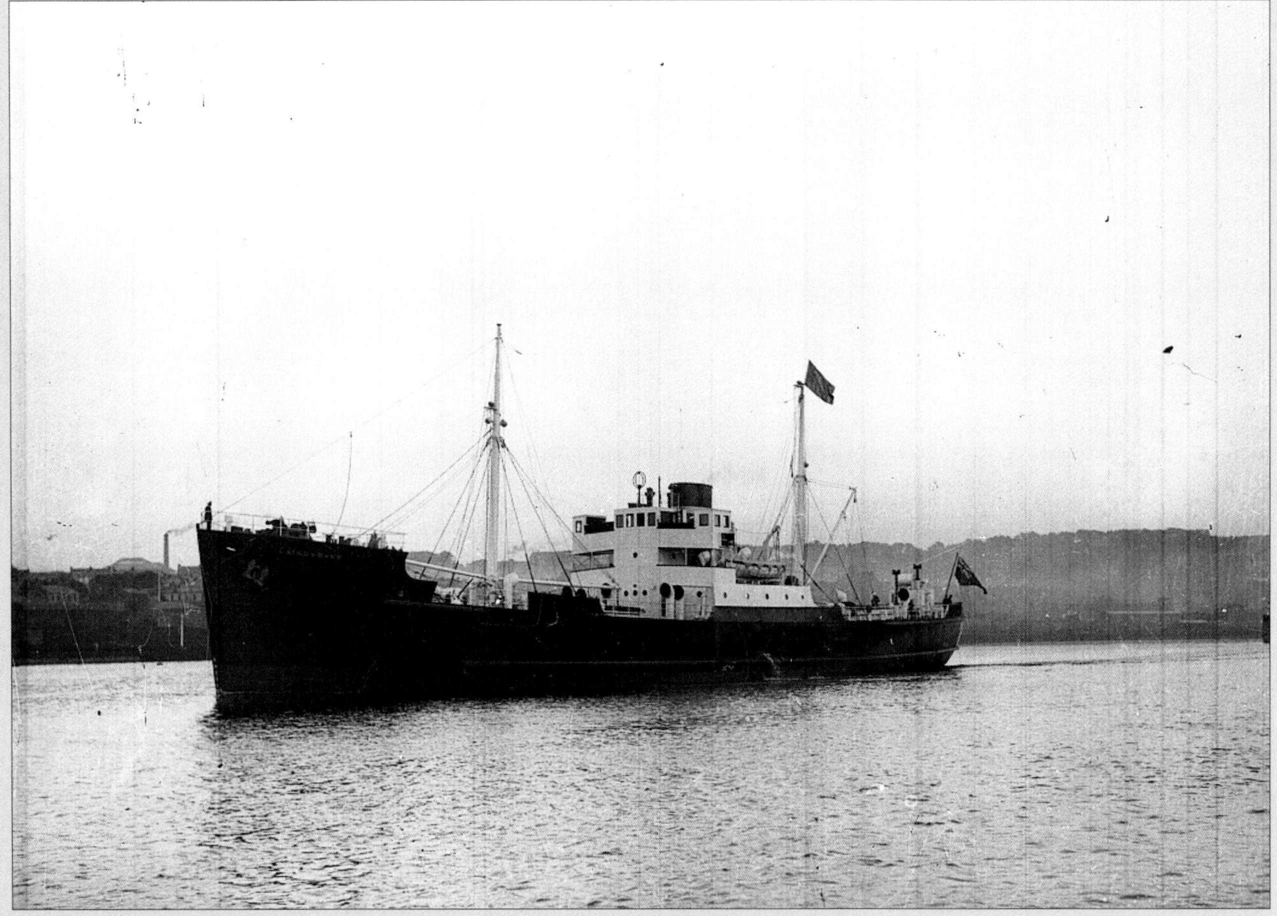

‘The new Burns & Laird Line cattle and general cargo boat, M.V. *Lairdsbank*, leaving Londonderry on her initial sailing to Heysham’ in September 1936. *(POR 16-8, 30 September 1936)*

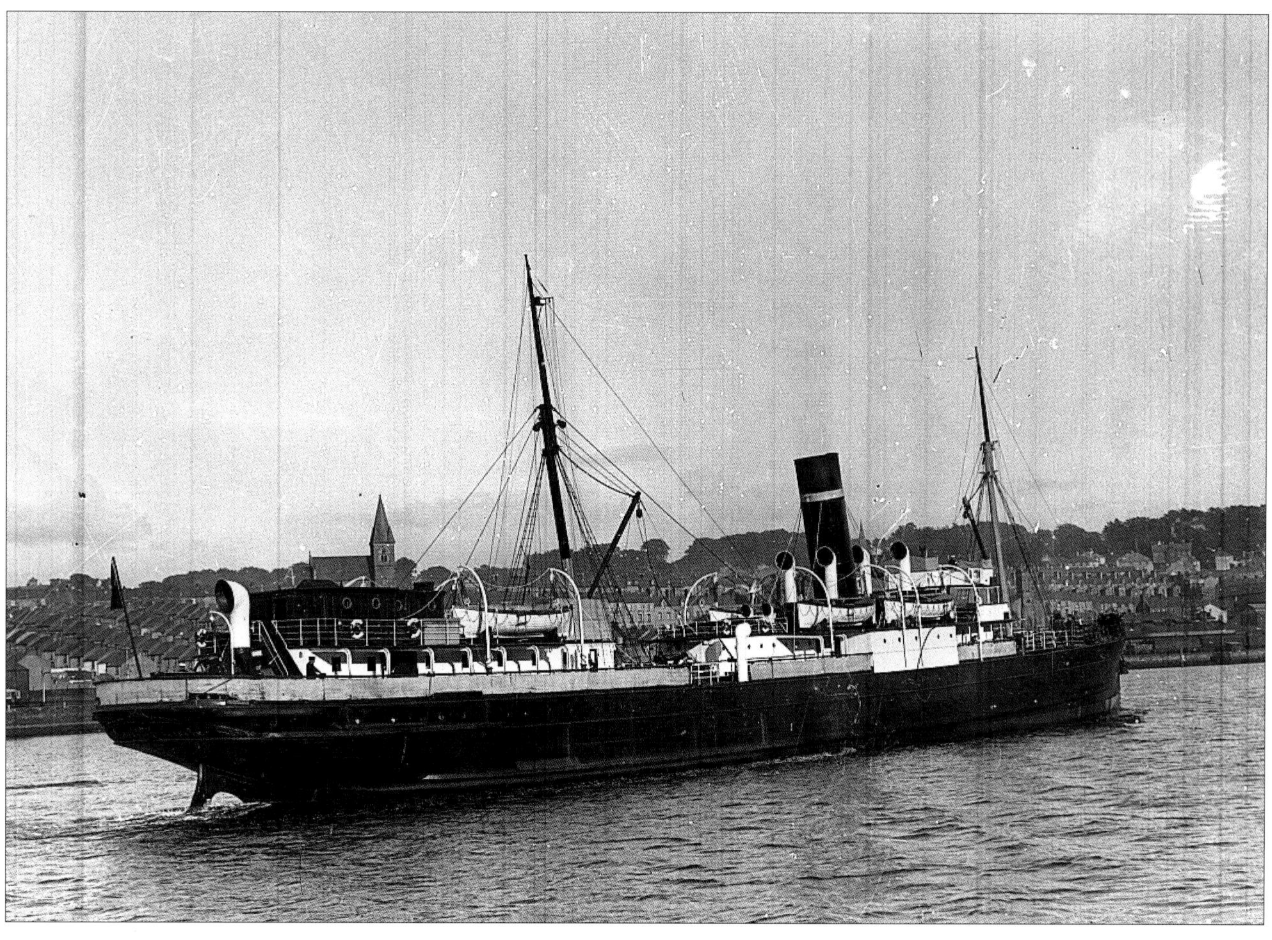

'The S.S. *Lairdsgrove*, which arrived at Derry Quay at eight o'clock and sailed in an hour's time with a full complement of Scottish Fair holidaymakers' on Monday night, 24 July 1939. In total, four thousand Scottish holiday-makers returned to Glasgow from Derry that night on three Burns & Laird vessels. The *Derry Standard* of 26 July 1939 reported that one of the intending passengers – Francis Boyle of Warwick Street, Glasgow – was taken into custody by detectives and 'charged with being in illegal possession of a revolver', which he got in a public house. 'He intended taking it home, as he thought it would be a useful weapon to frighten a "desperado" who was coming about the house.' *(POR 16-11, 26 July 1939)*

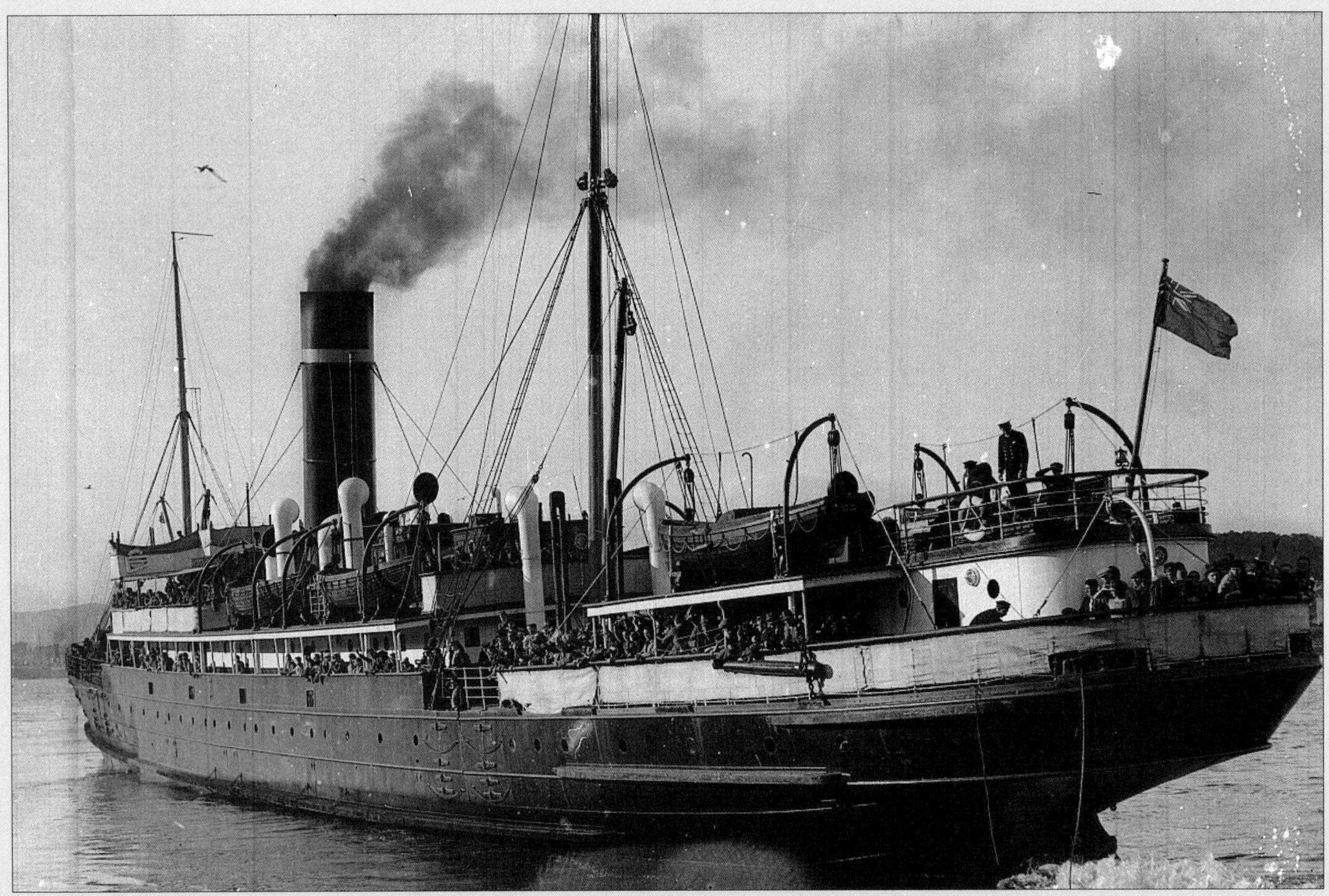

‘The Burns & Laird steamer *Lairdsrose*, one of the three boats leaving Derry on Monday night [24 July 1939] with Scottish Fair holidaymakers returning to Scotland.’ *(POR 16-12, 26 July 1939)*

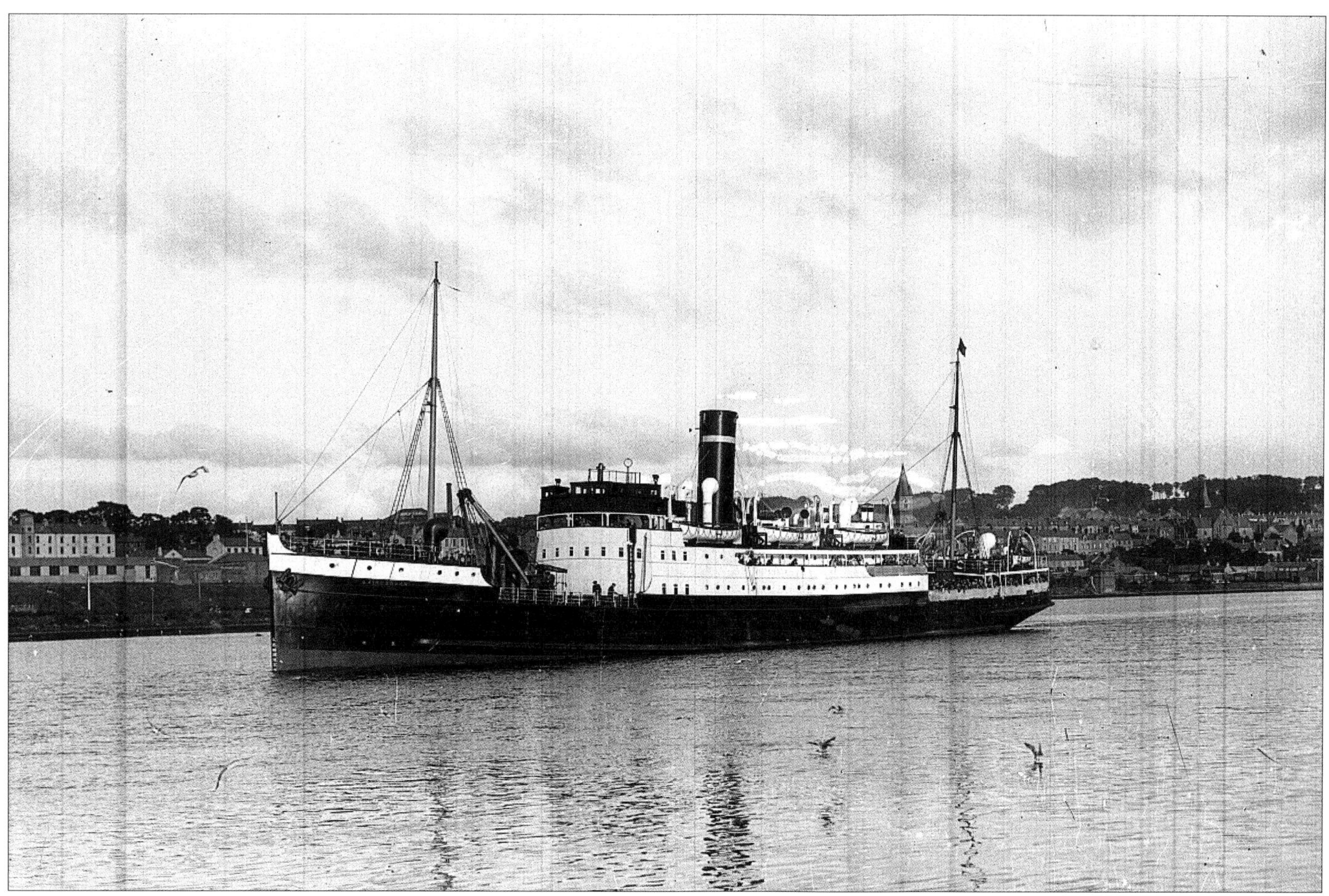

'The Burns & Laird Line steamer *Lairdsburn* leaving Derry Quay' in August 1939. In 1942, under the blackout regulations of the Second World War, the *Lairdsburn* struck and sank a tug, the SS *Romsey*, at Gourock on the Clyde. The tug had slipped moorings and drifted into the shipping channel with minimal lighting. Seventeen of its crew were killed in the accident. *(POR 16-7, 16 August 1939)*

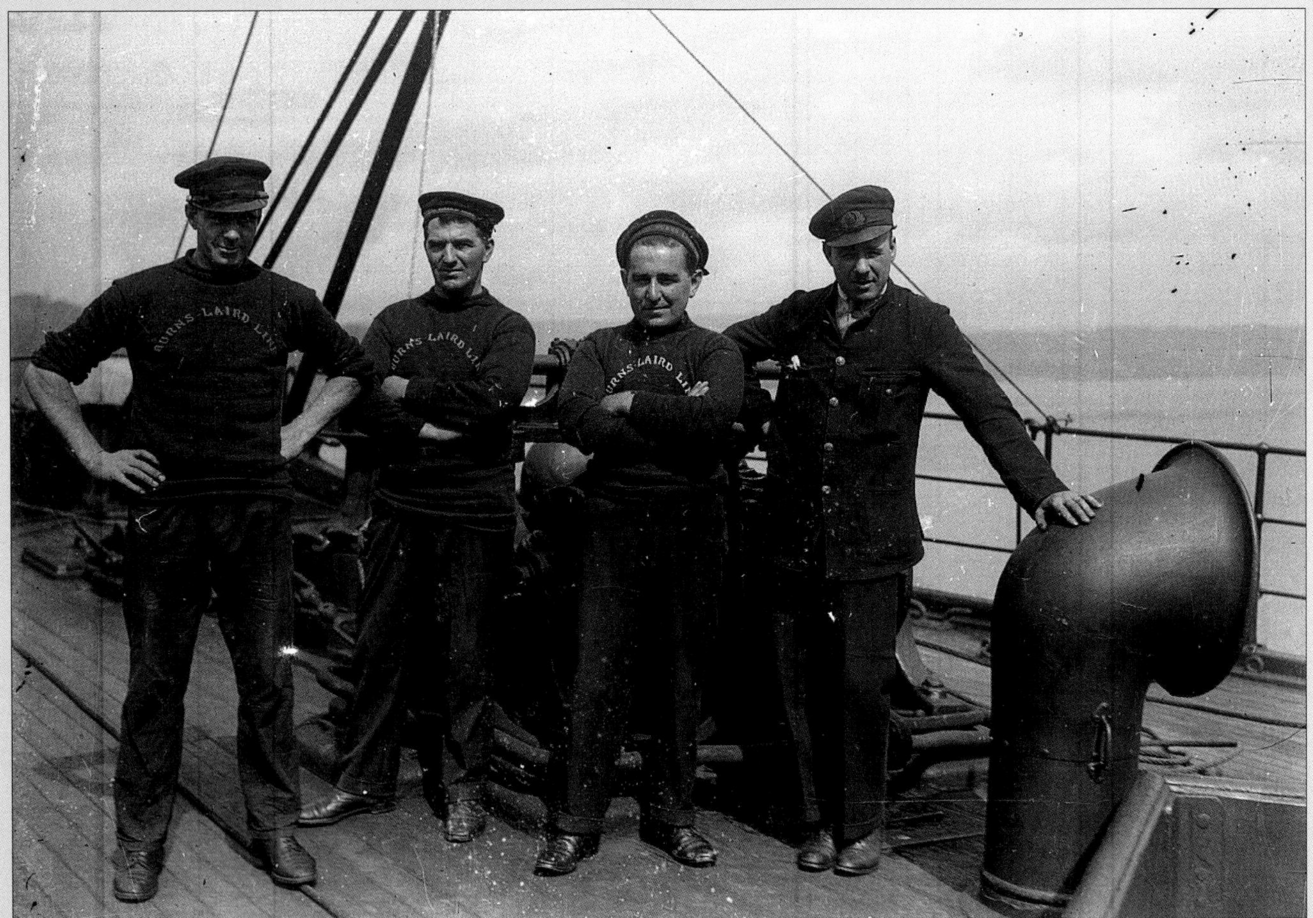


Burns & Laird Line crew members on board ship at Derry Quay. This company had been created by the amalgamation of two Glasgow companies, G&J Burns and Laird Line, in 1922. In 1930 Burns & Laird ships sailed from their Prince's Quay berth, every weekday at 6.30pm, for Glasgow. *(POR 16-4)*

## TRANSATLANTIC EMIGRATION

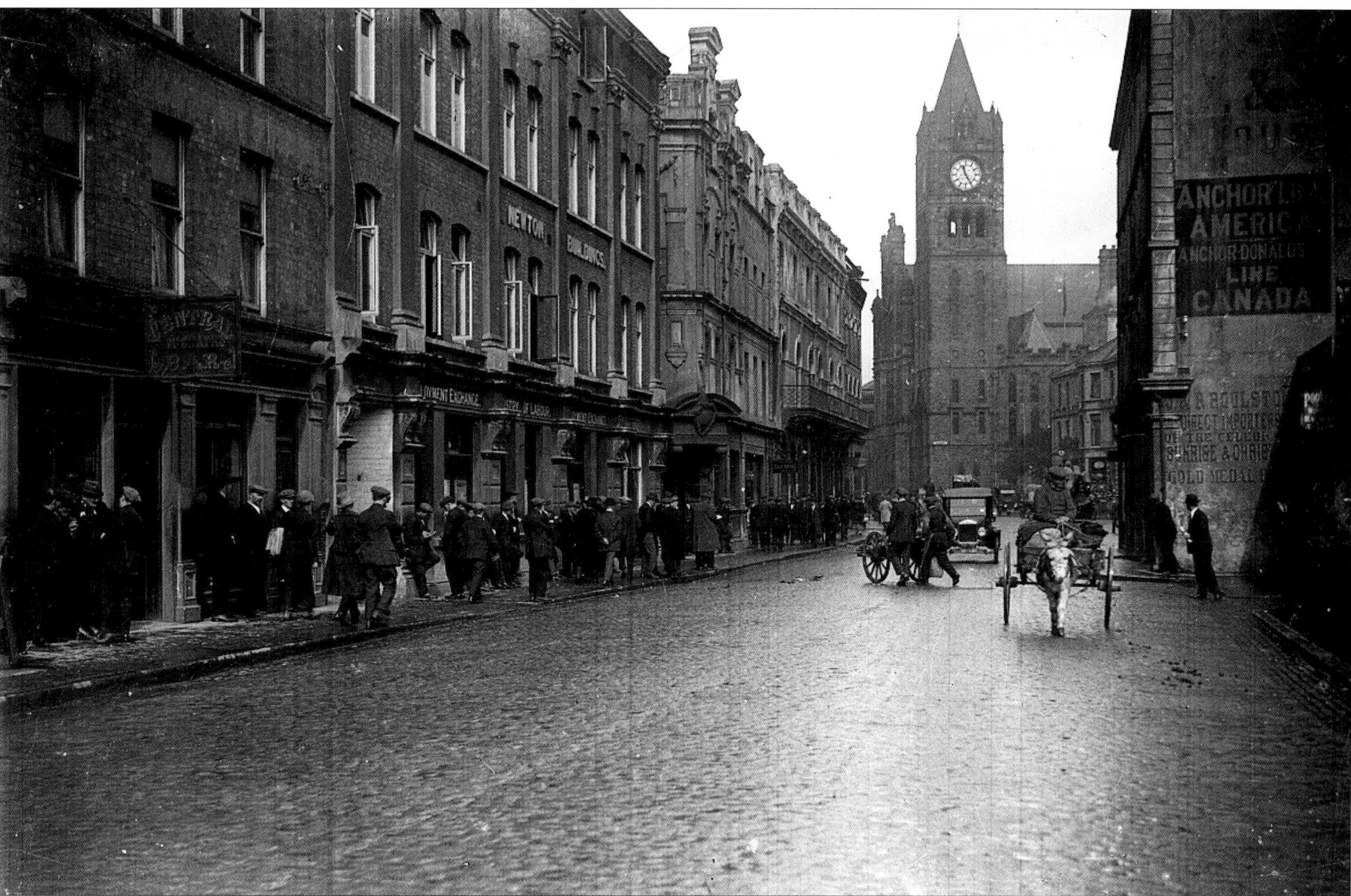


This photograph, dated 28 September 1927, summarises the push and pull factors that spurred young Irishmen and women to emigrate to North America. A large group of unemployed men are gathered outside the Labour Exchange, which was housed in Newton Buildings, Foyle Street and on the opposite side of the street is a billboard proclaiming 'Anchor Line America. Anchor Donaldson Line Canada.' In 1930 the Anchor Line were promoting their 'Londonderry & Belfast to New York' service on their 'New Oil-Burning Liners "California," "Caledonia," "Cameronia," "Tuscania," "Transylvania," – all 16,700 Tons'; and the Anchor–Donaldson Line their 'Londonderry and Belfast to Canada' service which sailed 'in Summer to Quebec and Montreal; in Winter to Halifax and St. John, N.B., or Portland, Maine'. *(DSS 4-3, 28 September 1927)*

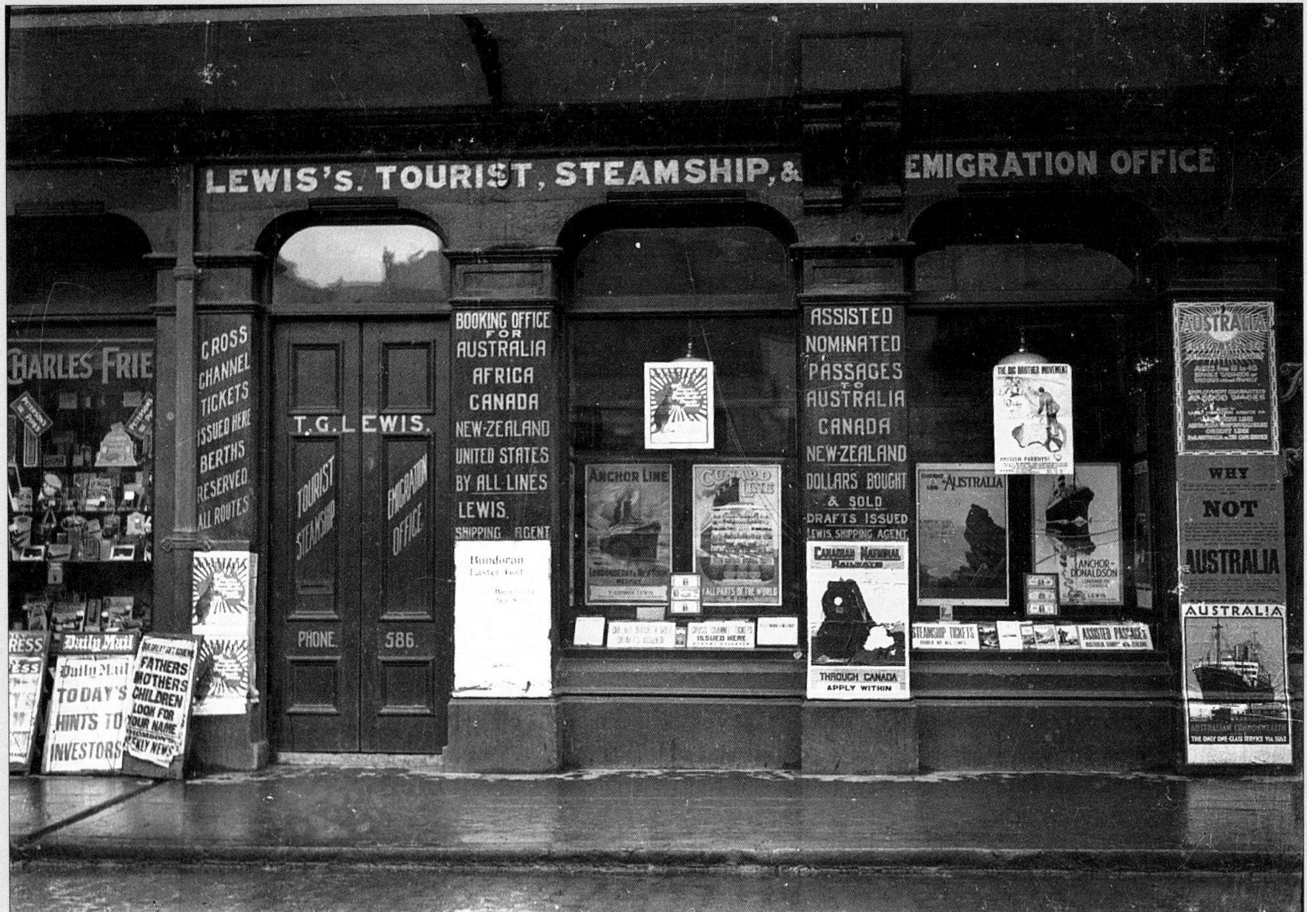


The office of TG Lewis, Emigration Agent of 27 Foyle Street, was located next door to the Labour Exchange. 'Lewis's. Tourist, Steamship & Emigration Office' offered 'Booking Office for Australia, Africa, Canada, New Zealand, United States by All Lines'. Anchor Line and Cunard Line posters are clearly visible on the window. *(S&B 10-4)*

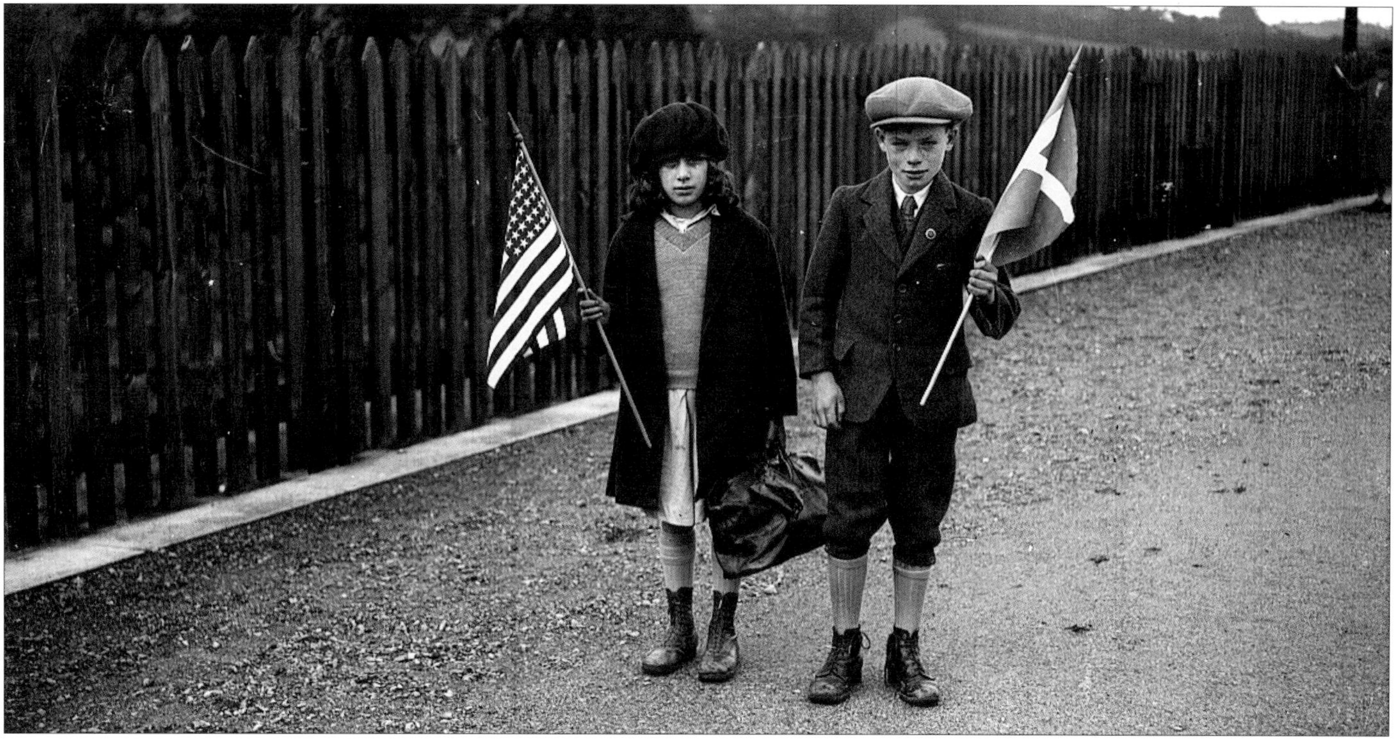

Destination New York. A young boy and girl, holding the US flag, wait at a railway station for a train to take them to Derry to connect with a transatlantic liner. The rail network that converged on Derry drew emigrants from the northern half of Ireland. Hence, the passenger manifests of transatlantic liners departing Derry, listed not only passengers from the city's traditional catchment areas of counties Derry, Donegal and Tyrone, but also emigrants from the other six counties of Ulster and from the northern counties of Connacht and Leinster.

Prior to 1924 emigrants destined for New York had to report to the Immigration Station at Ellis Island. Ellis Island was the gateway for 12 million immigrants to USA between 1892 and 1924, the busiest immigration station in USA. It is estimated that 10.5 million immigrants departed for points across the US from the Central Railroad of New Jersey Terminal located just across a narrow strait from Ellis Island.

With the passing of Immigration Act of 1924 no emigrant could enter the US without a valid immigration visa which was issued by an American consular officer in Ireland. Hence, from 1924, emigrants with valid paperwork didn't need to be inspected at Ellis Island on their way to New York. Today a visit to Ellis Island is seen by many Americans as a pilgrimage to honour immigrant ancestors. *(RLY 3-11)*

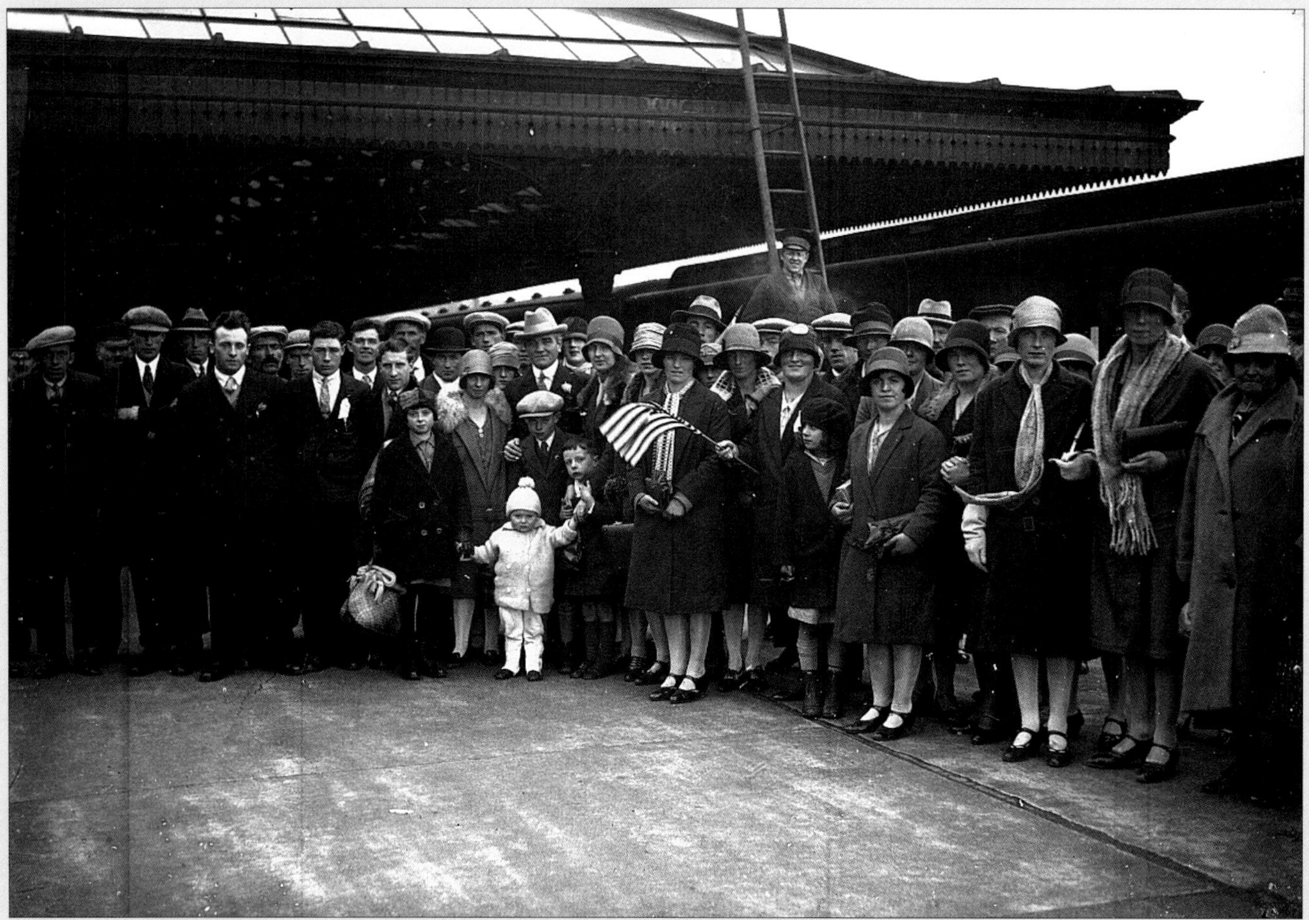

A party of emigrants (which includes the young boy and girl photographed on the previous page) from Cavan/Monaghan arrive at the Great Northern Railway station in Derry accompanied by Mr PJ Smith, Emigration Agent of Castleblayney, County Monaghan, who booked their passage. The Great Northern Railway Company connected Derry, via Strabane and Omagh, to both Belfast and Dublin from its terminus on Foyle Road. Every town and village in Ireland had an emigration agent who took bookings for sailings on transatlantic liners. *(RLY 2-6)*

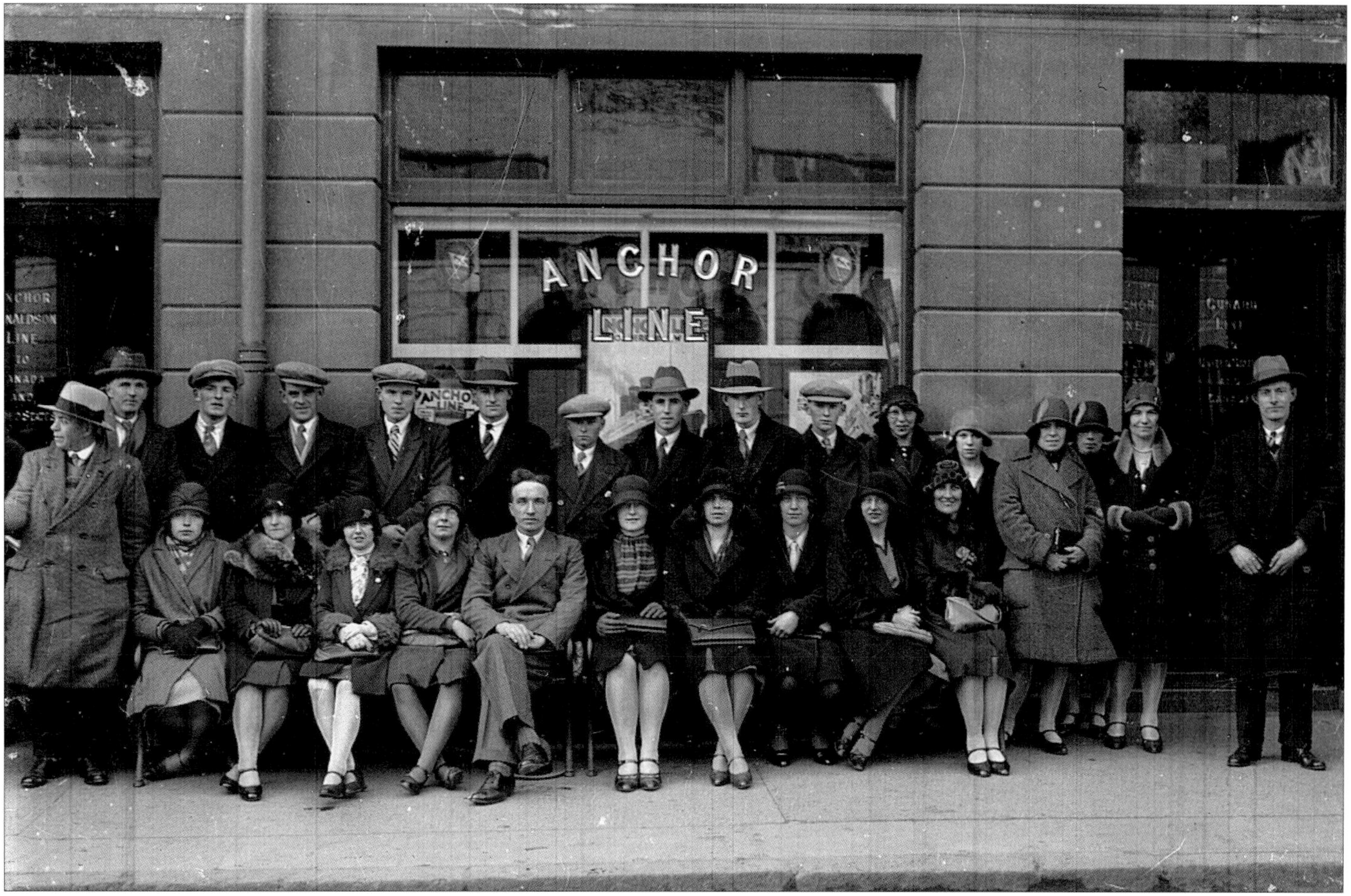

A party of emigrants are photographed outside the Anchor Line office at 111–113 Foyle Street before sailing for America. In 1911 the Anchor Line came under the control of the famous Cunard Line. In 1925 'Anchor, Anchor-Donaldson and Cunard Lines' office in Derry moved from 20 Foyle Street to these new premises at 111–113 Foyle Street, beside Hotel Metropole, at the junction with Bridge Street. For many emigrants the boarding houses and hotels in and around Bridge Street (such as the Metropole and the Canadian Hotel) was where they slept on their arrival, usually by train, in Derry. At the bottom of Bridge Street was the jetty, at the 'Transatlantic Tenders' shed on Abercorn Quay beside the Great Northern Railway station, where the tenders of the Moville Steamship Company and, from 1928, of the Anchor Line took emigrants to Moville to board the liners that left weekly for the USA and Canada. *(POR 14-12)*

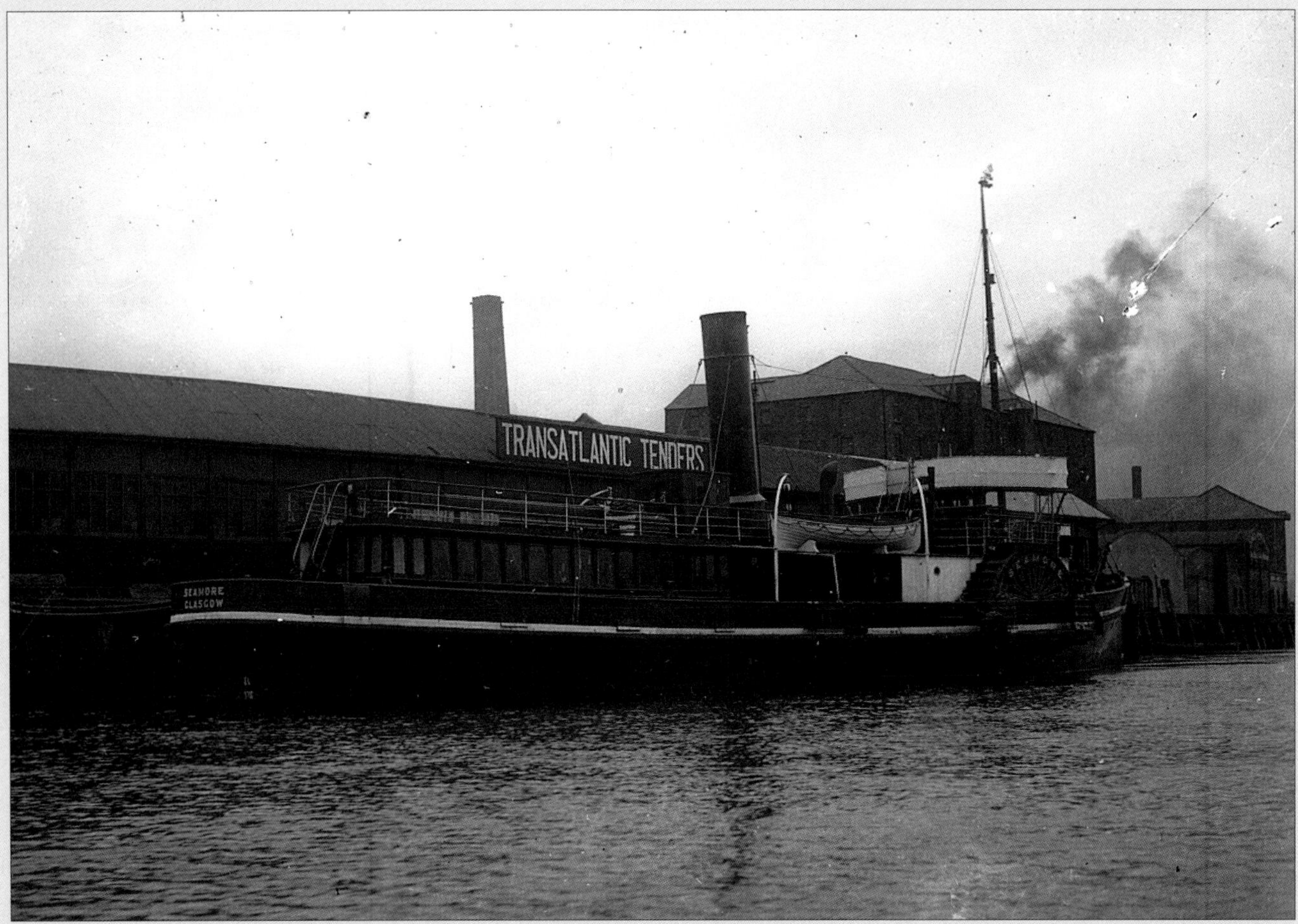


PS *Seamore* berthed at 'Transatlantic Tenders' shed (built 1904 and destroyed by fire in 1961) on Abercorn Quay. The *Seamore* was a typical tug-tender, an iron paddle steamer with one funnel and a small saloon for passengers on her after deck. In May 1928, the Anchor Line had acquired the Clyde Shipping Company's tug-tender *America* and renamed her *Seamore*. Until 1939, when transatlantic liners ceased calling in Lough Foyle, the *Seamore* ferried passengers, emigrants and tourists between Derry and Moville. *(POR 12-15)*

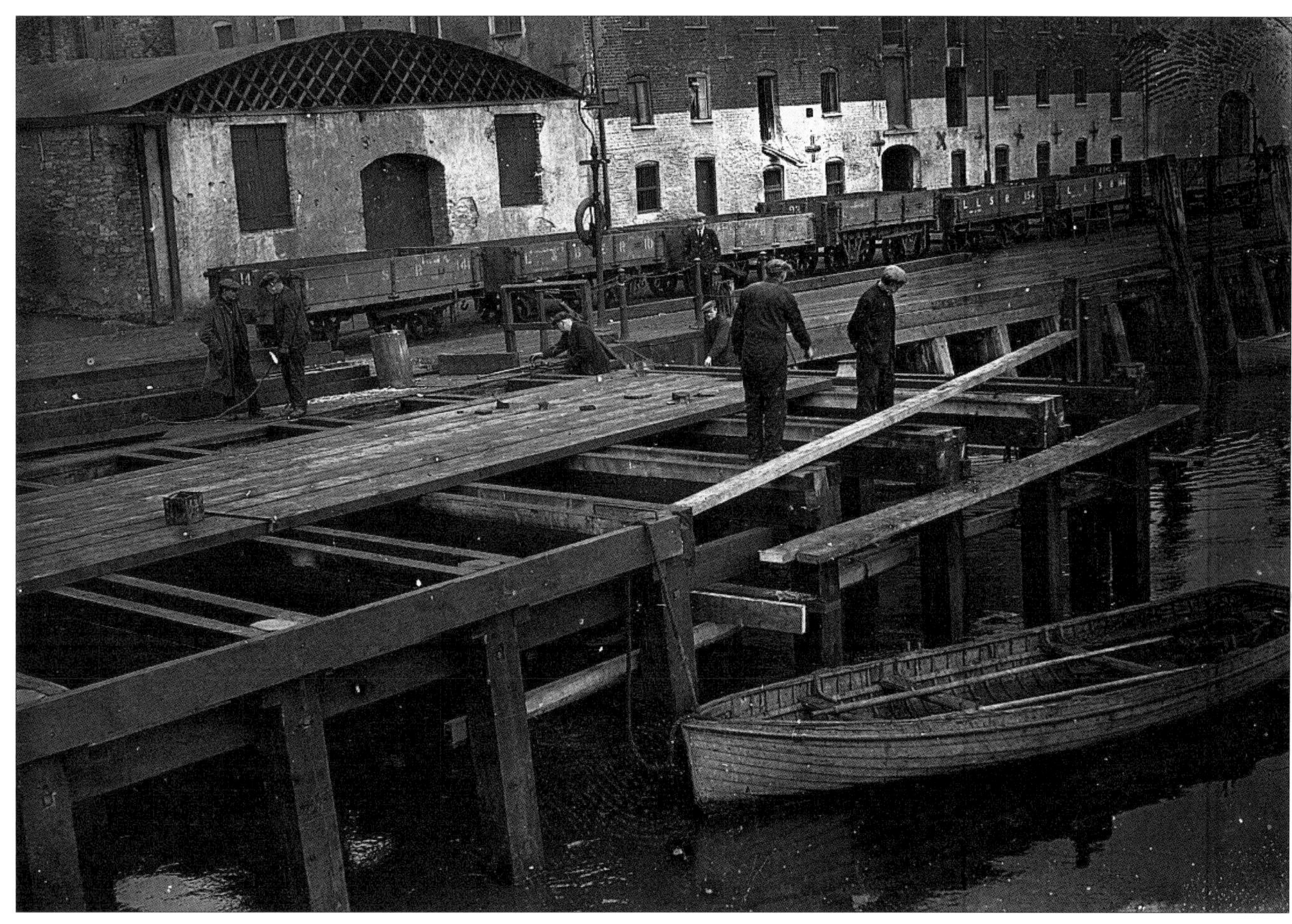

'Extending the Wharf at the Transatlantic Shed, Derry Quay' in March 1930. *(POR 8-6, 5 March 1930)*

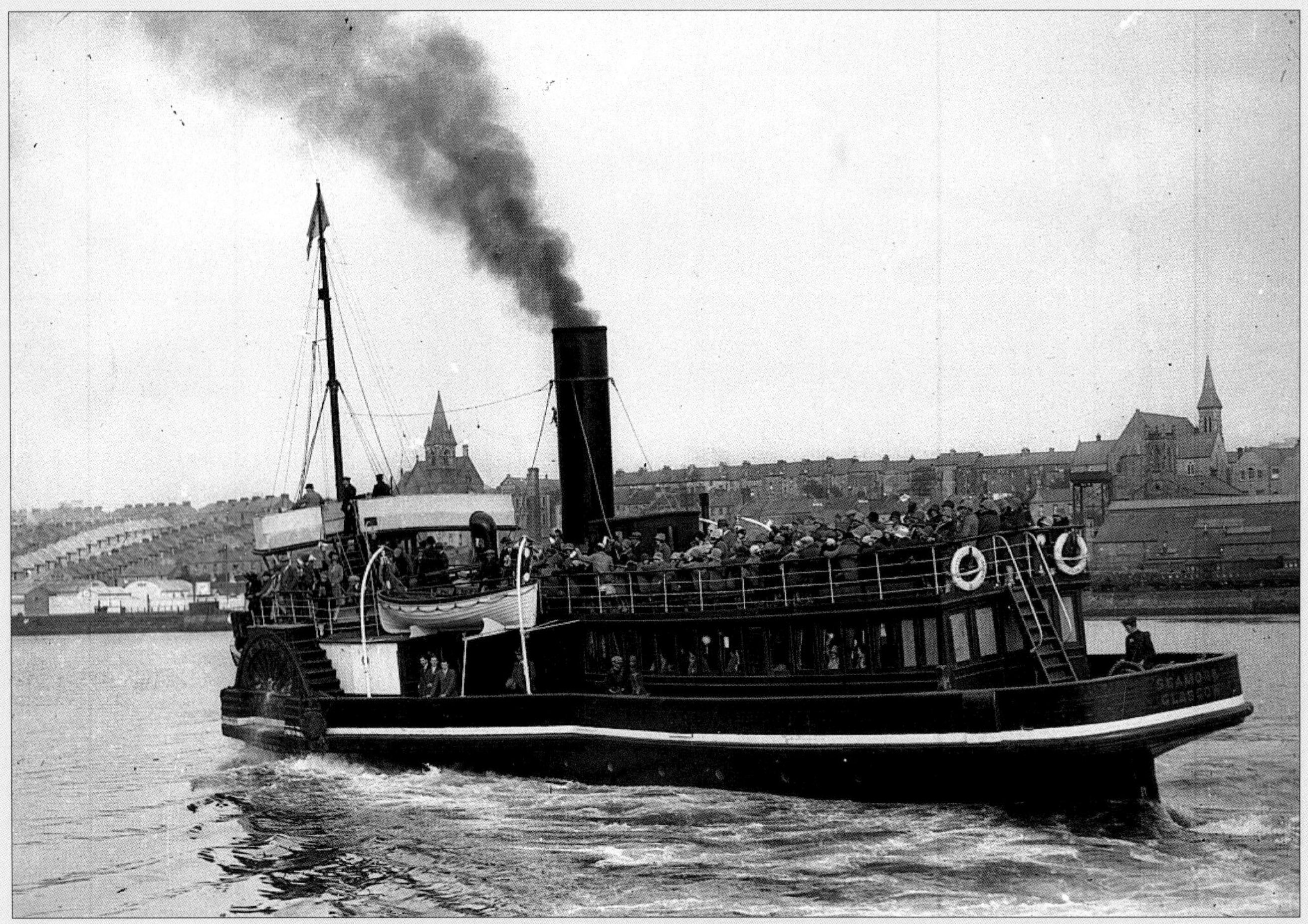

Tender *Seamore* leaves Derry quay with over 300 emigrants on Saturday 6 April 1929.
*(POR 13-3, 8 April 1929)*

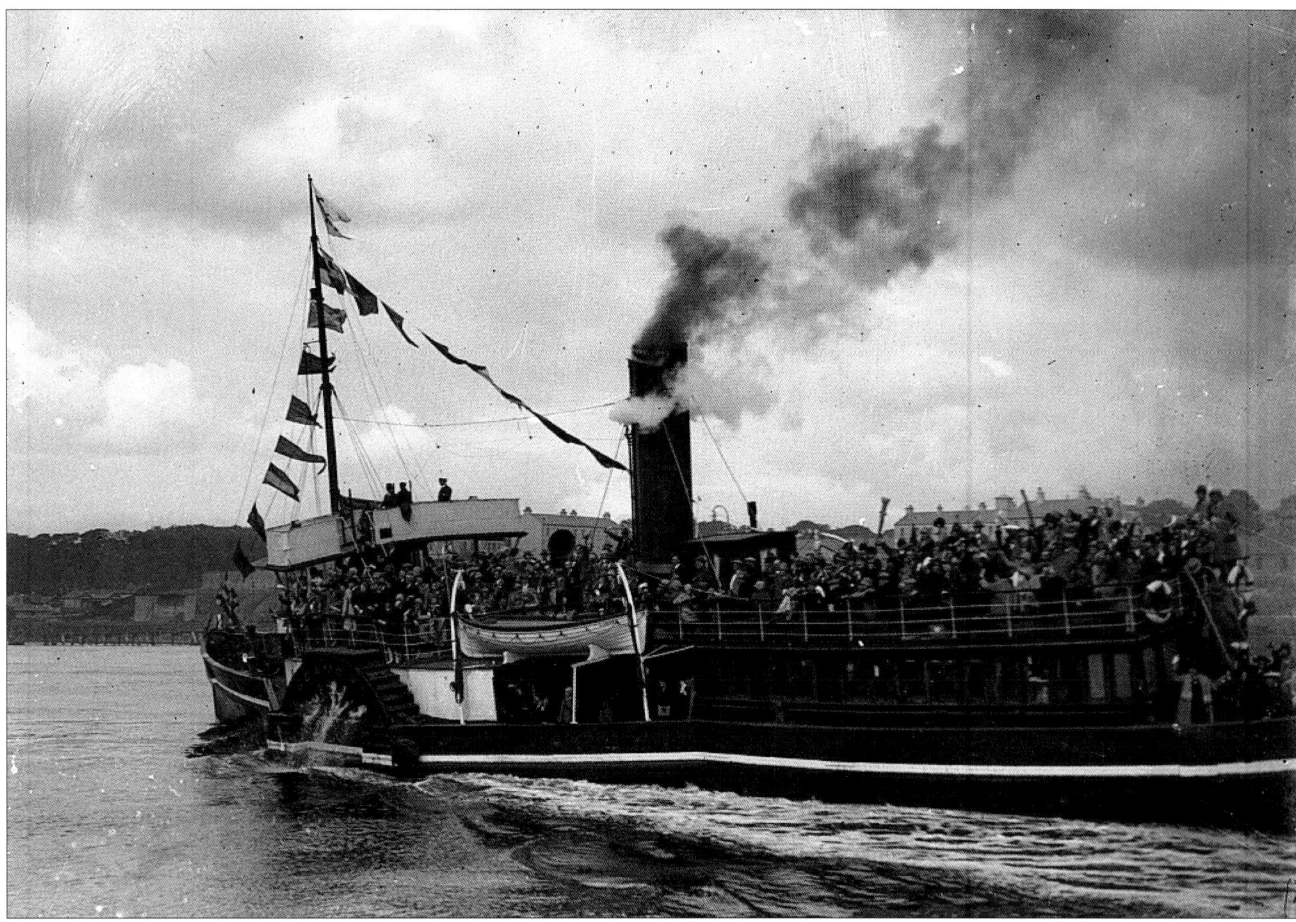

Tender *Seamore* gathers speed as it heads down the Foyle. During the summer, in particular, the *Seamore* would also have been a pleasure cruiser. In addition to day trips to Moville, some 18 miles downstream from Derry, the tender offered excursions to view visiting ships of the Royal Navy and military seaplanes. This photograph of the *Seamore*, with flags flying, may be dated to the summer of 1933 as it was reported in *Derry Standard* of 14 June 1933 that most of the shops and business premises in Derry were flying flags in honour of the Royal Navy's Fifth Flotilla of seven destroyers which arrived in Derry for a week's visit on 11 June 1933 and of the much-anticipated arrival of General Balbo's 'Italian Transatlantic Air Armada' which eventually landed in Derry on 2 July 1933. *(POR 12-5)*

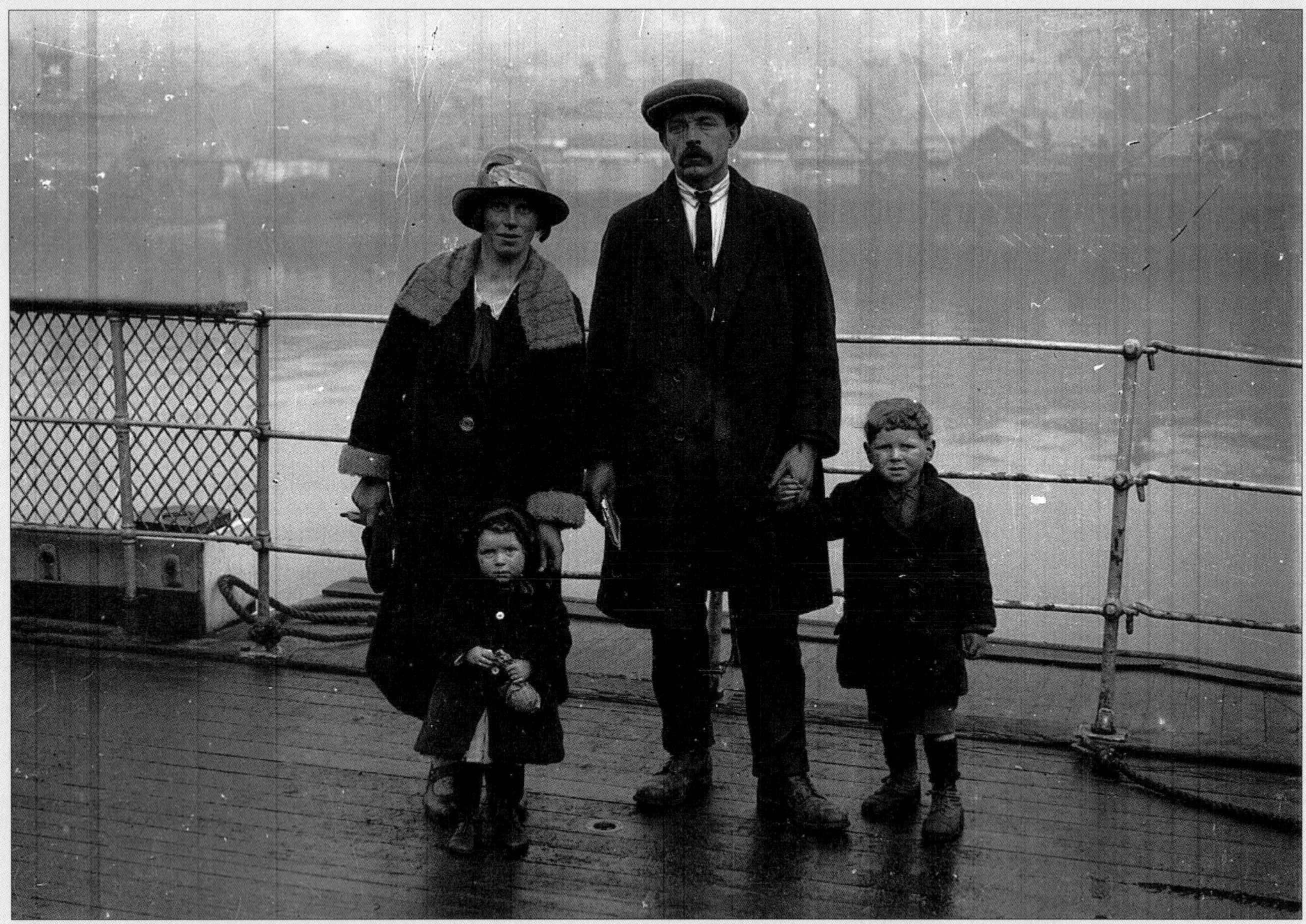

Family portrait on board tender *Seamore* of father, mother and their two young children just before setting off down the river for Moville. The *Derry Standard* photographer appears to have taken many photographs like this one, of departing families. These scenes would probably have been of poignant interest to the readers of the newspaper. *(POR 14-11)*

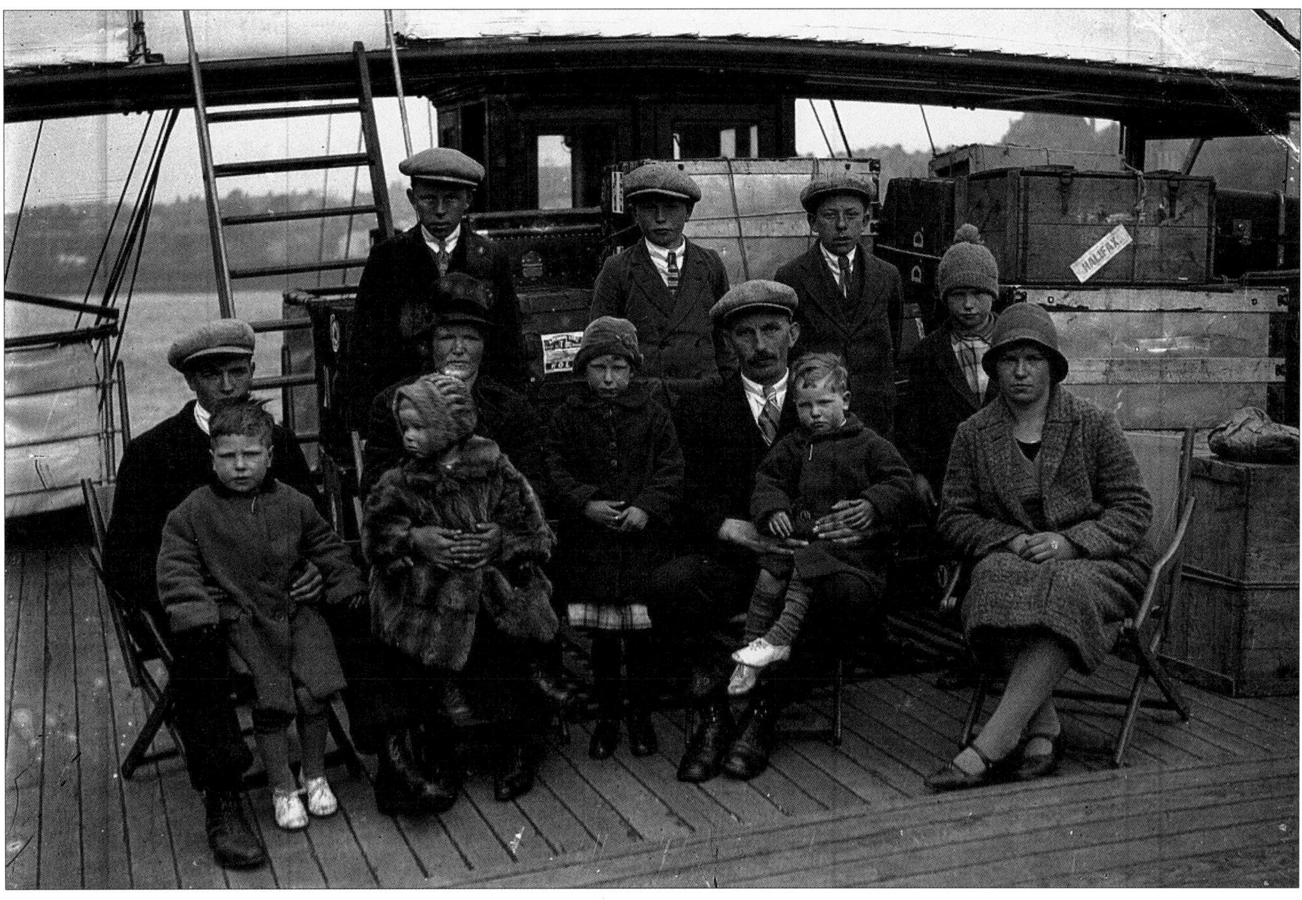


Family portrait of Monteith family of Castlederg, County Tyrone on board tender *Seamore* on Saturday 13 April 1929 as they head for Moville to connect with Anchor Line ship *California*, destined for Pier 21 in Halifax, Nova Scotia, Canada. Passenger manifests record that Joseph Monteith, age 32 and Rebecca Monteith, age 36 and children William (16), George (14), Joseph (12), Elizabeth (7), Ruby (6), Robert (4), Sarah (3) and Thomas Monteith (3) departed Derry for Halifax. Pictured with them, seated to the extreme left and right, are William Corry (16) and Mary Corry (14), relatives of Rebecca Monteith (neé Corry). The year before, on 8 March 1928, Pier 21, a new integrated ocean liner and railway facility, had opened in Halifax. Special immigrant passenger trains would take passengers from Pier 21 to towns across Canada. Between 1928 and 1971 Pier 21, Halifax, was the gateway to Canada for one million immigrants. Today Pier 21 hosts the Canadian Museum of Immigration, Atlantic Canada's only national museum. *(POR 14-9, 15 April 1929)*

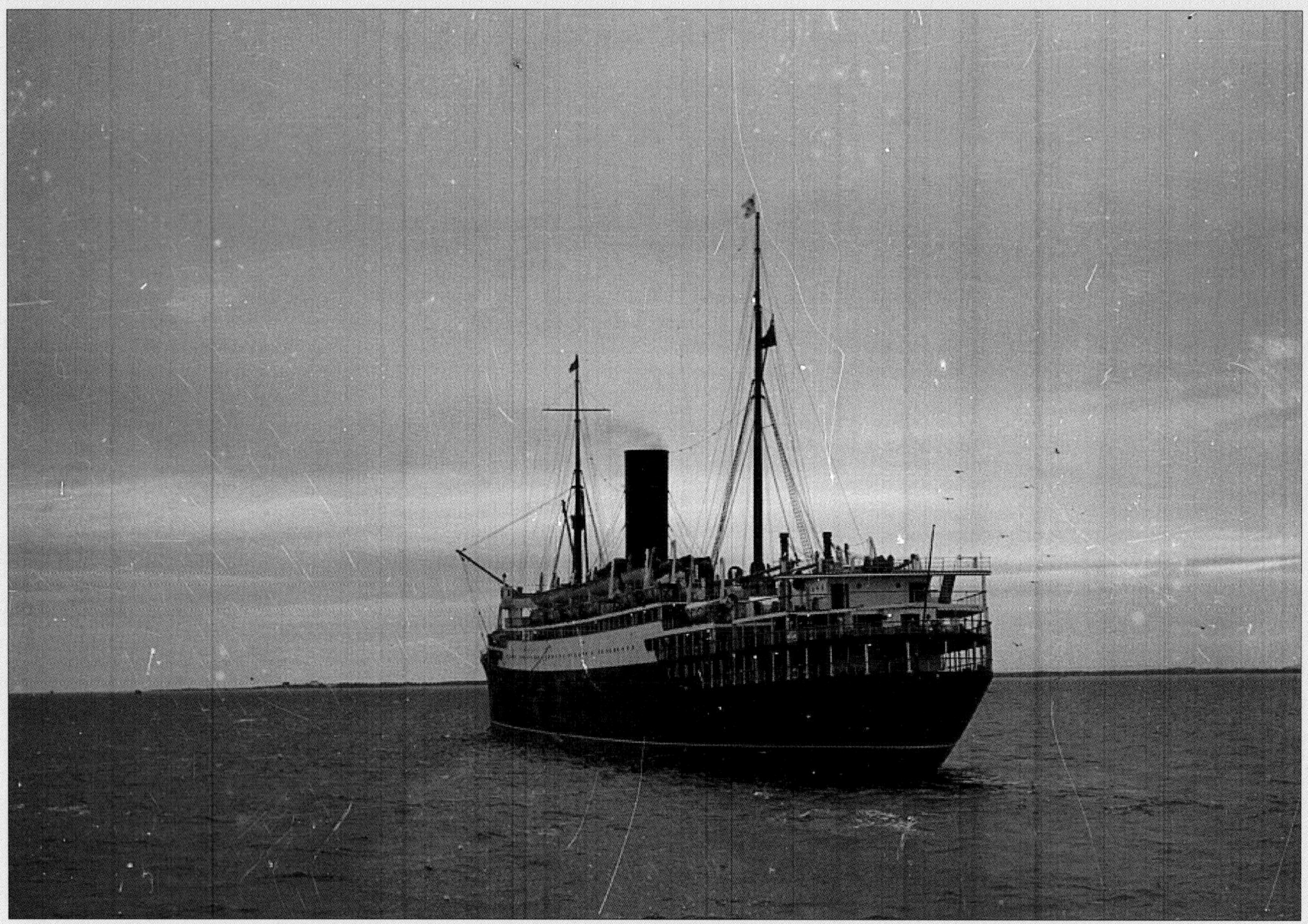

The Anchor liner *Cameronia* at anchor in Moville Bay on Saturday 10 September 1938. During the Second World War the *Cameronia* was requisitioned as a troopship and survived a torpedo attack. *(POR 15-6, 12 September 1938)*

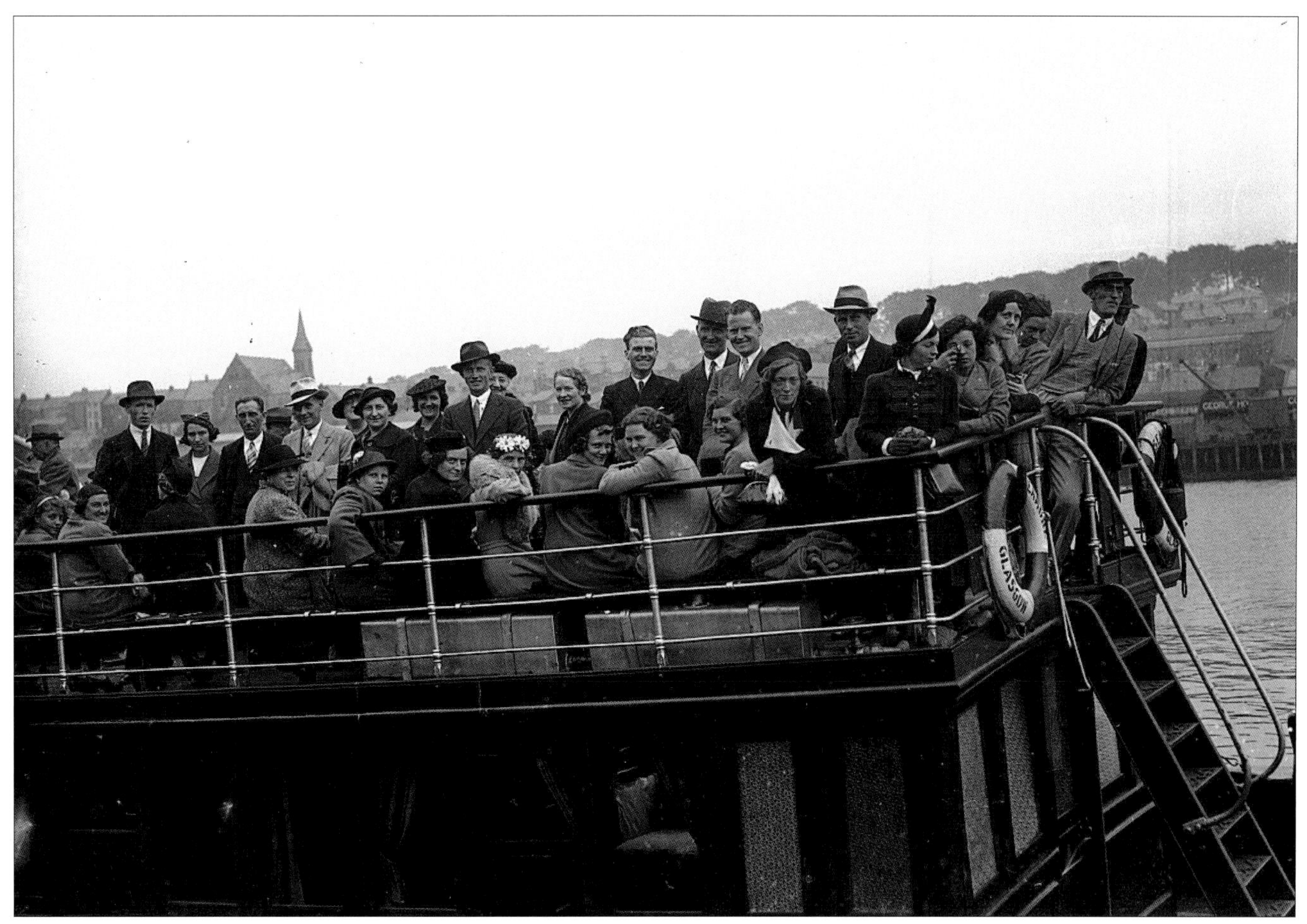

Tender *Seamore* prepares to leave Derry Quay on Saturday 10 September 1938 to connect with Anchor liner *Cameronia*. *(POR 13-6, 12 September 1938)*

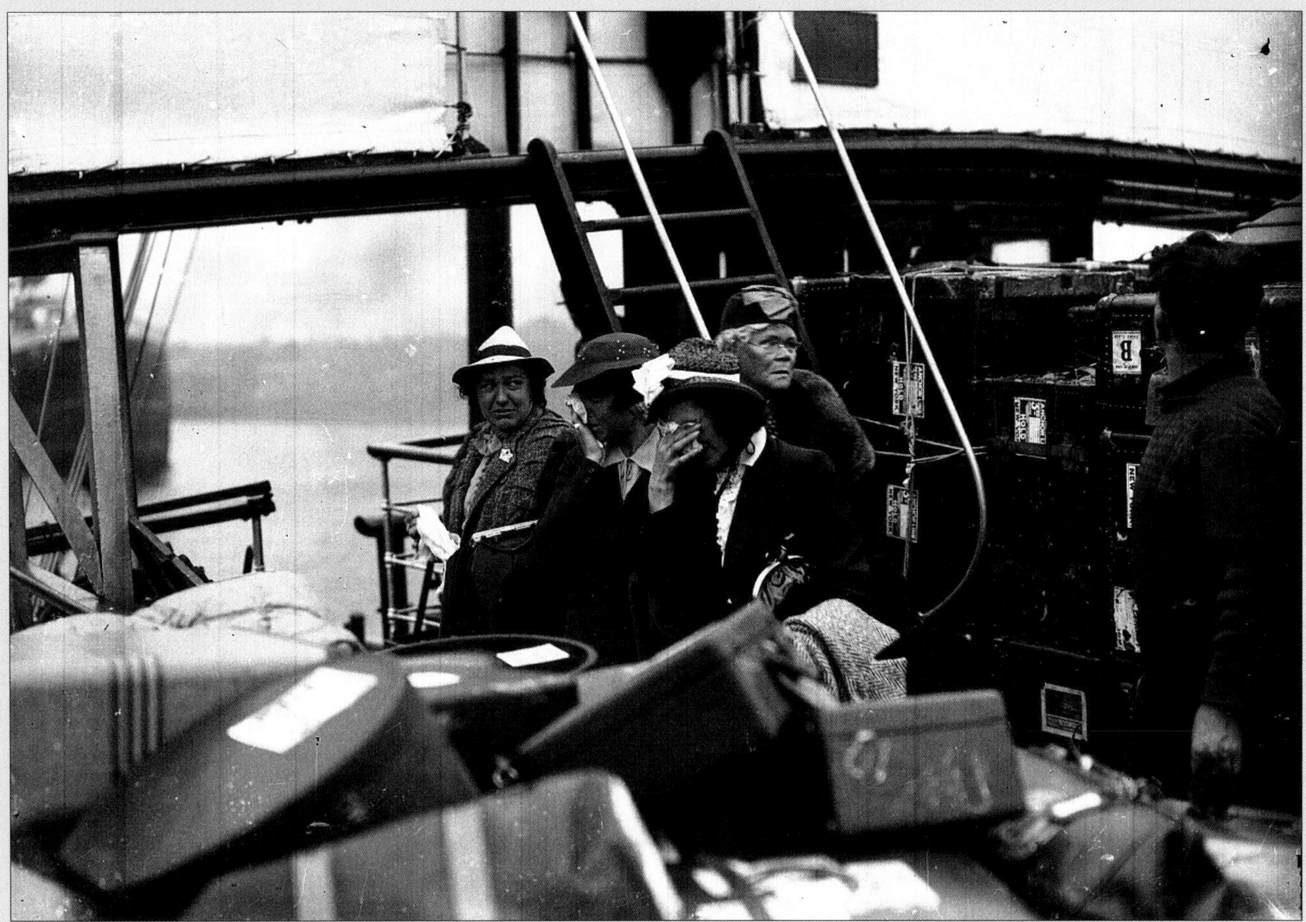

Some passengers were overcome with grief as tender *Seamore* moves off from Derry Quay on Saturday 10 September 1938. This photograph gives a good idea of the volume of luggage transported as well as passengers. *(POR 14-10, 12 September 1938)*

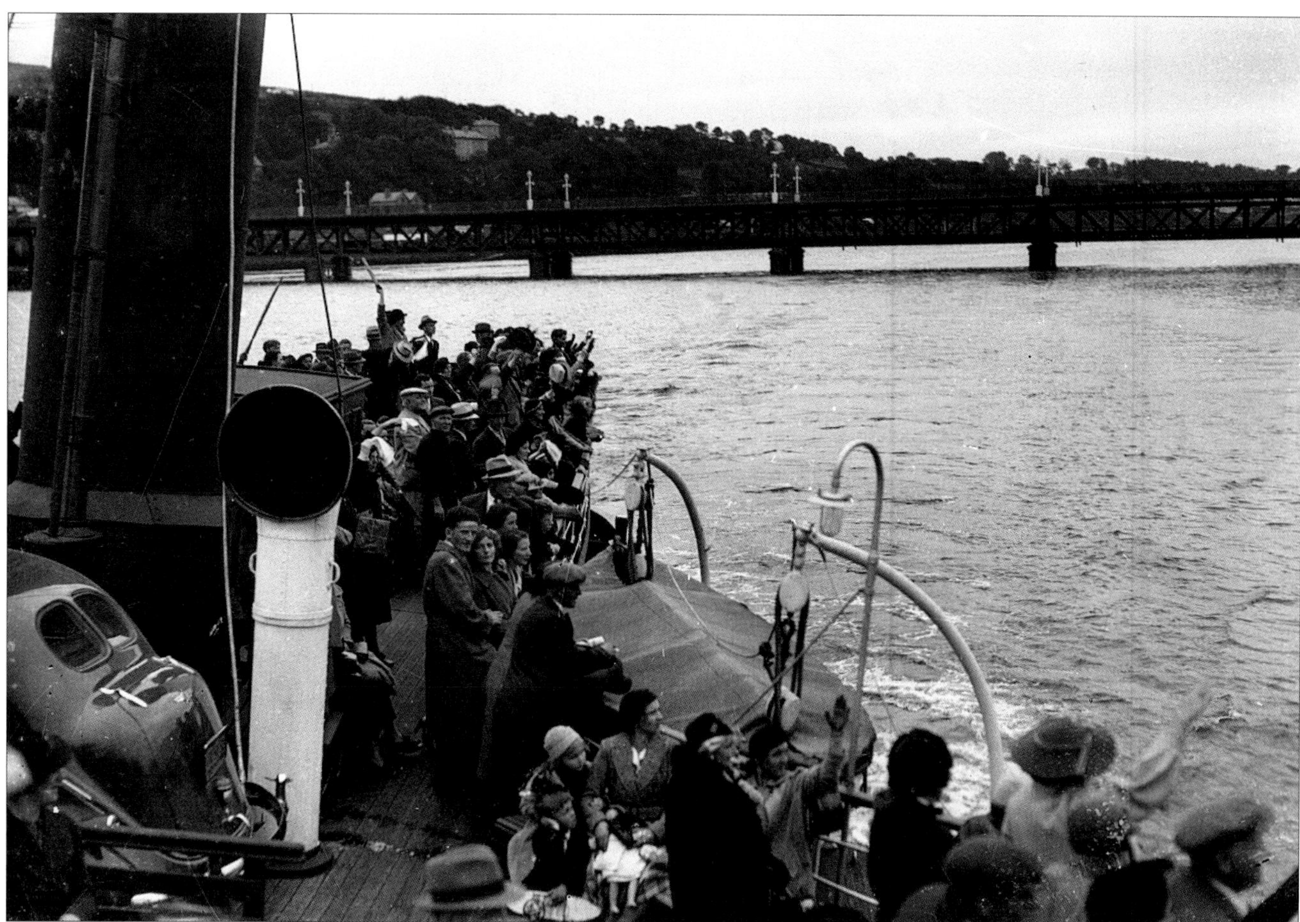

Some of the passengers wave farewell as the *Seamore* moves off from Derry Quay on Saturday 10 September 1938. Note the car on the lower left of the picture. Vehicles must have been difficult to manoeuvre between vessels at sea. *(POR 13-2, 12 September 1938)*

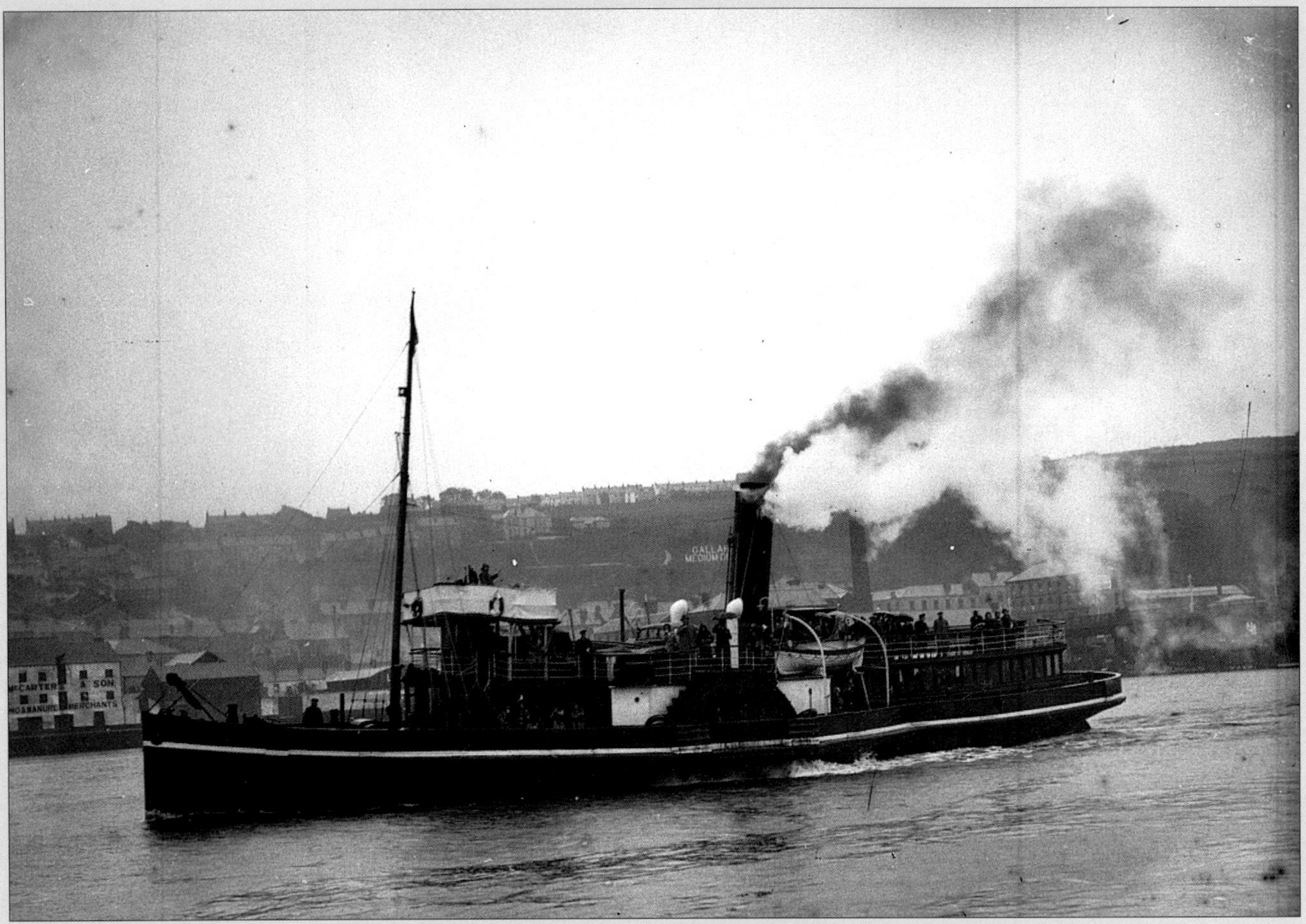

Another view of the *Seamore* leaving Derry Quay, this time on Saturday 8 October 1938, again to connect with Anchor liner *Cameronia*.
*(POR 12-9, 10 October 1938)*

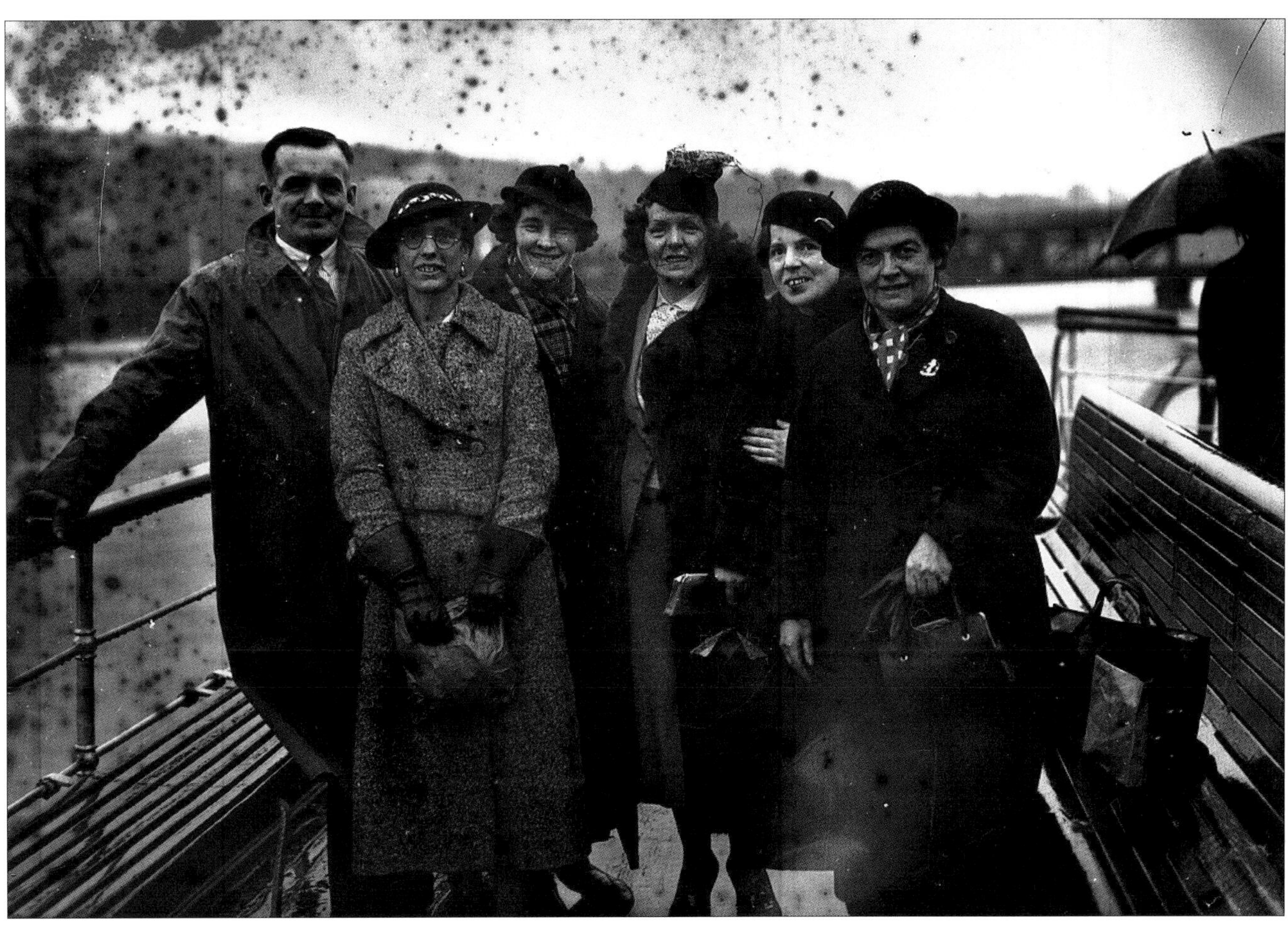

A happy group on the deck of tender *Seamore* on Saturday 8 October 1938 prior to boarding the *Cameronia*. *(POR 14-8, 10 October 1938)*

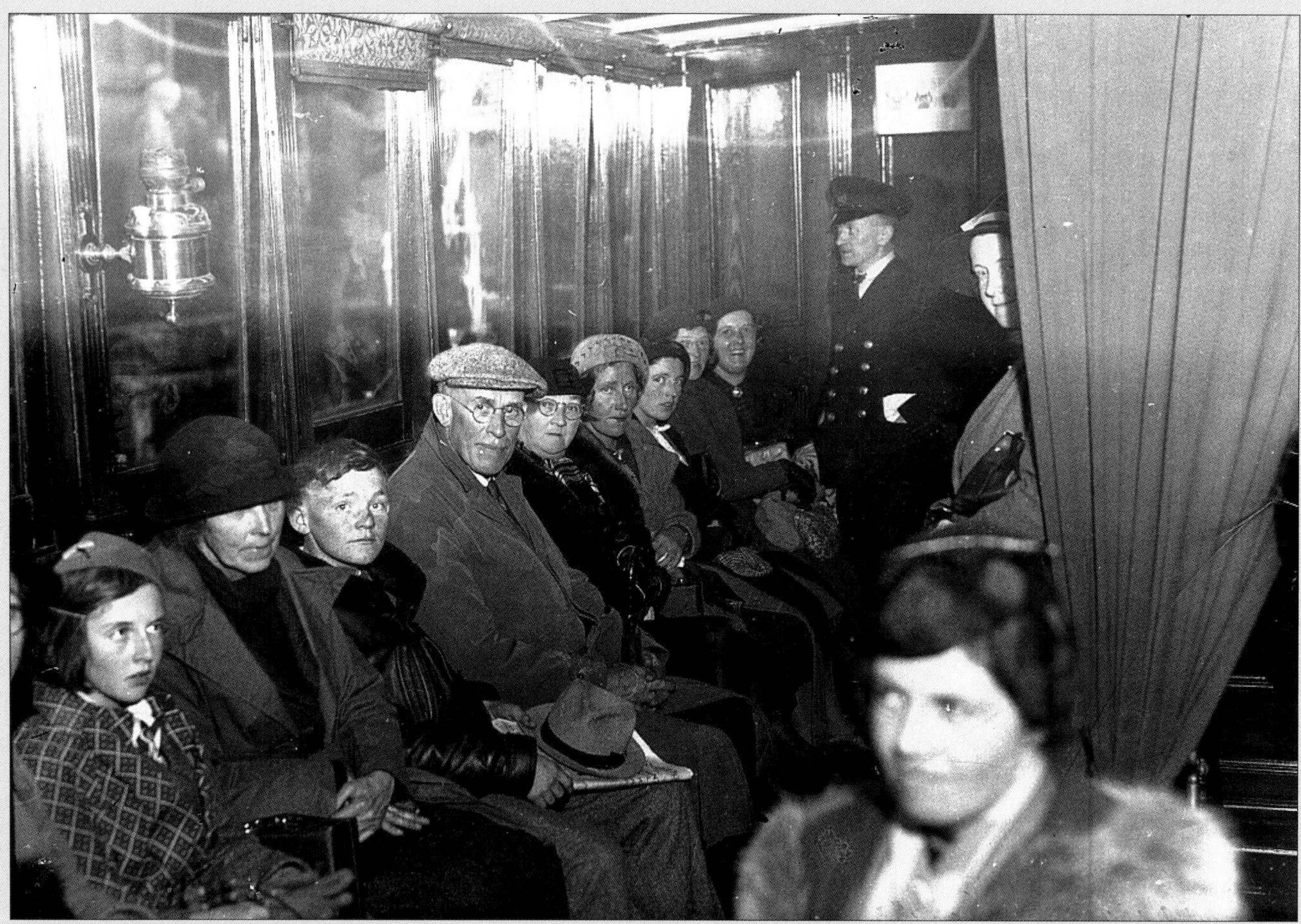

Some of the passengers photographed in the saloon on board the *Seamore* on Saturday 8 October 1938. Note the cramped conditions on the tender, compared with more spacious accommodation on the ocean liners. *(POR 12-10, 10 October 1938)*

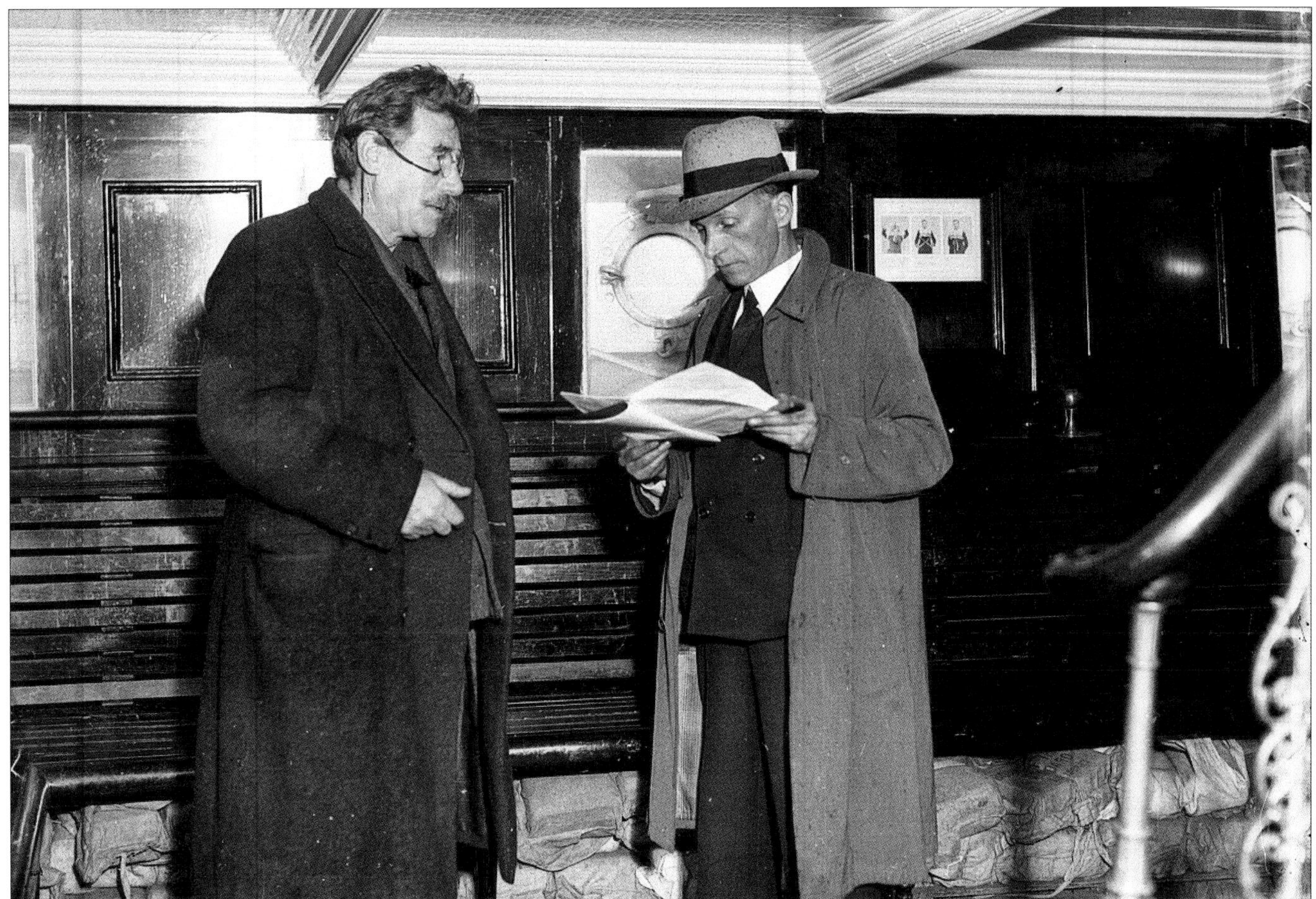

Seamus MacManus (left), playwright and actor, who is returning to New York, is photographed on Saturday 8 October 1938 with Mr S McClay, manager of Londonderry office of the Anchor Line, inside the saloon of the Anchor Line tender *Seamore*. Passenger manifests record that Seamus MacManus, age 69, sailed from Derry, on Saturday 8 October 1938, for New York on the Anchor Line ship *Cameronia*. Seamus MacManus, who was born at Mountcharles (near Donegal town) was considered 'by many to be the last great *seanchaí* or storyteller of the ancient oral tradition. He wrote down and interpreted traditional stories so that they would not be lost to future generations.' He believed that 'tales were made not for reading, but for telling. They were made and told for the passing of long nights, for the shortening of weary journeys, for entertaining of traveler-guests, for brightening of cabin hearths.' (*POR 14-15, 10 October 1938)*

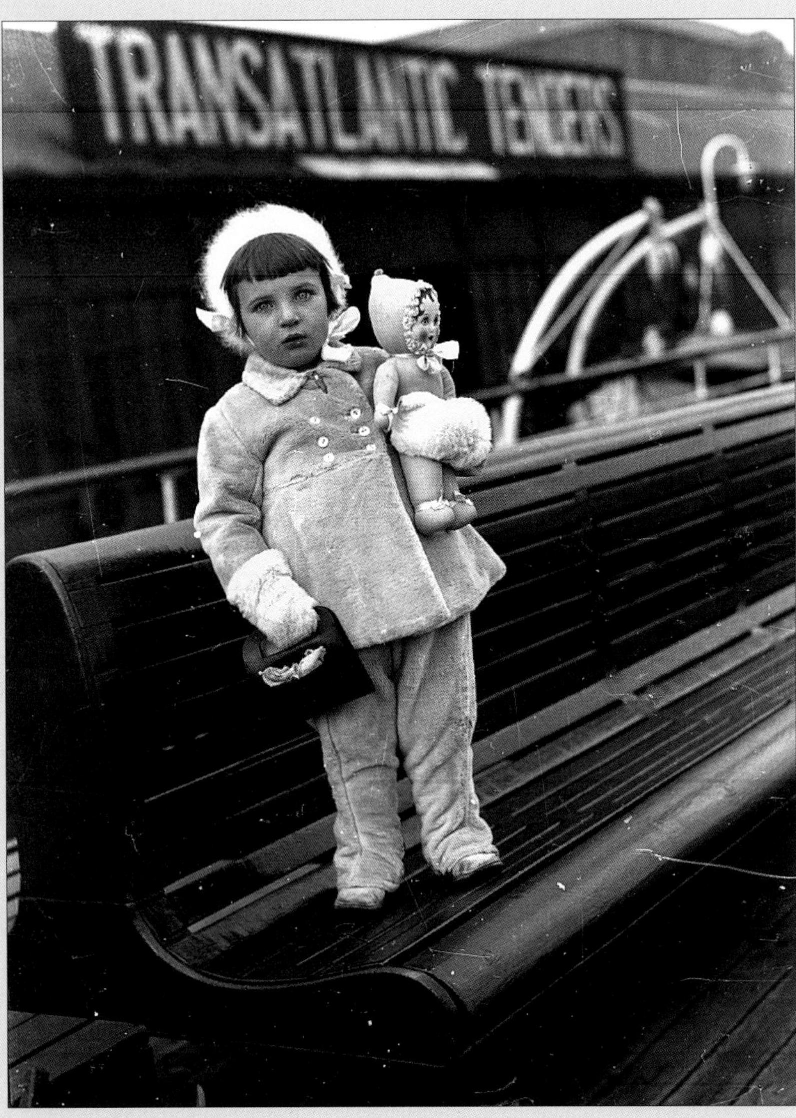


Joan Markey, aged two years, clutching a doll in one hand and a handbag in the other, is photographed on tender *Seamore* prior to departing Derry quay on Saturday 22 October 1938 to connect with the *Caledonia* and onwards to New York. She was travelling alone to join her parents in Brooklyn. It would appear that unaccompanied children were be taken care of by other female passengers on board. Joan had been staying in Derry with her aunt, Grace Duffy. Passenger manifests record her address as 107 Foyle Street and the *Derry Almanac* records that this house was the property of Grace Duffy. The US Federal Census of 1940 records Joan now living with her sisters Muriel and Grace and parents James and Rose Markey in Kings County, Brooklyn. *(POR 14-14, 24 October 1938)*

## TRANSATLANTIC TOURISM

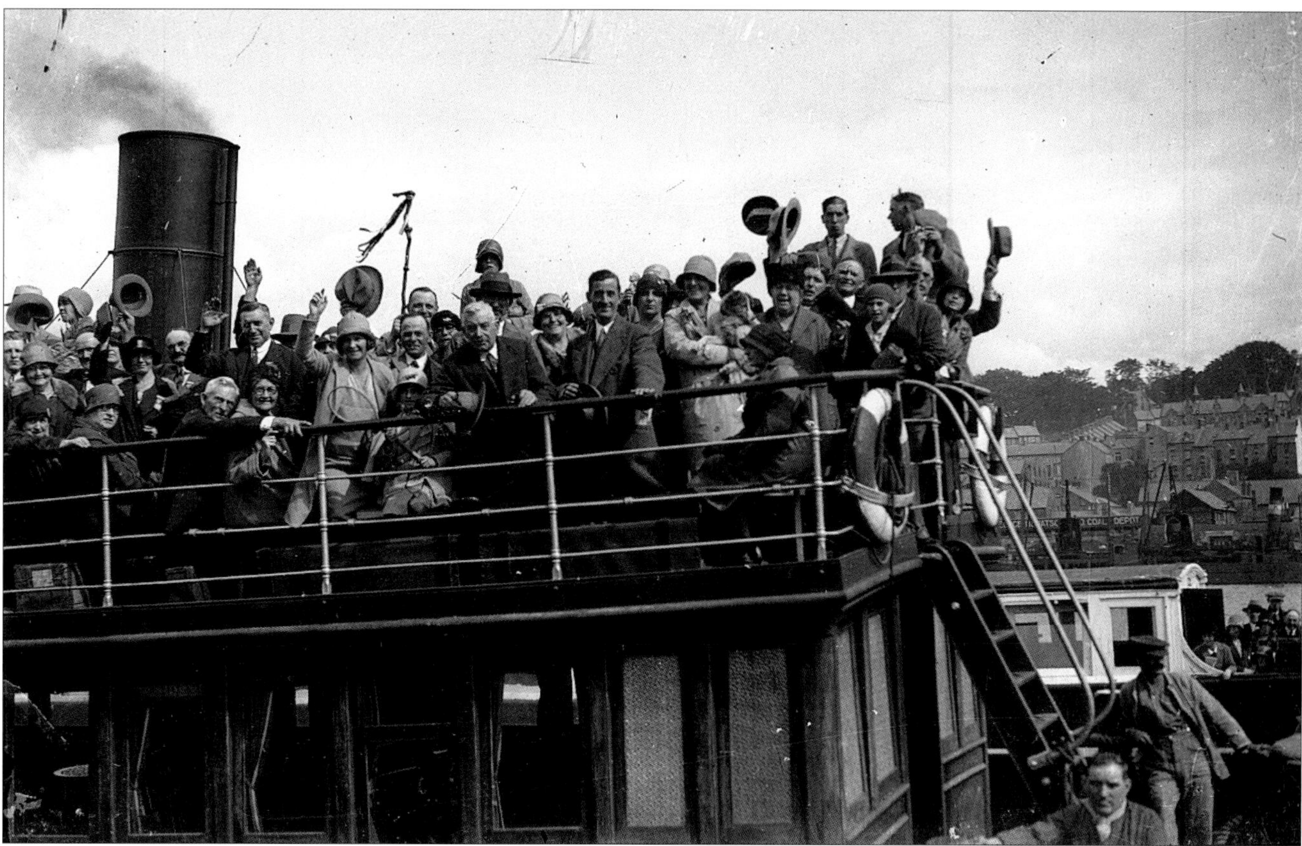

A happy party of American Orangemen leaving Derry Quay on tender *Seamore* in August 1929 to connect with Anchor Line ship *Caledonia*, departing Moville for New York. Another photograph of 'the Americans marching to the Quay' states 'thousands lined the route and gave them a cordial send-off.' The tender *Cynthia*, also with passengers, can be seen in the background.

When the overall reduction in European emigration led shipping companies to turn to tourism to fill their vessels, Derry's position as an Irish transatlantic hub became an asset. The shipping companies emphasised the style and romance of the ocean liners to encourage holidays abroad. Soon 'Tourist third cabin' took over from 2nd class accommodation as liners were adapted to meet the new requirements of passengers as tourists as opposed to emigrants. Indeed many of the tourists were in fact former emigrants, revisiting their homeland and making contact with friends and relatives. *(POR 12-12, 16 August 1929)*

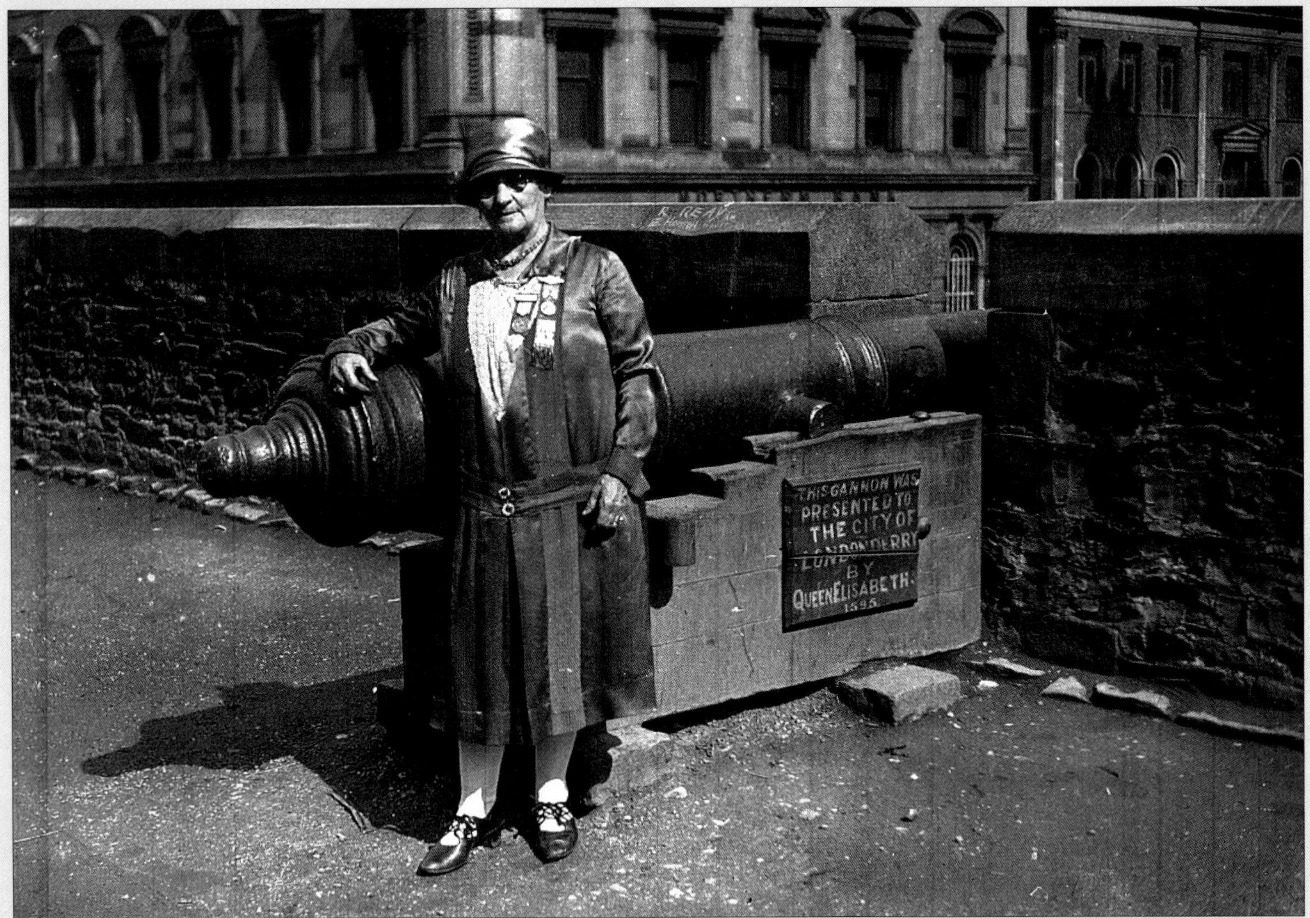


Ellen McCreedy, Supreme District Mistress of the Princess Loyal Orange Lodge Number 10, Boston, is photographed in August 1929 'at one of the old Siege guns on Derry Walls' overlooking Shipquay Place. She was part of the contingent of 'American Orangemen' taking part in Relief of Derry celebrations on 12 August 1929. Passenger manifests record that Ellen McCreedy, age 65, sailed home on Anchor liner *Caledonia*. *(PGU 6-1, 16 August 1929)*

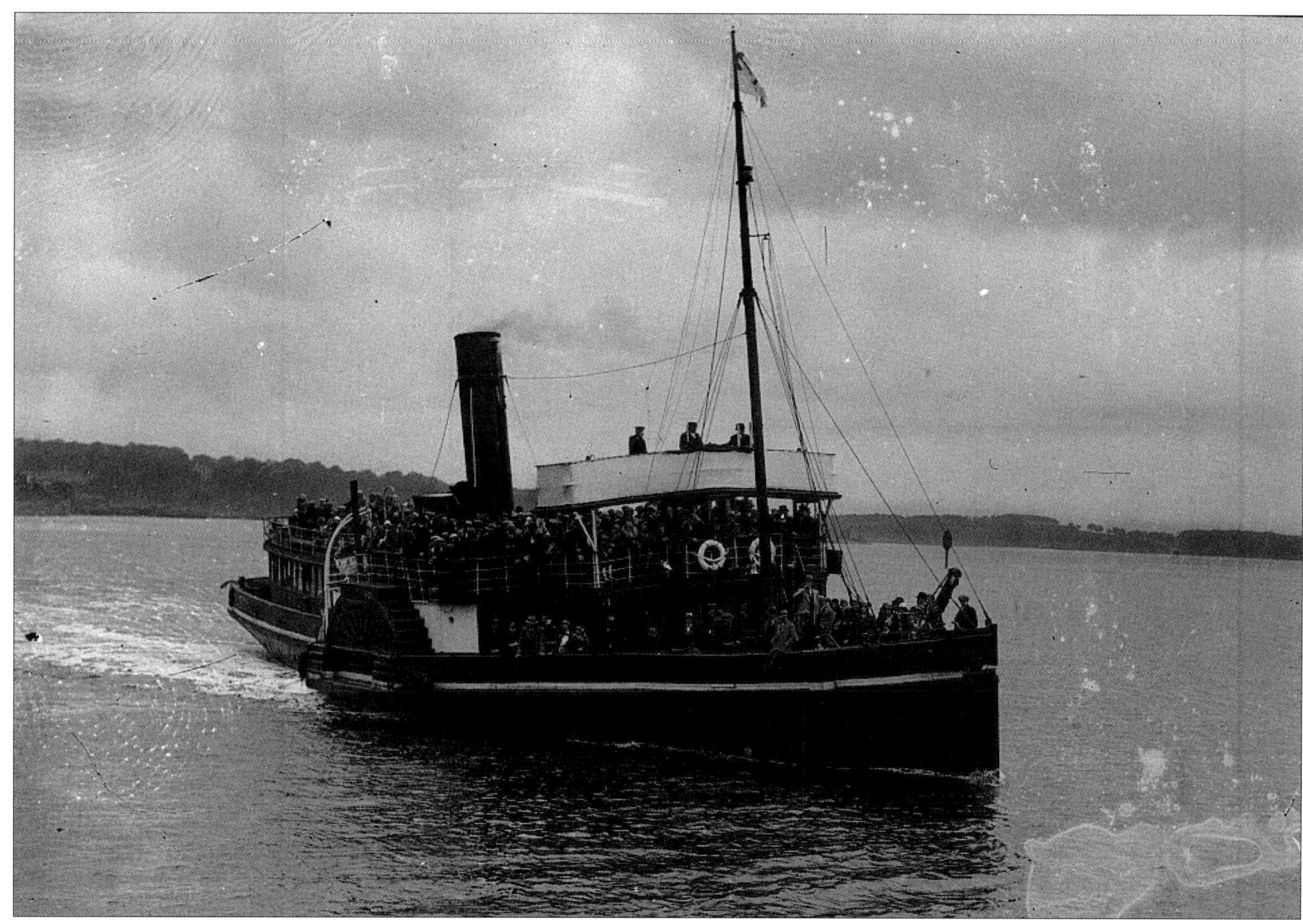

'The tender Seamore coming alongside the wharf' in May 1932 with 400 American passengers who had disembarked from the Anchor liner at Moville. It is clear that the *Seamore* was at full capacity, with all decks crammed with passengers. *(POR 12-4, 18 May 1932)*

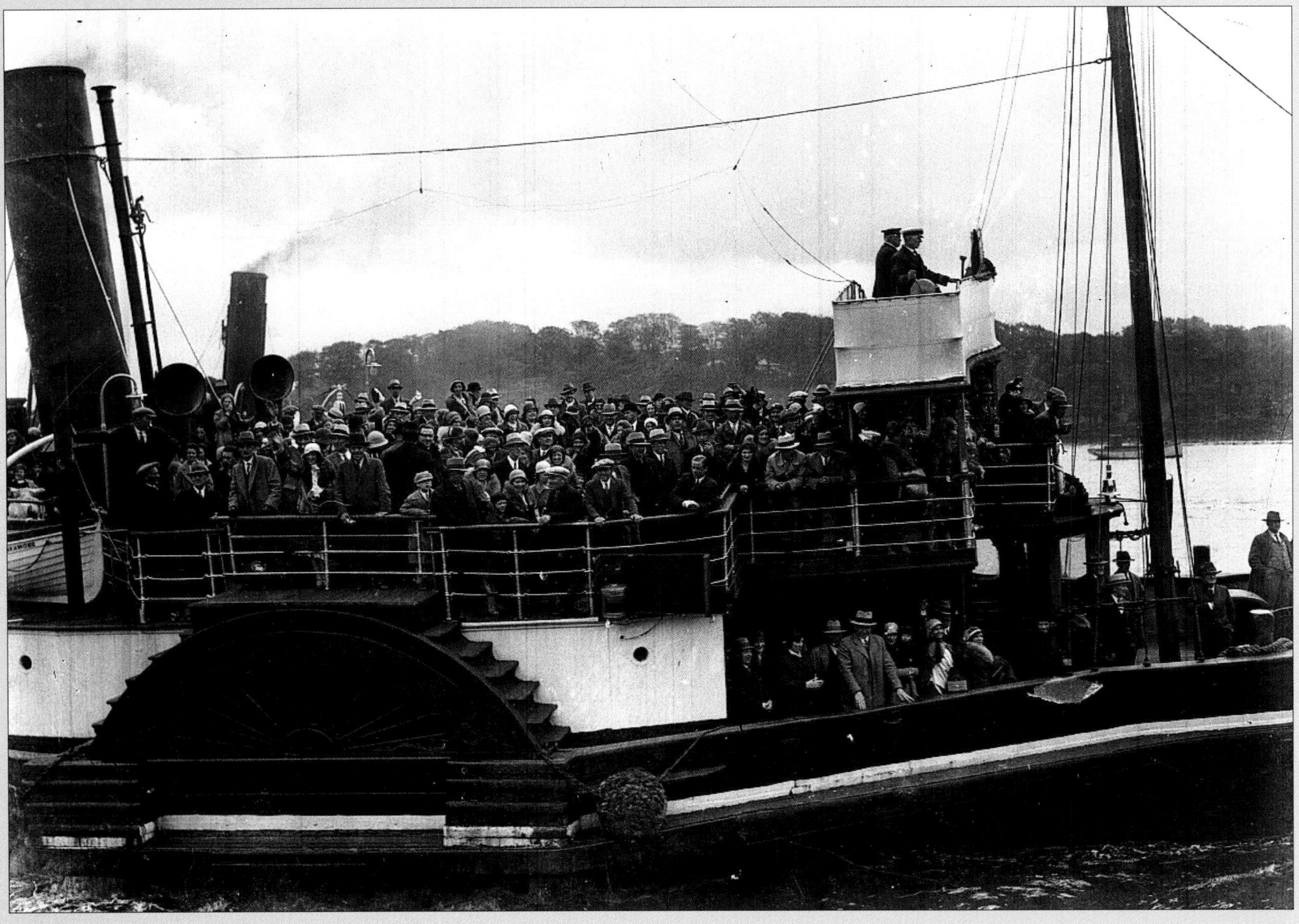

Another view of the *Seamore* as it arrives at Derry quay in May 1932. There seems to be much delight amongst the passengers at their arrival and a few are waving, presumably greeting friends or relatives at the dock. *(POR 13-8, 18 May 1932)*

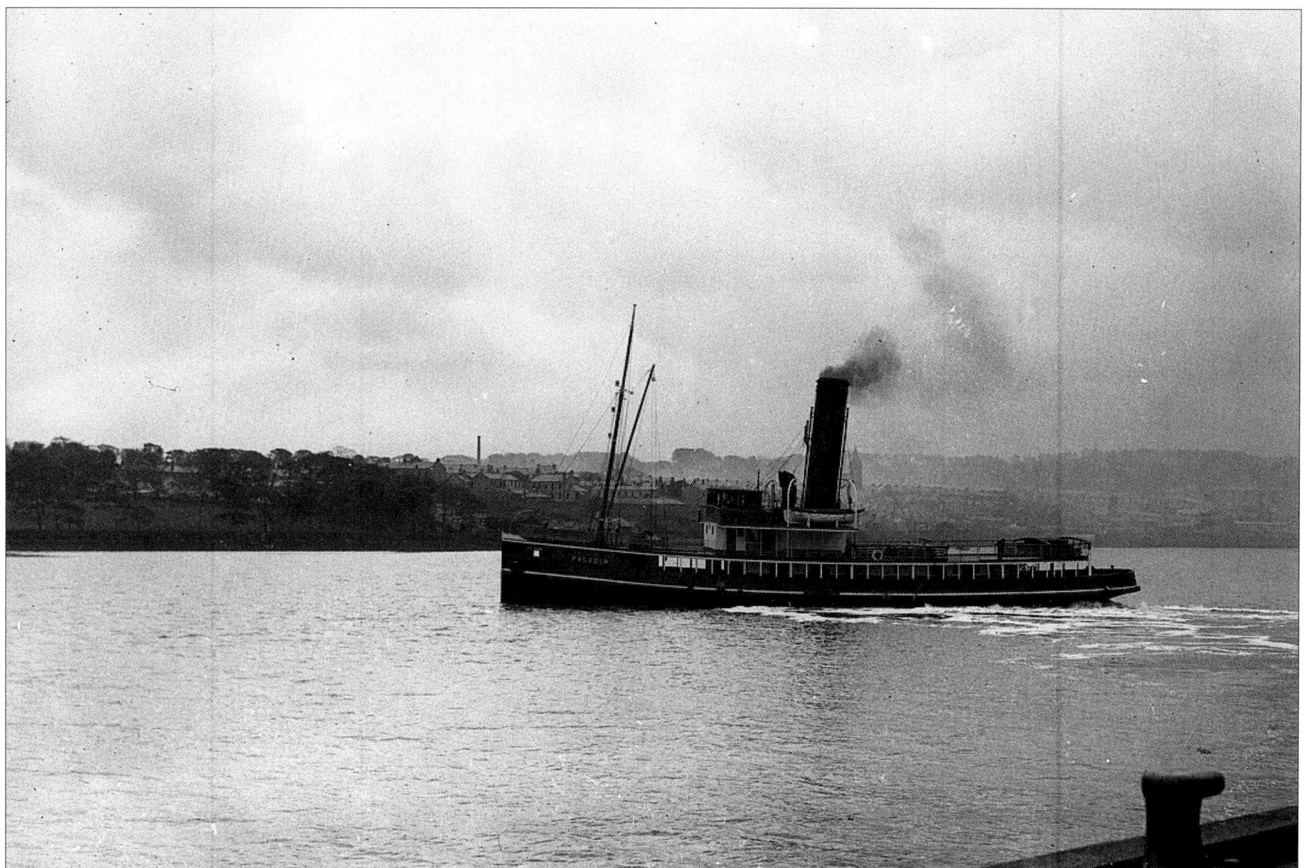

'The tender *Paladin* returning to Glasgow after discharging the luggage' belonging to the 400 American visitors who had just arrived in Derry on tender *Seamore* in May 1932. *Paladin*, owned by Anchor Line, with twin-screw propulsion as opposed to paddle wheels, was stationed on the Clyde but, if a larger number of passengers than usual were expected to embark or disembark at Derry, she was then sent over to act as relief tender to the *Seamore*, with baggage on one tender and passengers on the other. *(POR 12-6, 18 May 1932)*

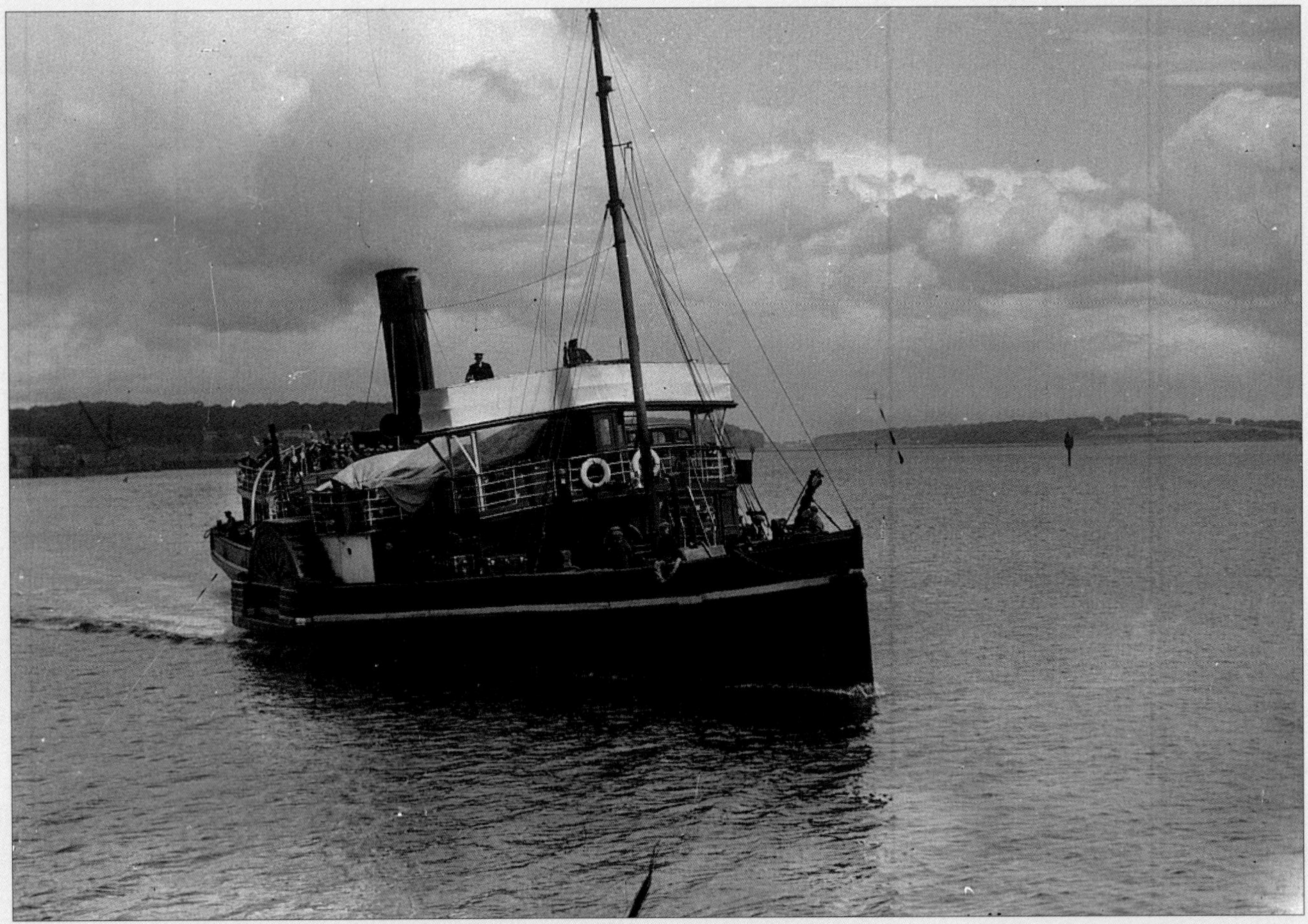

The Anchor Line tender *Seamore* approaches Abercorn Quay 'with a large number of passengers' in June 1935. *(POR 13-5, 14 June 1935)*

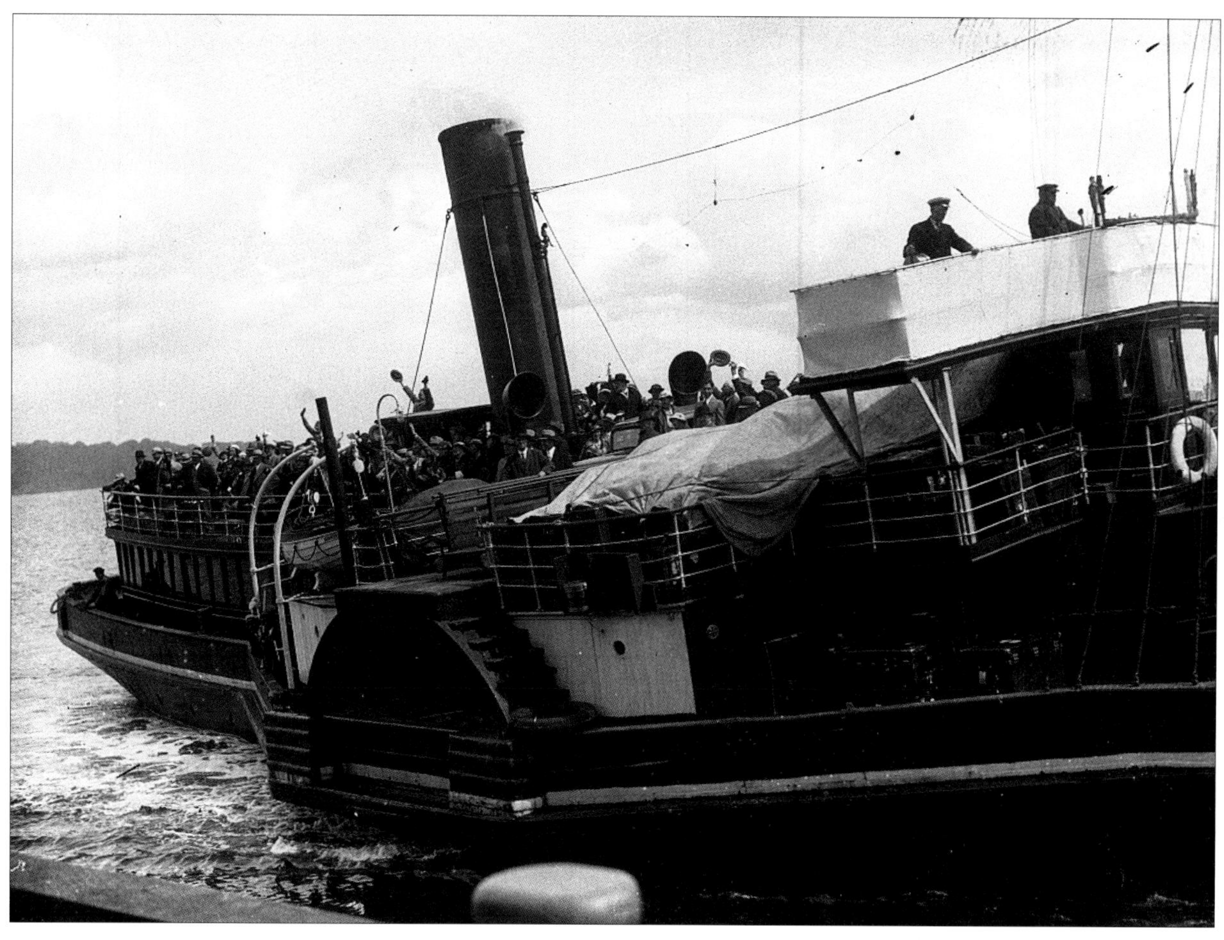

The *Seamore* 'coming alongside the wharf' at Abercorn Quay in June 1935. Again it appears to be at full capacity and many passengers are greeting onlookers with enthusiasm from the crammed deck. *(POR 13-1, 14 June 1935)*

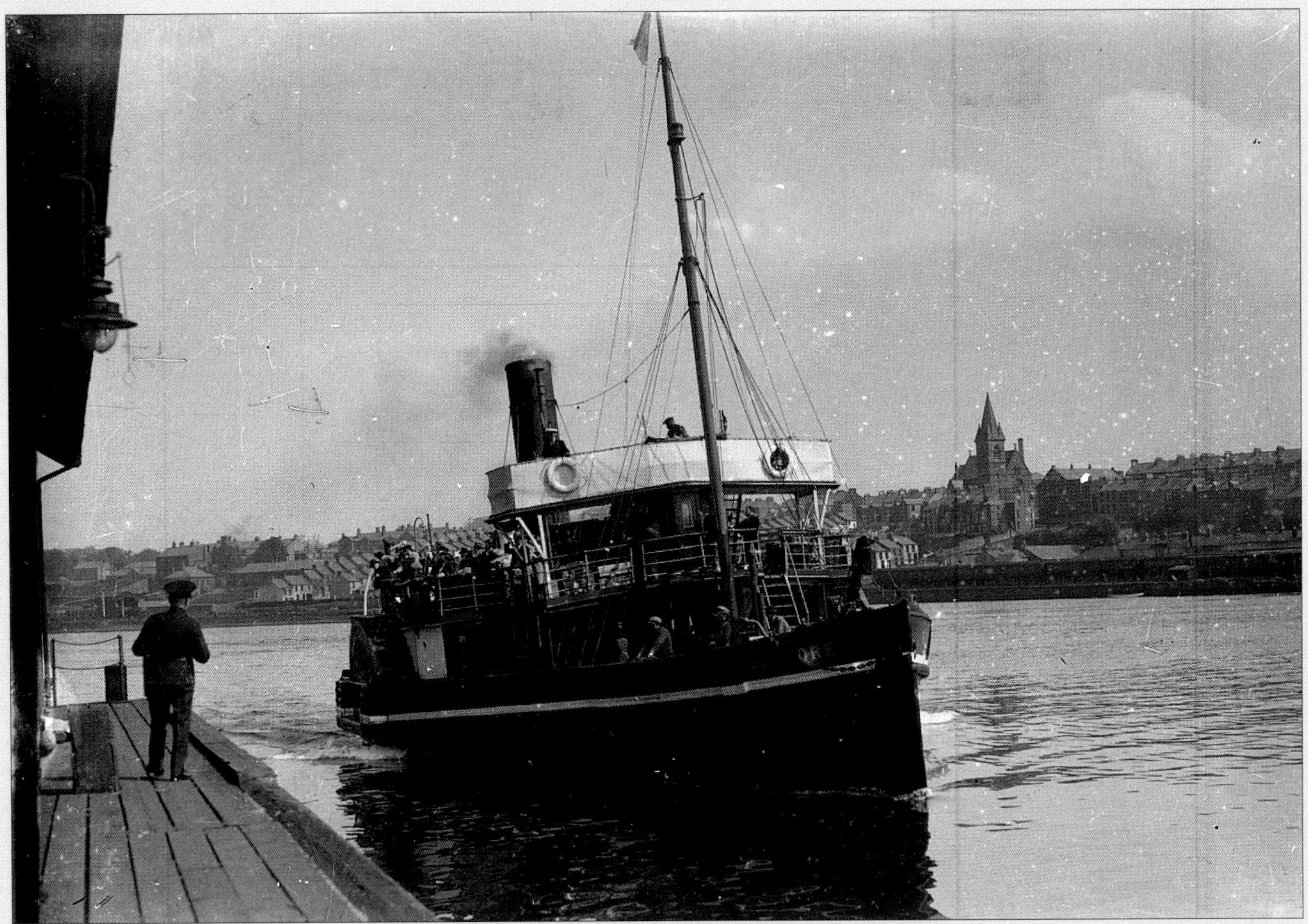

Another view of the *Seamore* approaching the wharf at Abercorn Quay 'with a large number of passengers', this time on 2 May 1937. The large building in the background is All Saints Clooney Church of Ireland. *(POR 13-4, 3 May 1937)*

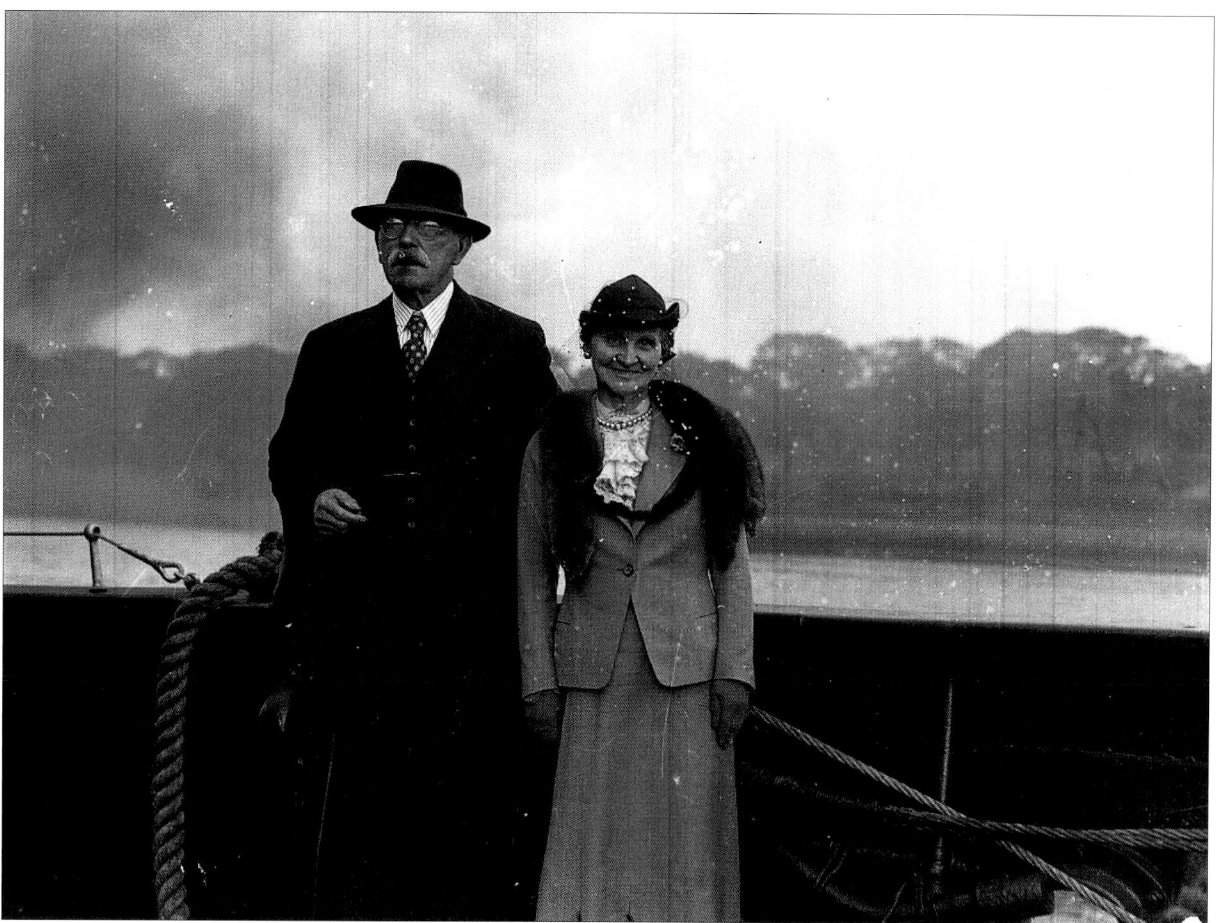

'Dr. Irwin and Mrs. Irwin, who are returning to America after their annual visit to Bushmills.' Passenger manifests record that they sailed from Moville for New York on Saturday 24 September 1938 on the *Caledonia*. The Irwins are obviously well-to-do; Mrs Irwin is wearing what is probably an expensive fur. Many returning emigrants could demonstrate their success in America by being well dressed, as they were unlikely to have been on the way out. *(POR 15-8, 26 September 1938)*

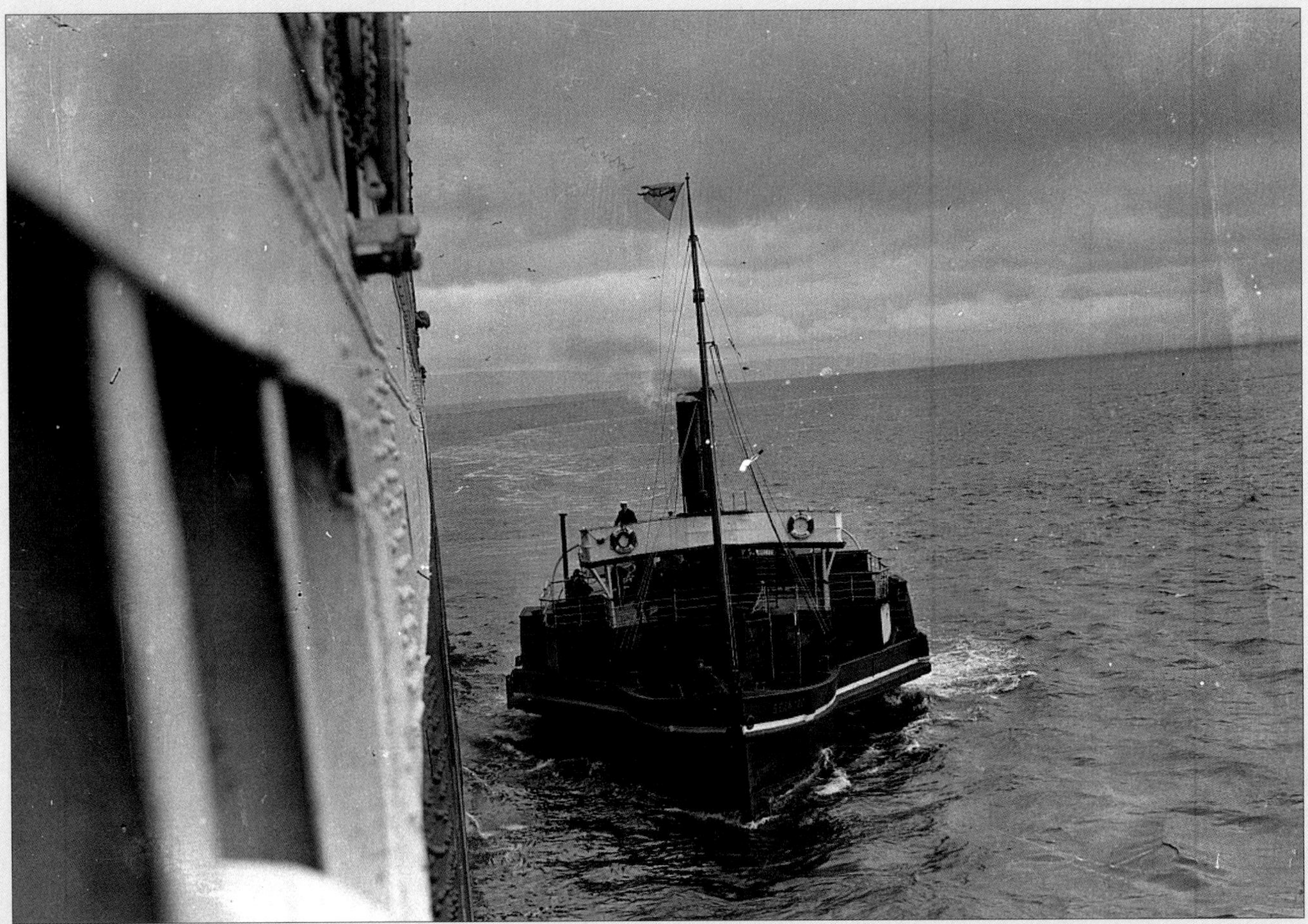

Tender *Seamore* approaches Anchor Line ship *Caledonia* on Saturday 2 July 1938. *Derry Standard* of Monday 4 July 1938 devoted one page, consisting of 12 photographs, to 'Pictures by the "Derry Standard" Photographer on a trip from Belfast to Moville on the Anchor Liner *Caledonia*'. Several are reproduced on the following pages. *(POR 12-11, 4 July 1938)*

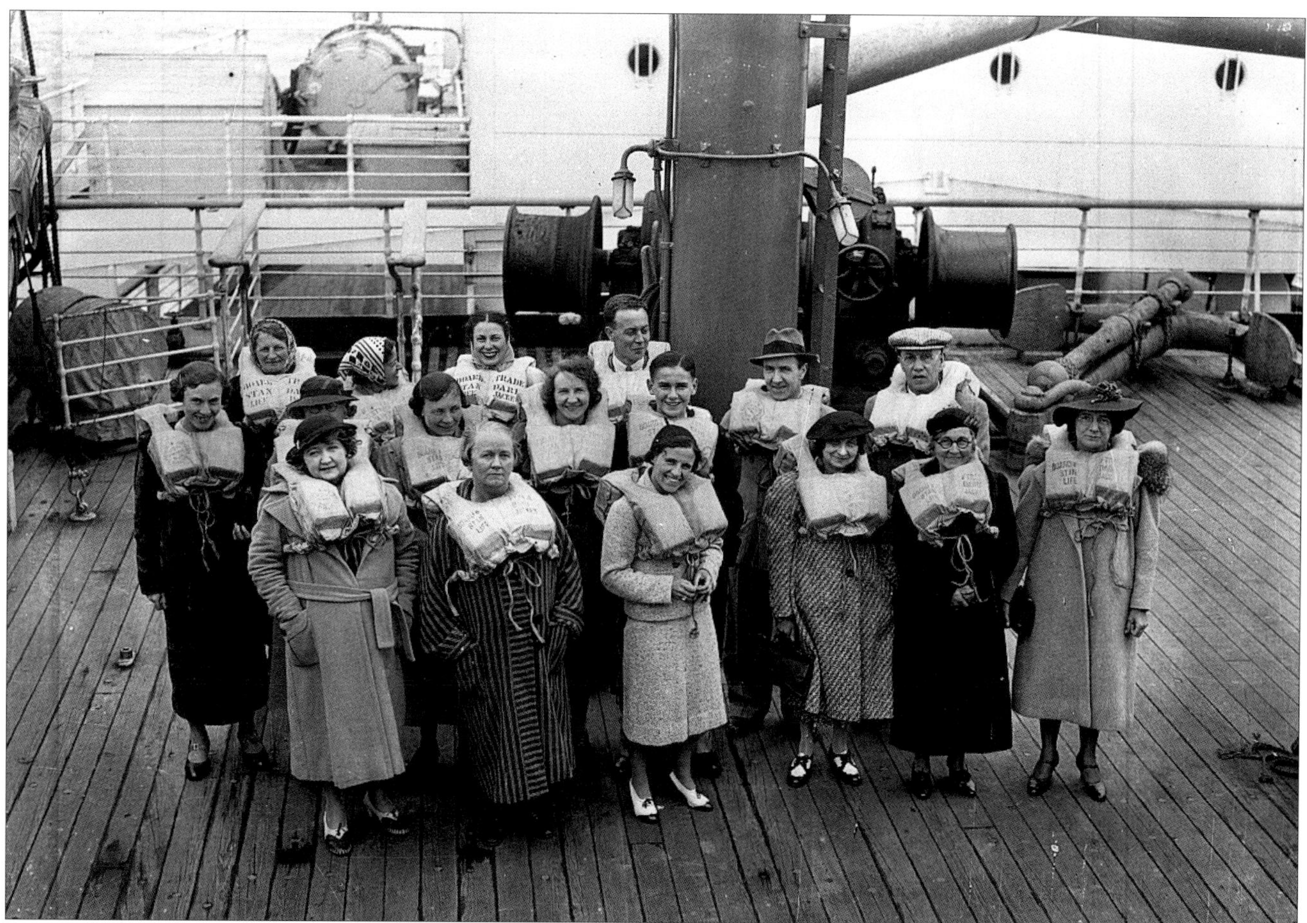

Lifeboat Drill on the *Caledonia*, 2 July 1938. This happy group are obviously wealthier travellers, perhaps tourists returning to America. The absence of children is notable, although perhaps children, such as the girl in the next photograph, were given their own drill. *(POR 15-2, 4 July 1938)*

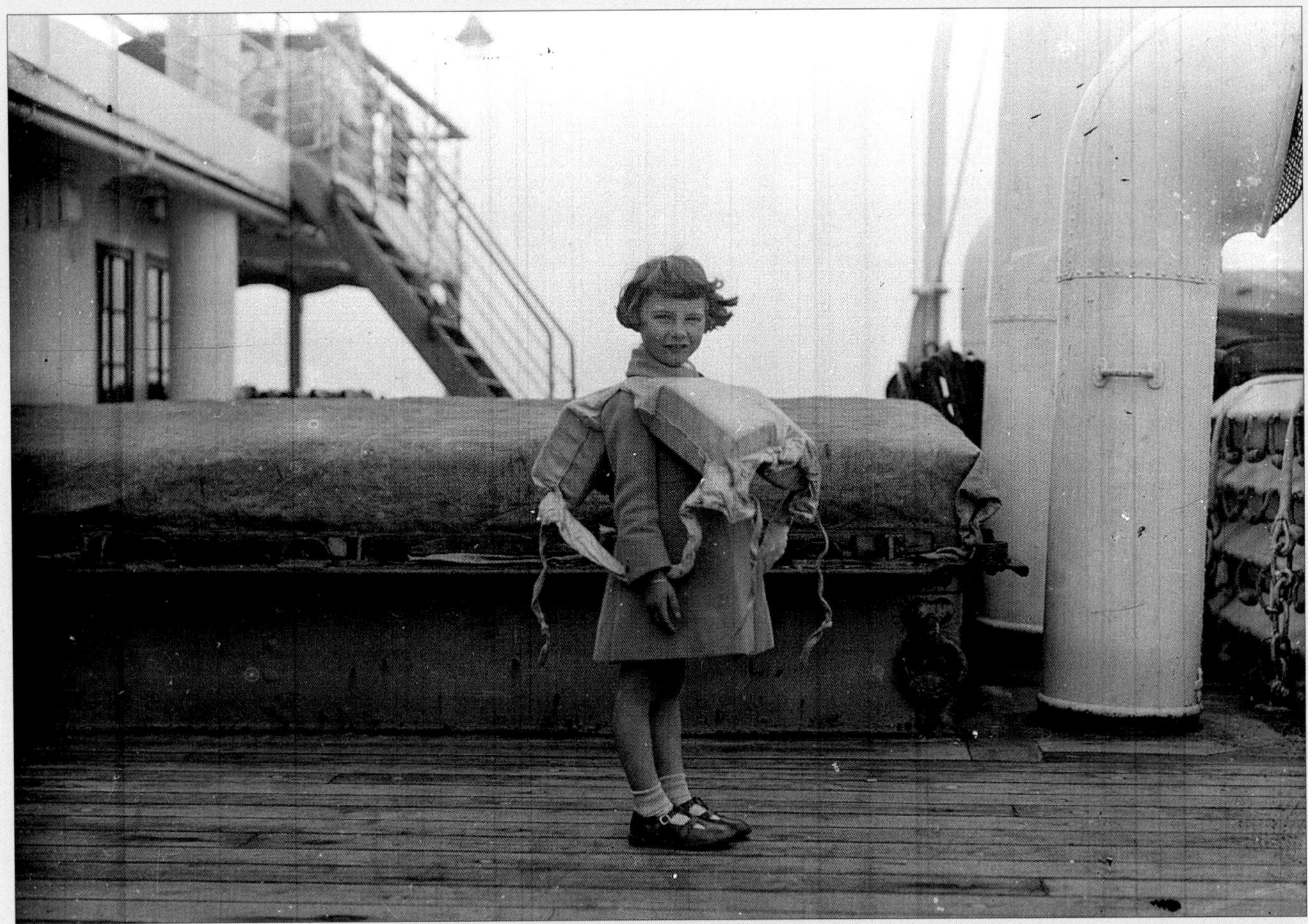

A young girl at her boat station on *Caledonia*, 2 July 1938. At the outbreak of the Second World War, the *Caledonia* served as an armed merchant cruiser and was eventually sunk by a German submarine in June 1940. Hindsight adds poignancy to this photograph taken only two years earlier. *(POR 15-13, 4 July 1938)*

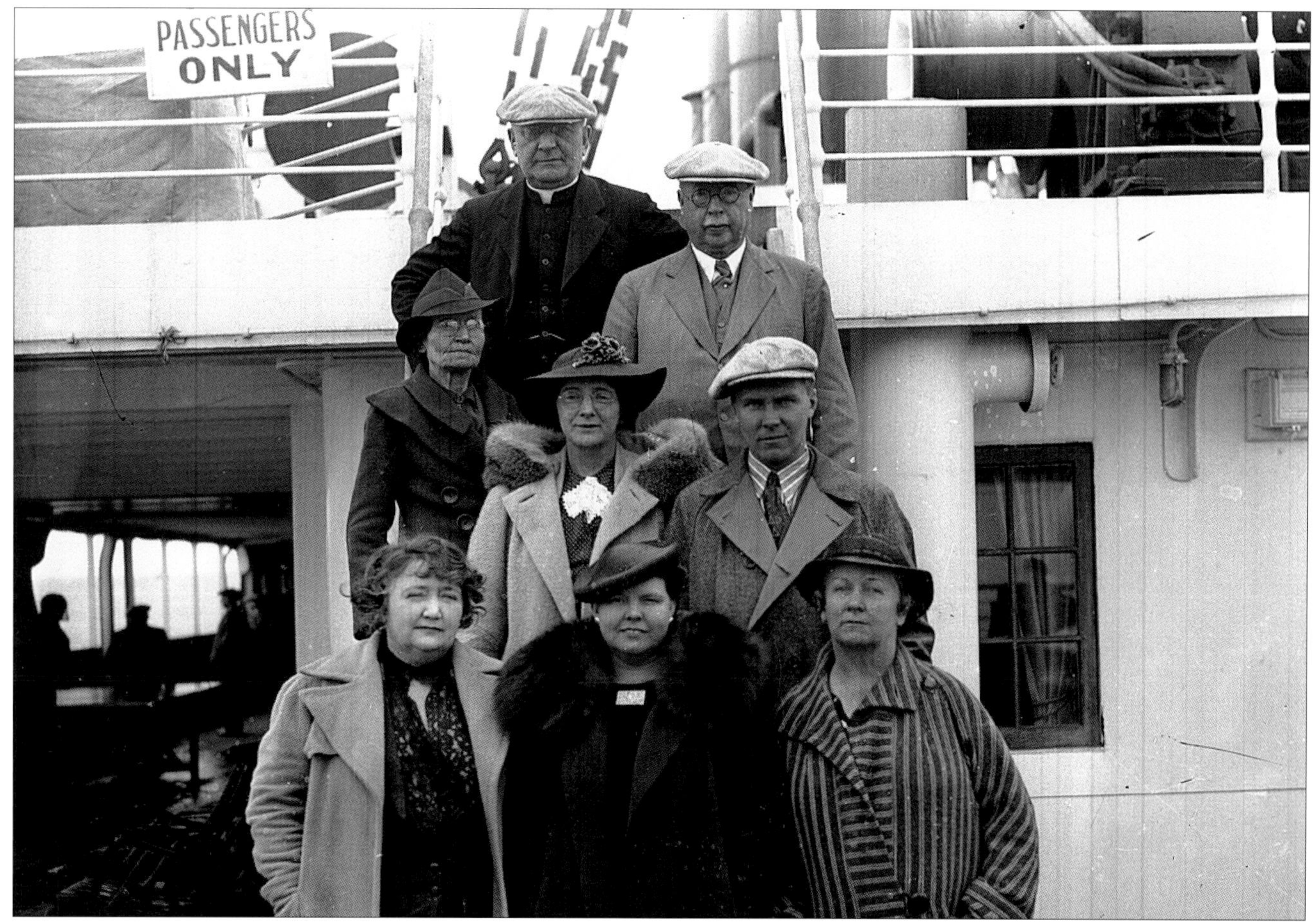


Party of James Boring Co of Chicago on board *Caledonia*, 2 July 1938. These passengers, complete with fur collars, were obviously wealthy. One wonders if these passengers had any inkling of the dangers that lay just over a year in the future, when the outbreak of war made crossing the Atlantic extremely dangerous. *(POR 15-12, 4 July 1938)*

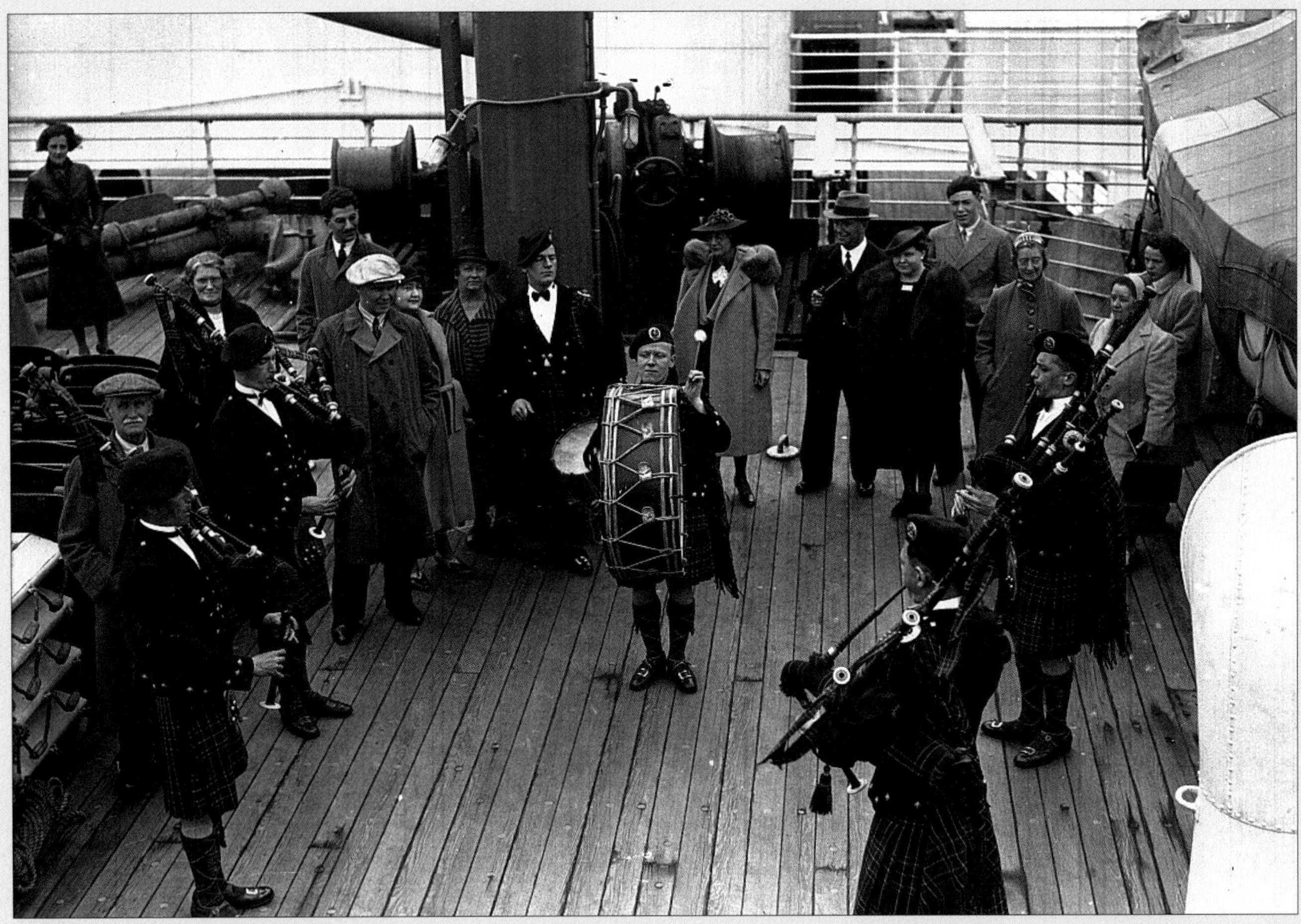

An appropriately Scottish pipe band playing on the deck of the *Caledonia*, 2 July 1938. Several of those watching are from the party of James Boring Co seen in the previous photograph. *(POR 15-9, 4 July 1938)*

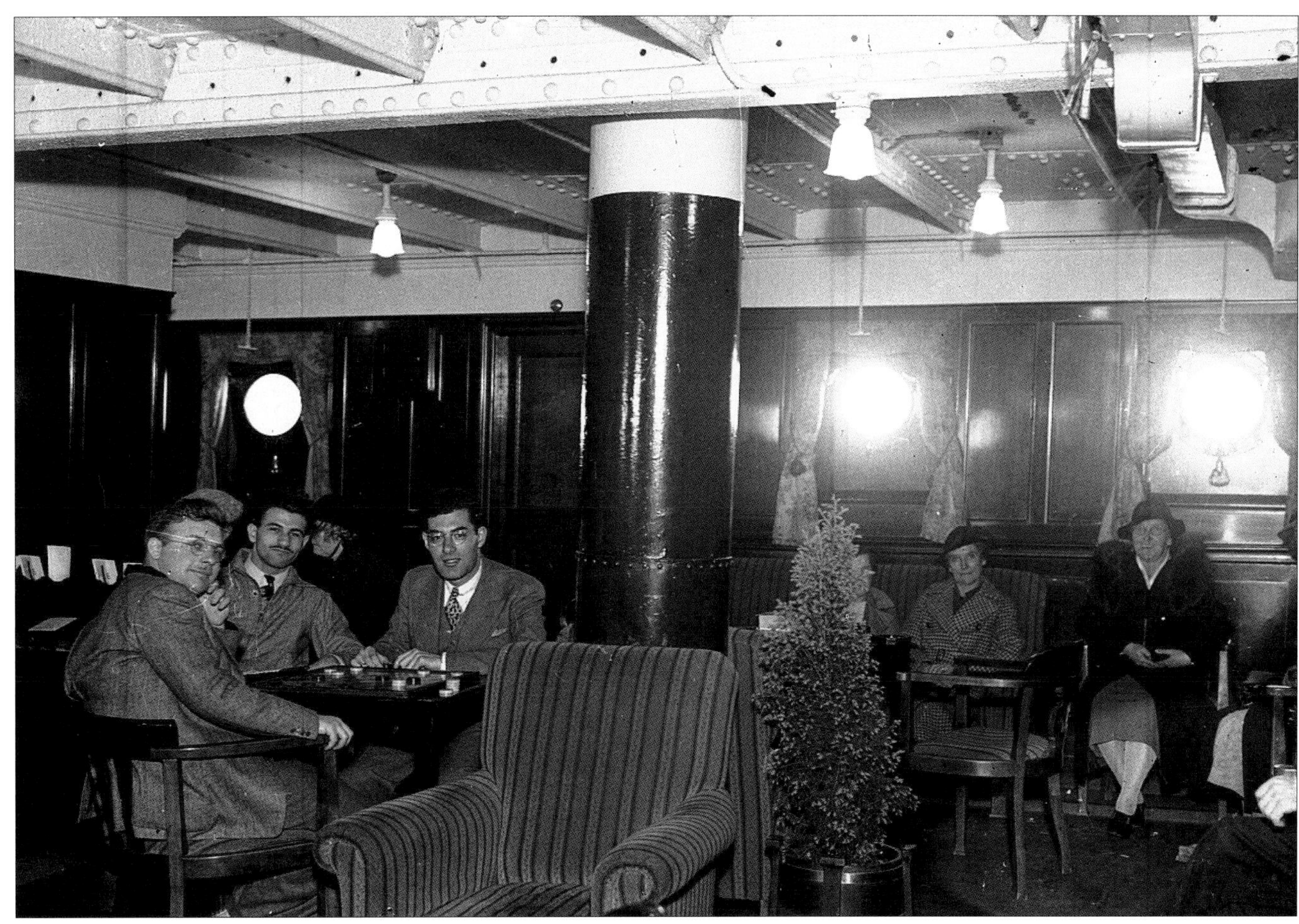

Enjoying a game of draughts in a comfortable saloon on board *Caledonia*, 2 July 1938. *(POR 15-4, 4 July 1938)*

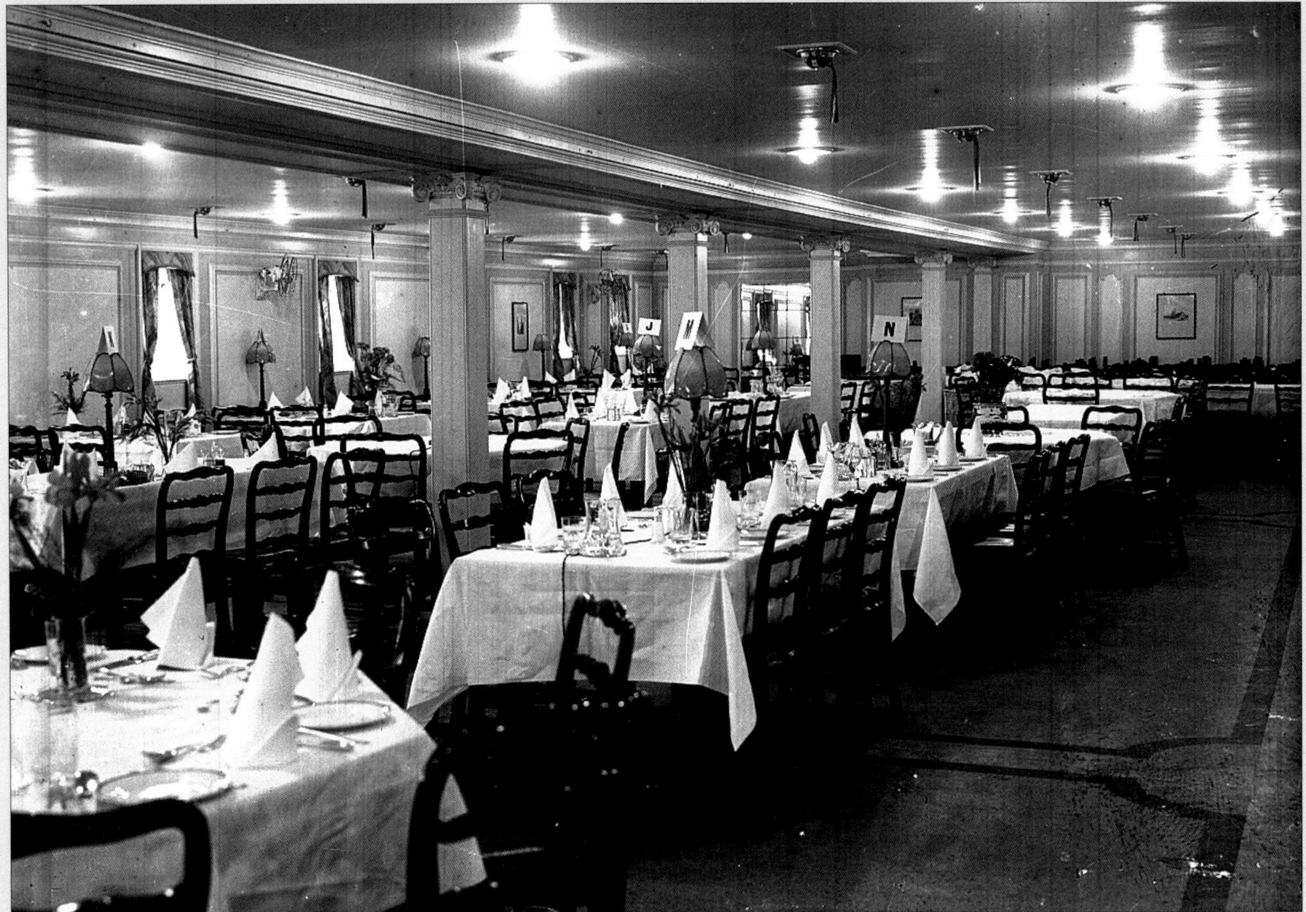


Tourist Class Dining Room on board *Caledonia*, 2 July 1938. This beautifully laid out dining room gives some idea of the number of Tourist Class passengers the ship carried. Note the letters on the lamps assigned to many of the tables. *(POR 15-11, 4 July 1938)*

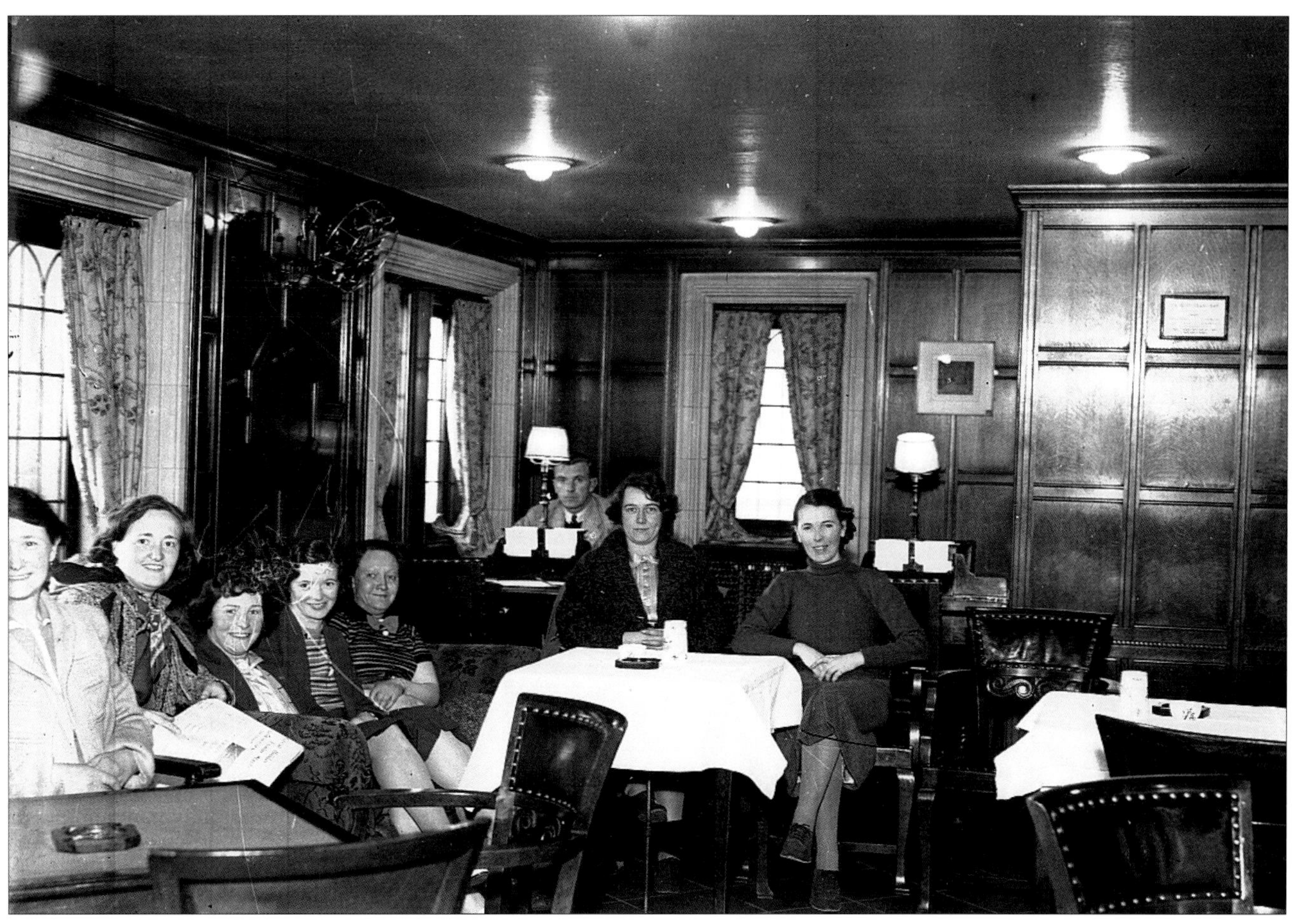

Tourist Class Smoke-room on board *Caledonia*, 2 July 1938. (POR 15-15, 4 July 1938)

## TUG-TENDERS

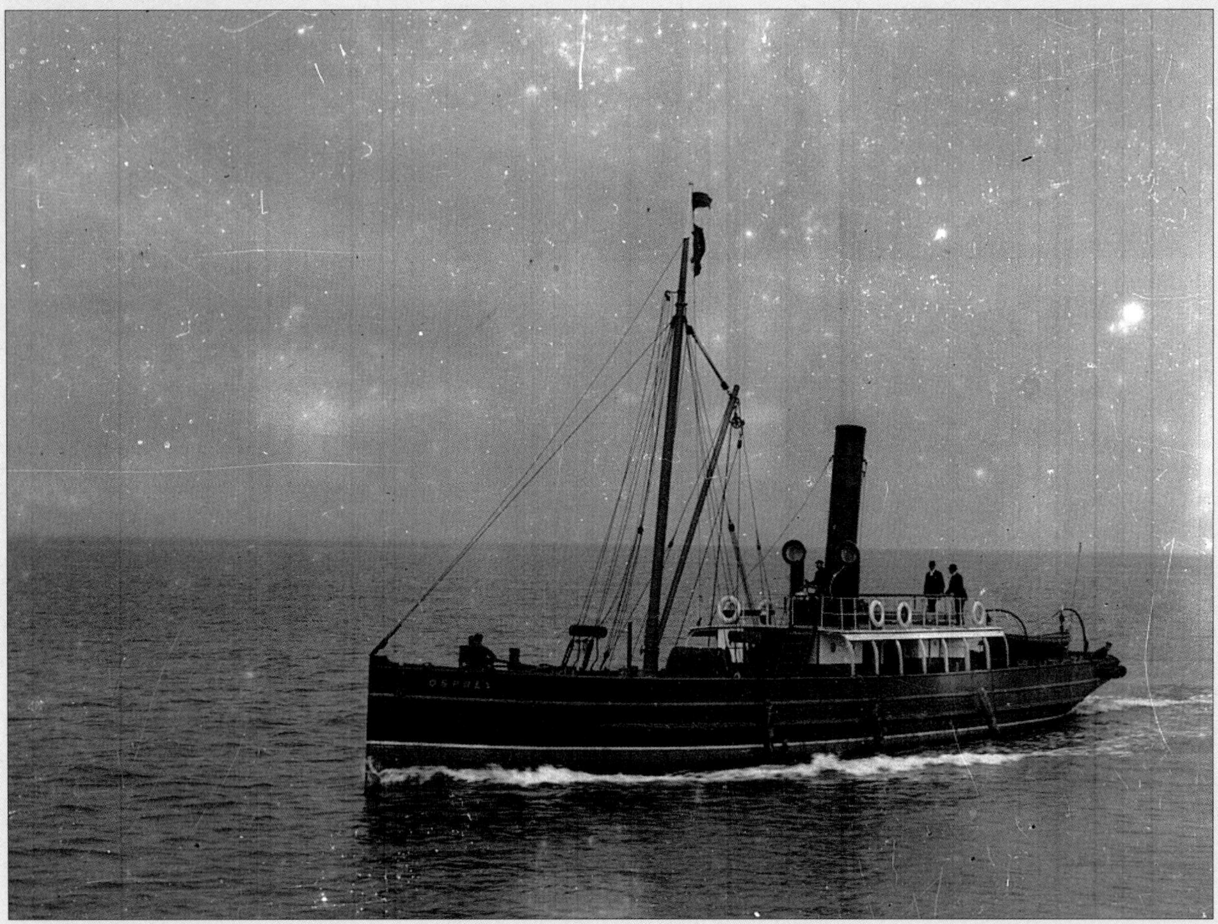

Photographed in 1906, the tug-tender *Osprey,* with single-screw propulsion as opposed to paddle wheels, operated on Lough Foyle prior to the First World War, ferrying passengers and emigrants between Derry and Moville. *(POR 13-10, 26 February 1930)*

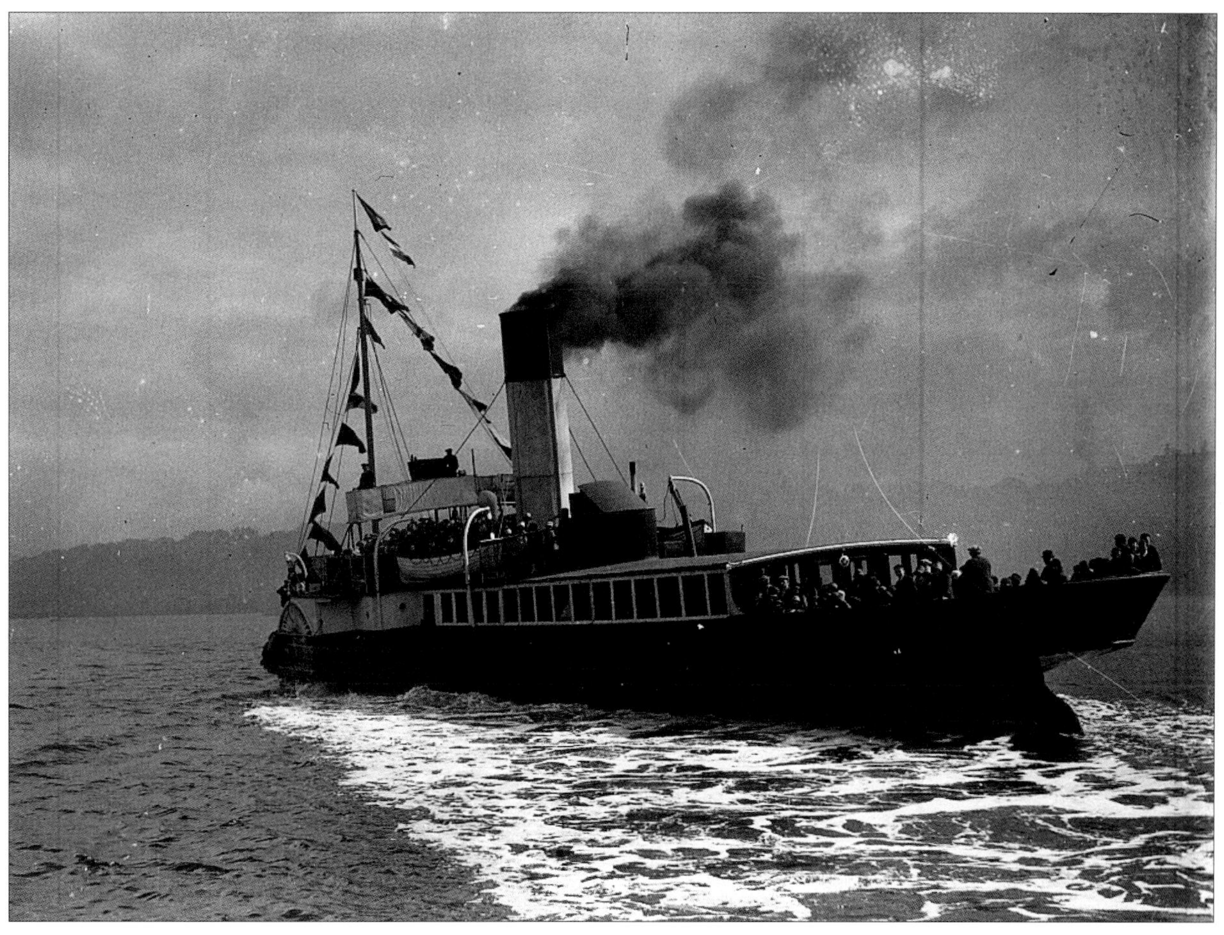

*Cynthia*, a paddle steamer, was purchased by Anchor Line in 1928 when Moville Steamship Company went out of business. She operated as a tug-tender on the Foyle, ferrying passengers and emigrants between Derry and Moville, until Anchor Line sold her in 1931. *(POR 12-7)*

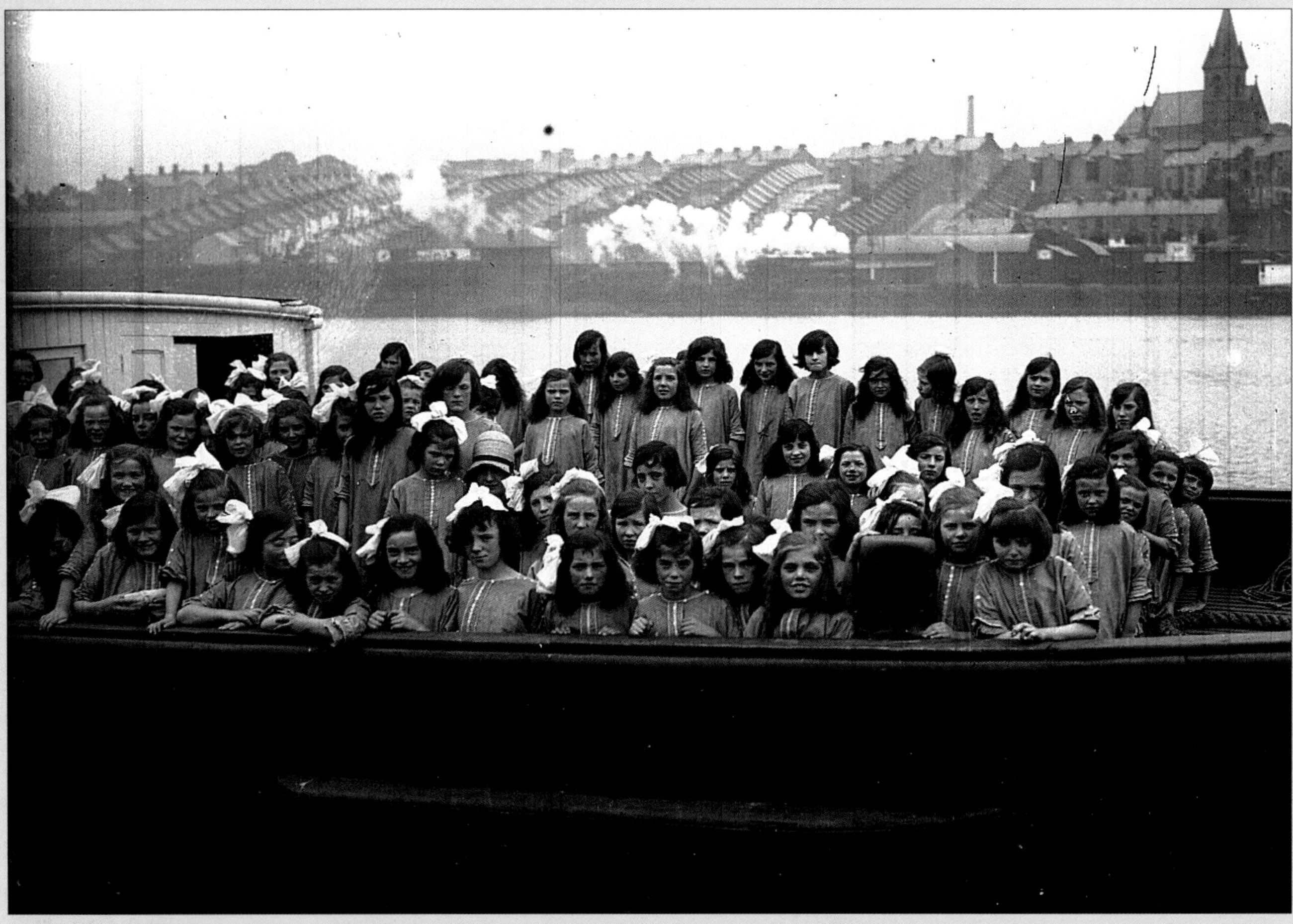

'Children from the Nazareth Home and St. Joseph's Home, Derry, photographed on the Moville Steamer, *Cynthia*, kindly lent by the Anchor Line, Ltd., before leaving on a trip to Moville' in July 1930. St Joseph's was a boys' home, so if they are also on board there must have been a policy of segregating the boys from the girls, even on outings like this. *(POR 13-9, 9 July 1930)*

# ROYAL NAVY

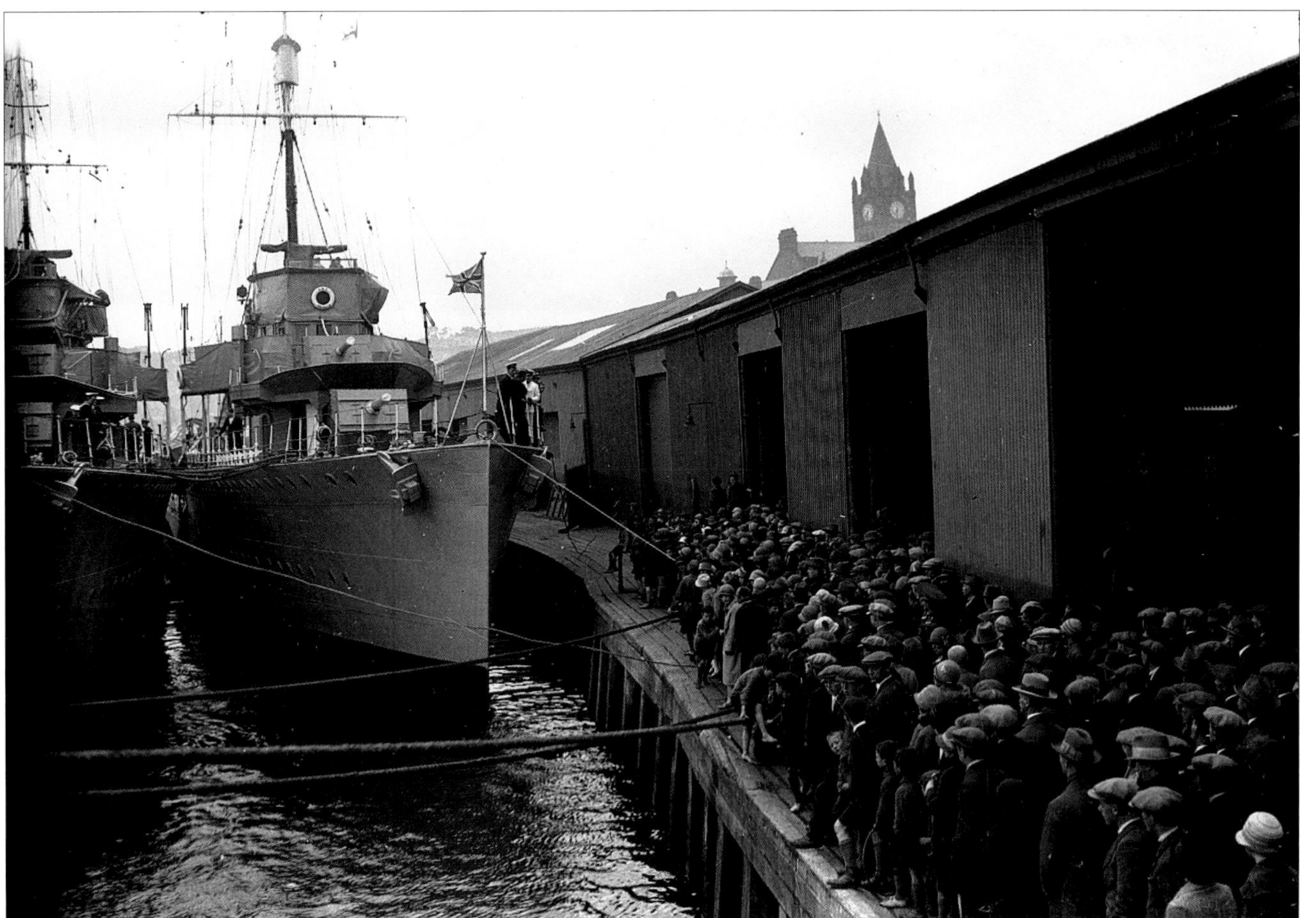

Large crowds thronged the quay on Friday evening, 17 June 1927, to give a 'hearty send-off' to the four destroyers – *Westcott*, *Walpole*, *Wolfhound* and *Valhalla*, the flagship of Commander Porter – of the Royal Navy's Sixth Destroyer Flotilla which had arrived on a visit the previous Sunday.

The Royal Navy were regular visitors to the port and their ships drew big crowds eager to inspect them. The port and its facilities were, therefore, very familiar to the Royal Navy when the Admiralty took the decision in September 1940 to develop the port as a major convoy-escort, refuelling and repair base. As the most westerly base of the allies during the Second World War (1939–1945) Derry played a crucial role in the 'Battle of the Atlantic' as an escort base. Its function was to shield convoys of merchant ships from U-boat attack. *(POR 9-11, 20 June 1927)*

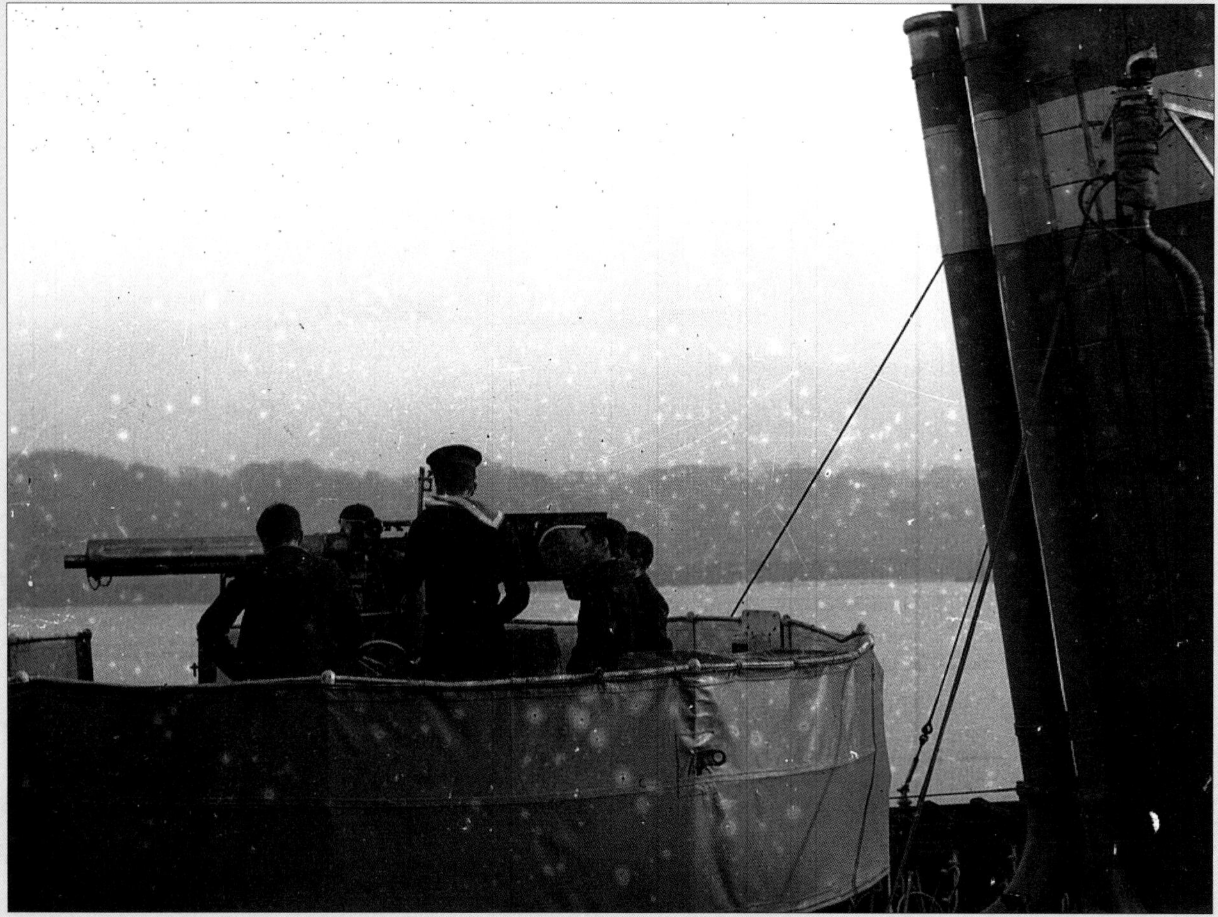

Schoolboys inspect the anti-aircraft gun on the Royal Navy's HMS *Walker* which visited Derry in December 1932. This W-class destroyer of the Royal Navy – 1,100 tons, 300 feet in length and top speed of 34 knots – saw service in the final months of the First World War, in the Russian Civil War in 1919 and in the Second World War. She was sold for scrap in 1946. *(POR 9-9, 2 December 1932)*

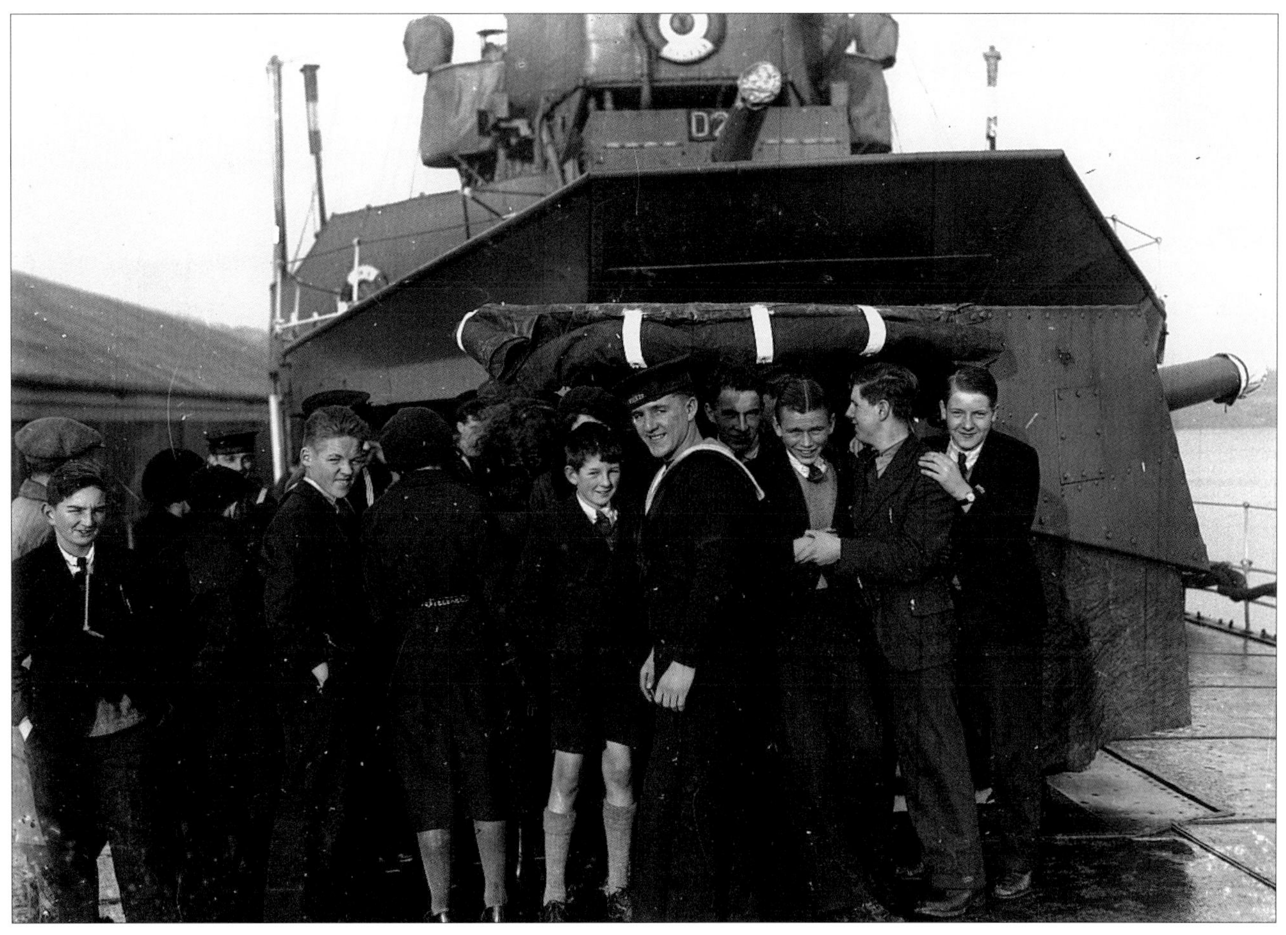

More visitors on board HMS *Walker* at Derry Quay in December 1932. *(POR 9-8, 2 December 1932)*

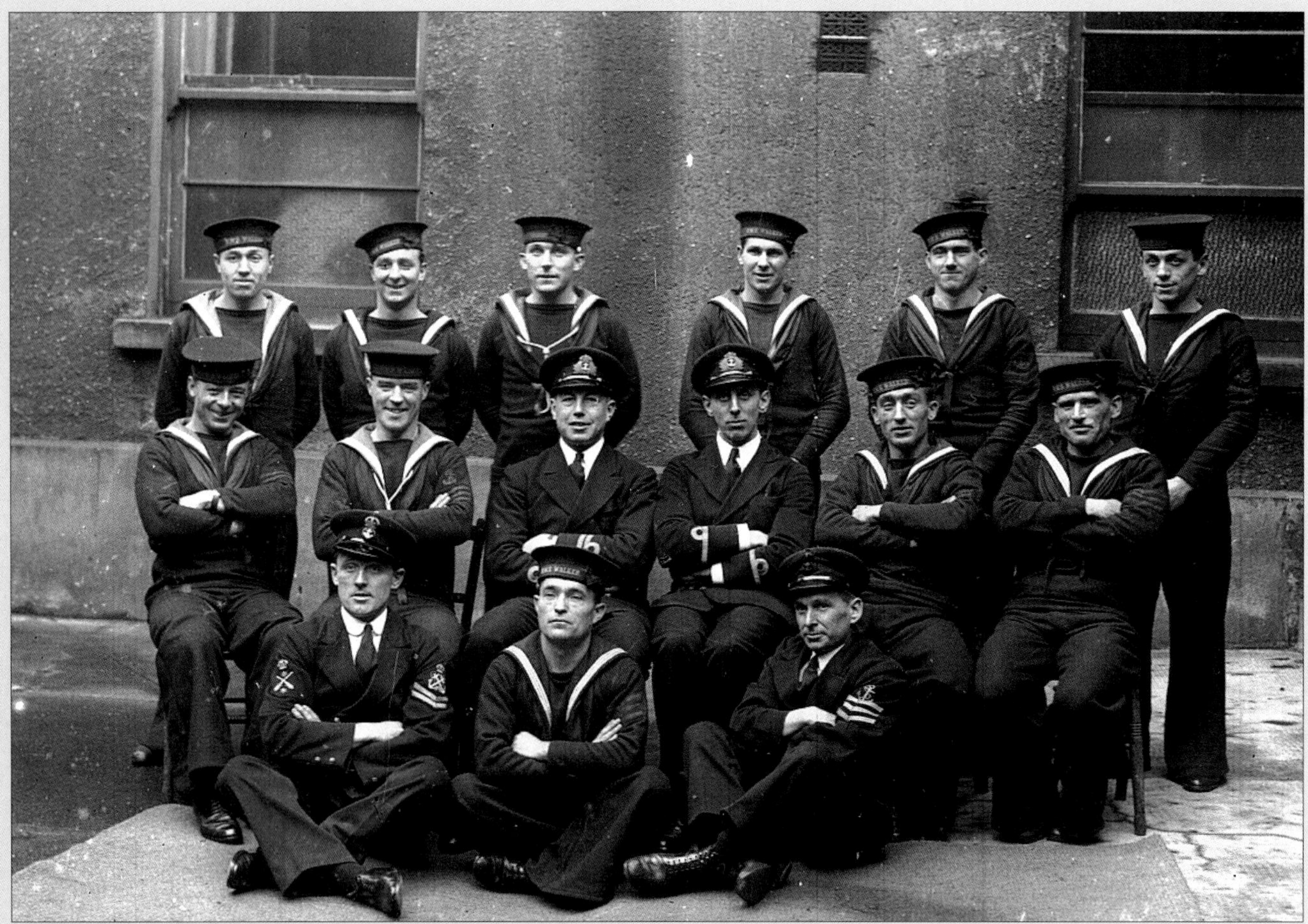

Concert Party from HMS *Walker* in Derry in December 1932. The *Derry Standard* of 2 December reported: 'Before a large and appreciative audience in Derry Y.M.C.A. a concert party from H.M.S. *Walker*, which is now on a visit to Derry, gave a most enjoyable and highly-successful entertainment... The programme included sketches, choruses, and community singing.' *(POR 9-10, 2 December 1932)*

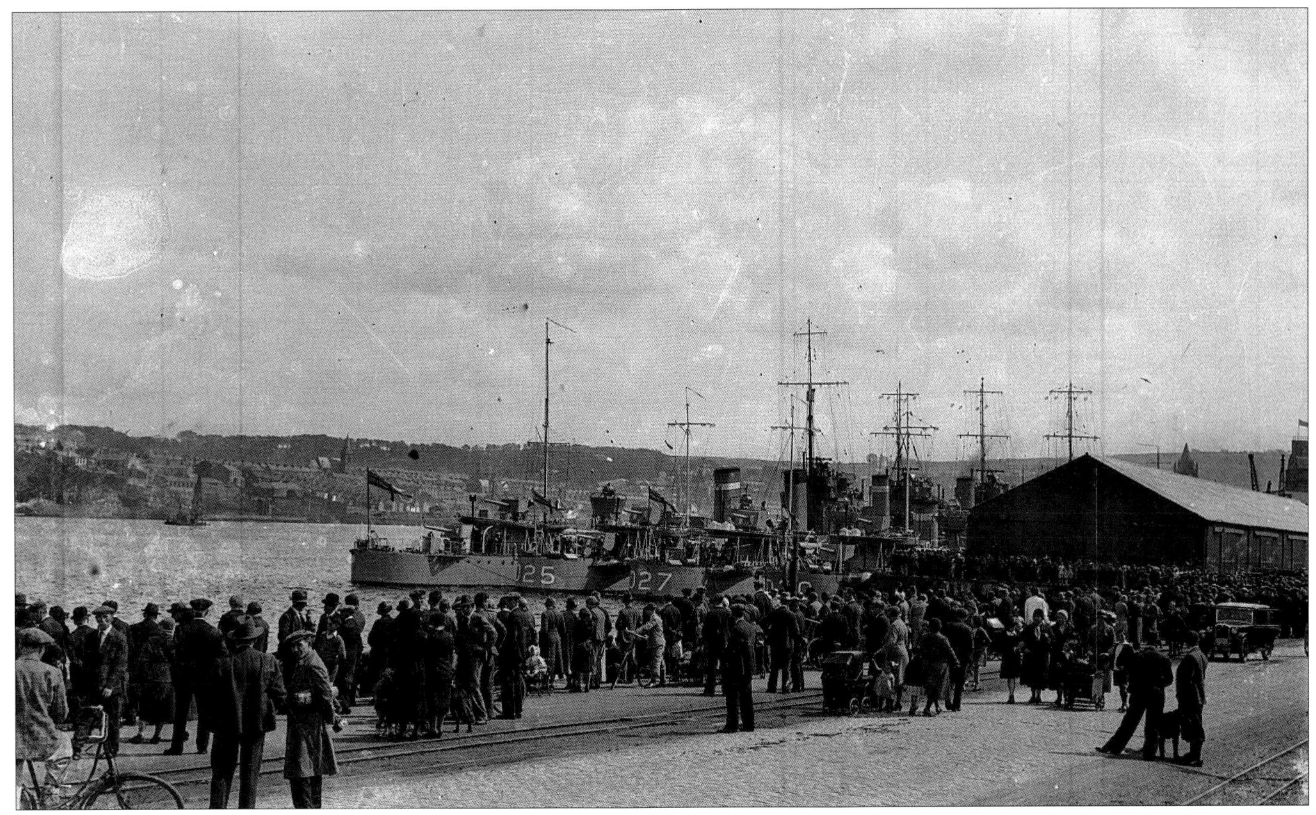

The crowd beginning to gather for departure of the Royal Navy's Fifth Flotilla of seven destroyers which had arrived in Derry for a week's visit on Sunday 11 June 1933. The pennant numbers of two of the destroyers are clearly visible D25 (HMS *Warwick*) and D27 (HMS *Walker*). *Derry Standard* of 14 June 1933 reported: 'Derry has assumed a gala appearance during the past few days, and most of the shops and business premises are flying flags in honour of the Royal Navy and the visiting aviators.' The visiting aviators refers to the much-anticipated arrival of 24 seaplanes led by General Balbo, the Italian Air Minister. *(POR 10-2, 21 June 1933)*

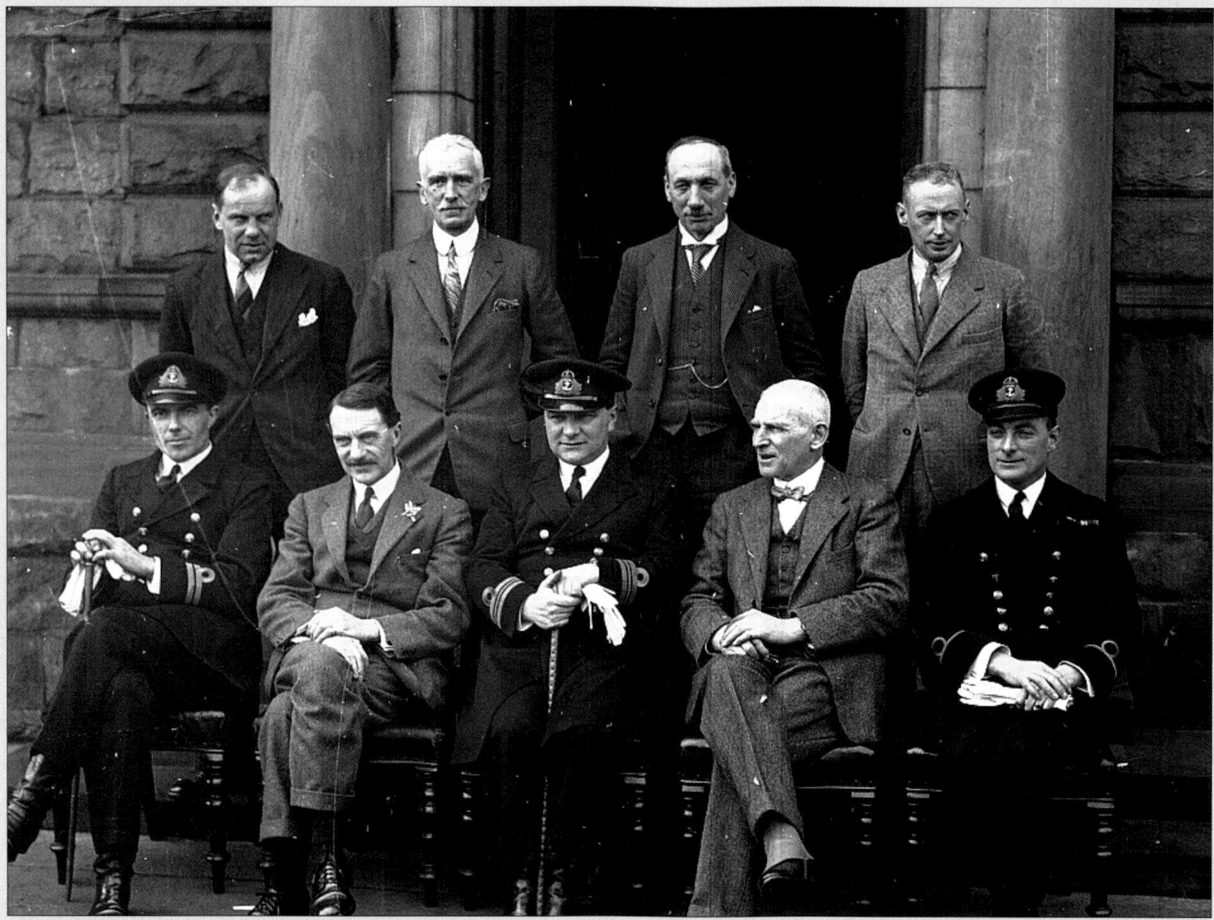

A reception for visiting Royal Navy officers at Harbour Office by Londonderry Port and Harbour Commissioners. Such courtesy calls were common. *Derry Standard* of 14 June 1933 published a similar photograph, taken at the entrance to the Harbour Office, of the officers of Royal Navy's Fifth Flotilla with the Harbour Commissioners. *(POR 9-5)*

# FRENCH NAVY VISIT

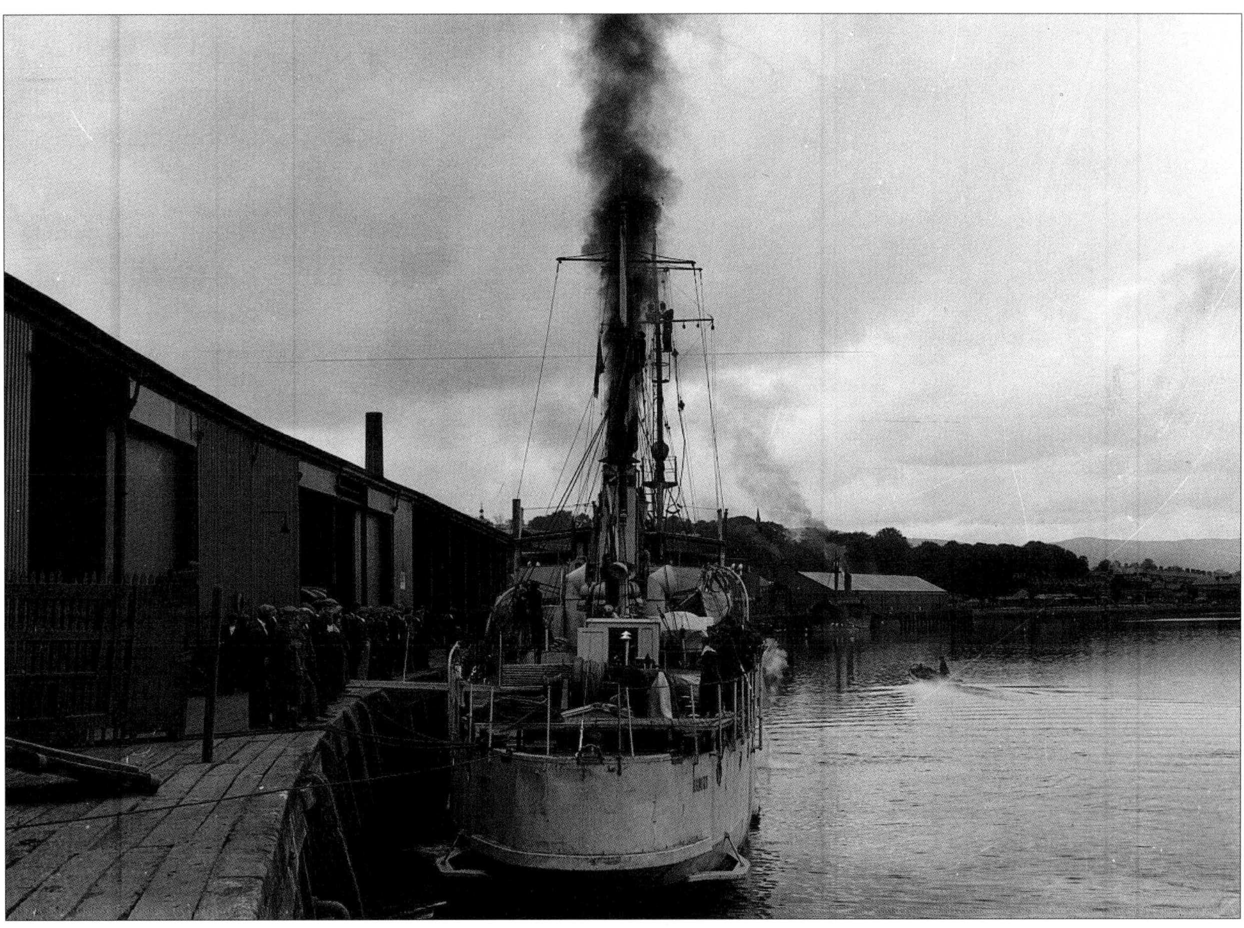

The French gunboat *Ardent* at Derry Quay in May 1933. *Derry Standard* of 17 May 1933 reported that 'the *Ardent,* a French fishing patrol gunboat, is in Derry at present, the main object of the visit being to give the crew a rest. The *Ardent*, which is under the command of Lieutenant Daynac, and has a crew of 58, is at present carrying out a survey of the fishing grounds around the Irish coast, principally the South and West... The *Ardent* is probably the first French man-o'-war to visit Derry.' The *Standard* also carried a photograph of the crew of the *Ardent* 'leaving Lewis's Travel Office for a motor bus trip to Portrush, Causeway and Ballycastle.' *(POR 4-5, 17 May 1933)*

# INTERNATIONAL INCIDENT: SPANISH CIVIL WAR

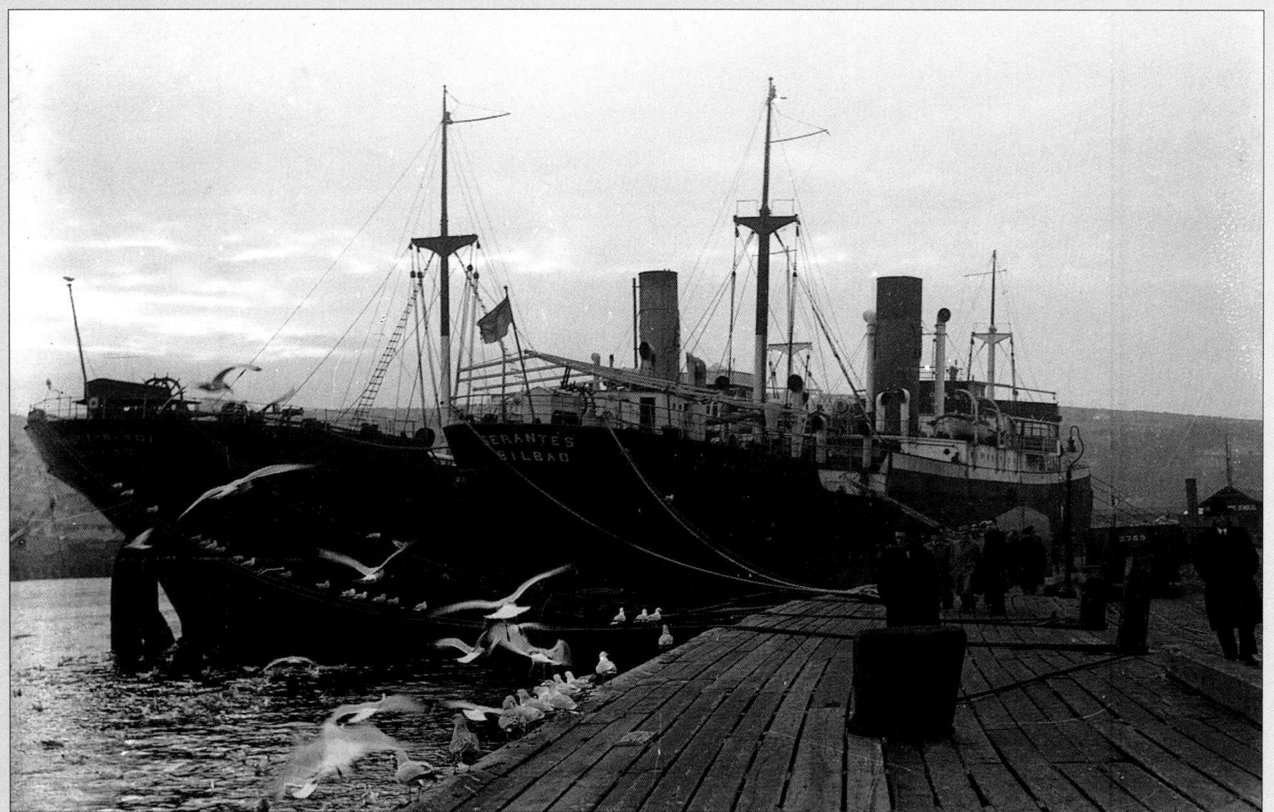

Two of the three 'arrested' Spanish ships at Derry Quay in February 1938. *Derry Standard* of 9 February 1938 reported that three Spanish ships, *Serantes*, *Gorbea Mendi* and *Atalaya*, lying in Derry since July 1937, were the centre of a legal battle over the ownership of the ships, which were claimed by the Spanish Republican Government under their 'nationalisation of shipping' scheme. The vessels had been 'arrested' at the instigation of the owners.

By February 1938 the owners were seeking an order to release the vessels and *Derry Standard* of Monday 7 February 1938 reported that 'forty-four men from Dublin arrived by special train in Derry' to 'man the vessels if their release is granted.' It was believed that these sailors were 'members of General O'Duffy's brigade.' General O'Duffy refers to Eoin O'Duffy (1892–1944), leader of the Monaghan Brigade of IRA during the Irish War of Independence and Chief of Staff of IRA in 1922. An anti-communist, in 1936 he raised the Irish Brigade to fight for Franco and defend the Roman Catholic church during the Spanish Civil War (1936–1939). *(POR 1-15, 9 February 1938)*

# HARBOUR COMMISSIONERS: DIVERS

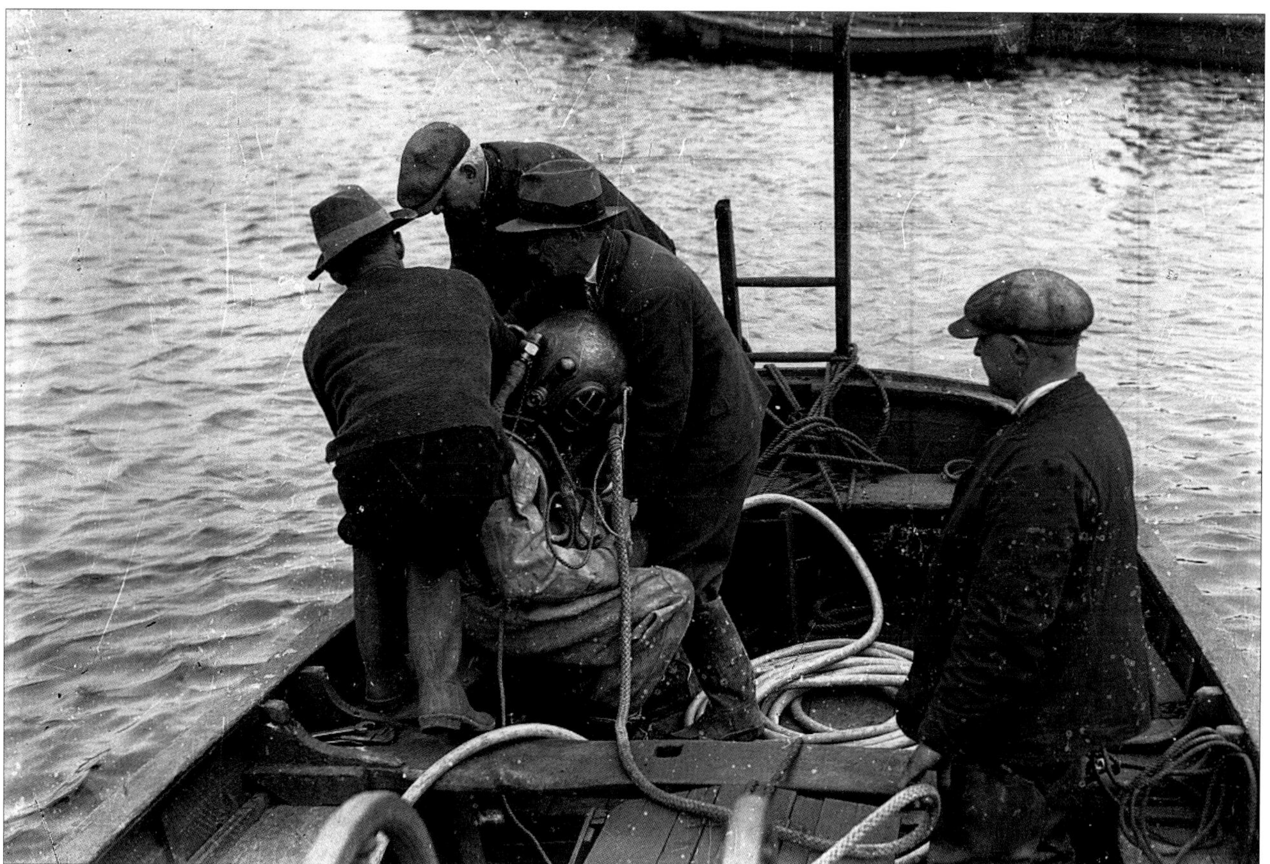

The Londonderry Port and Harbour Commissioners' diver 'receiving attention before descending to fasten the couplings of the pipes in the River Foyle' for the Banagher Water Scheme in August 1930. The city, with its large shirt industry, was in need of a new water supply source. Banagher Glen, 18 miles southeast of Derry in the Sperrin Mountains, was identified as an ideal site for a new reservoir. An access road, three miles long, was built between 1918 to 1926 and construction of the dam over the Altnaheglish Burn took place between 1931 and 1935. *(POR 7-13, 1 September 1930)*

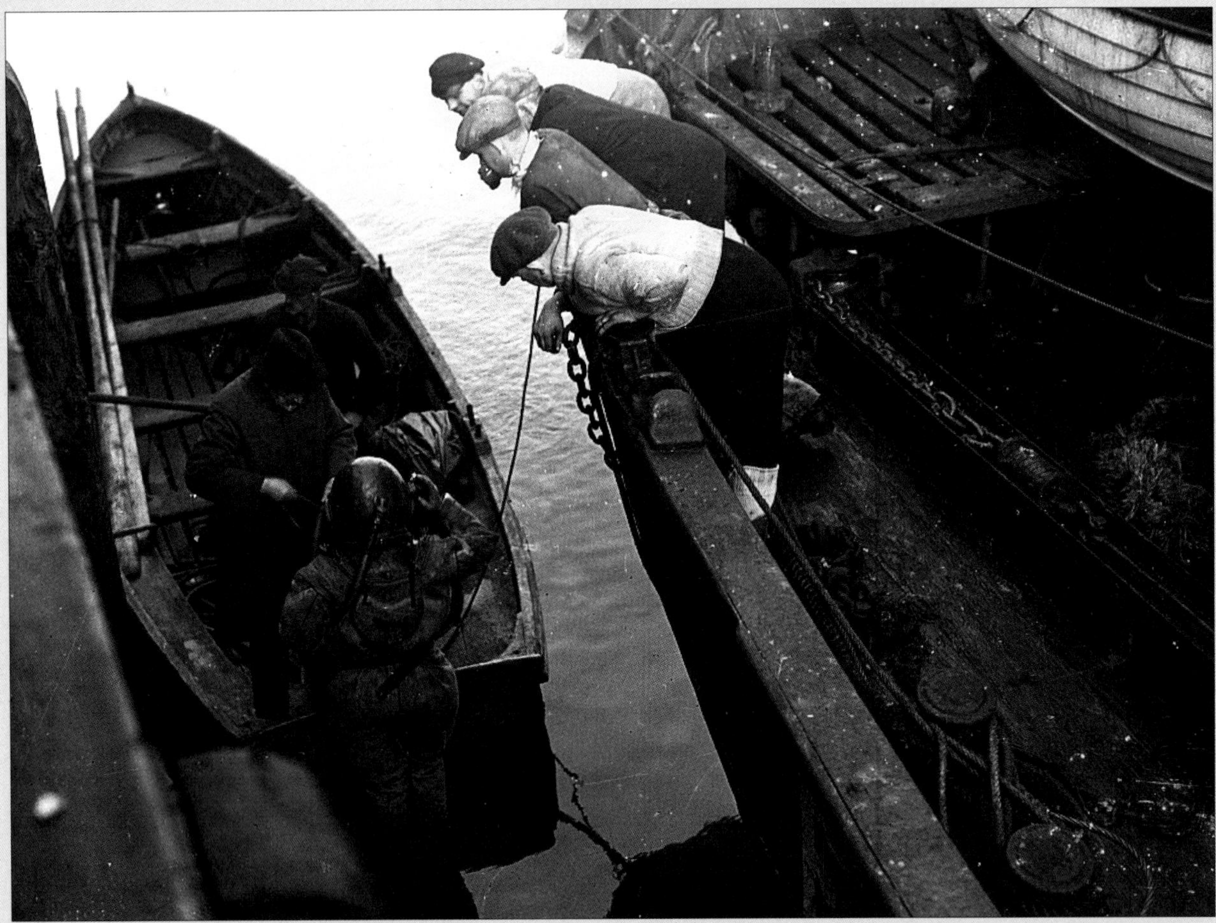

'The Derry Port and Harbour diver about to go down to release a wire rope which fouled the propeller of the fishing trawler *Wigan*, now lying at Derry Quay' in February 1938. *(POR 6-5, 4 February 1938)*

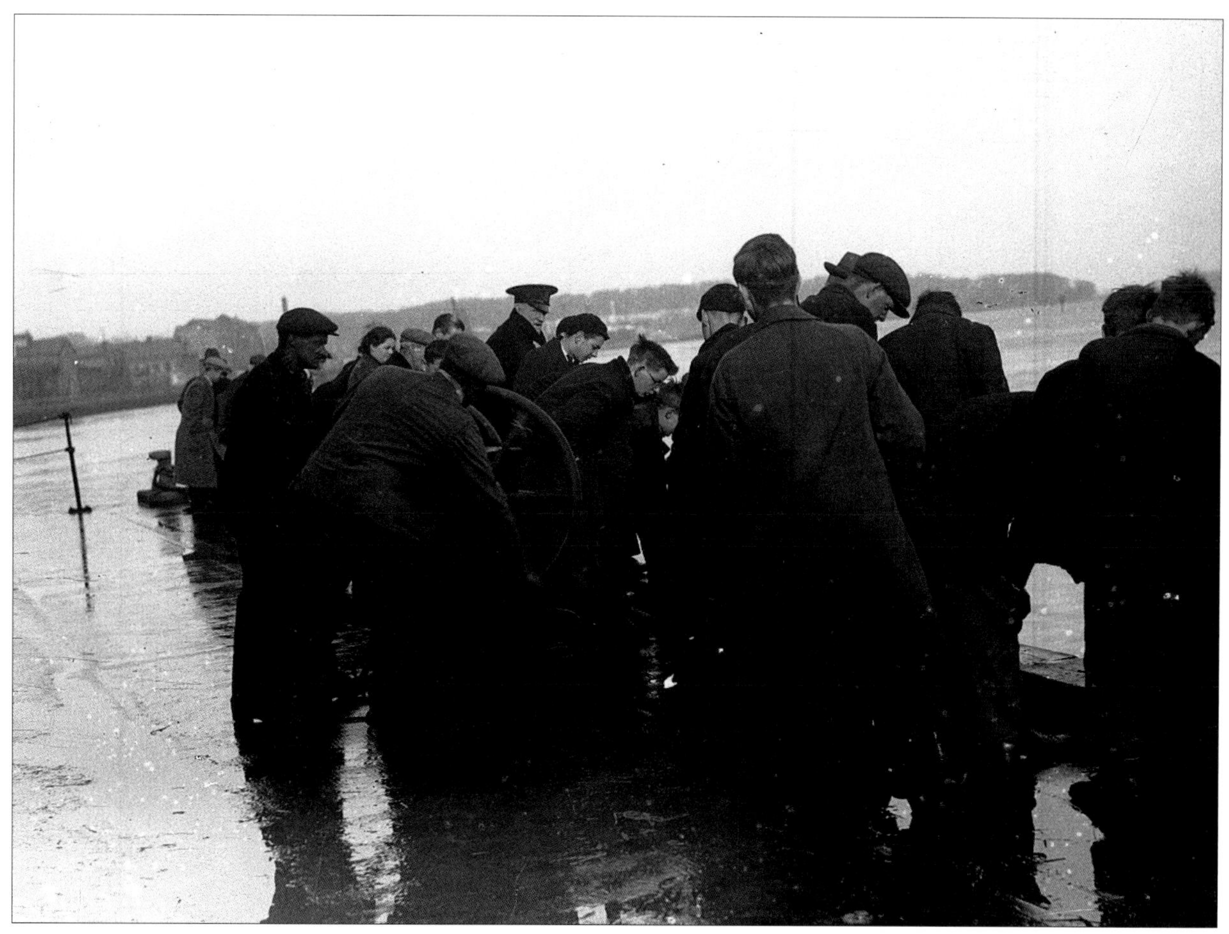

'Workmen pumping air to the diver when he is engaged under the water,' attempting to release the wire rope. *(POR 7-14, 4 February 1938)*

## HARBOUR COMMISSIONERS: DREDGER *HERCULES*

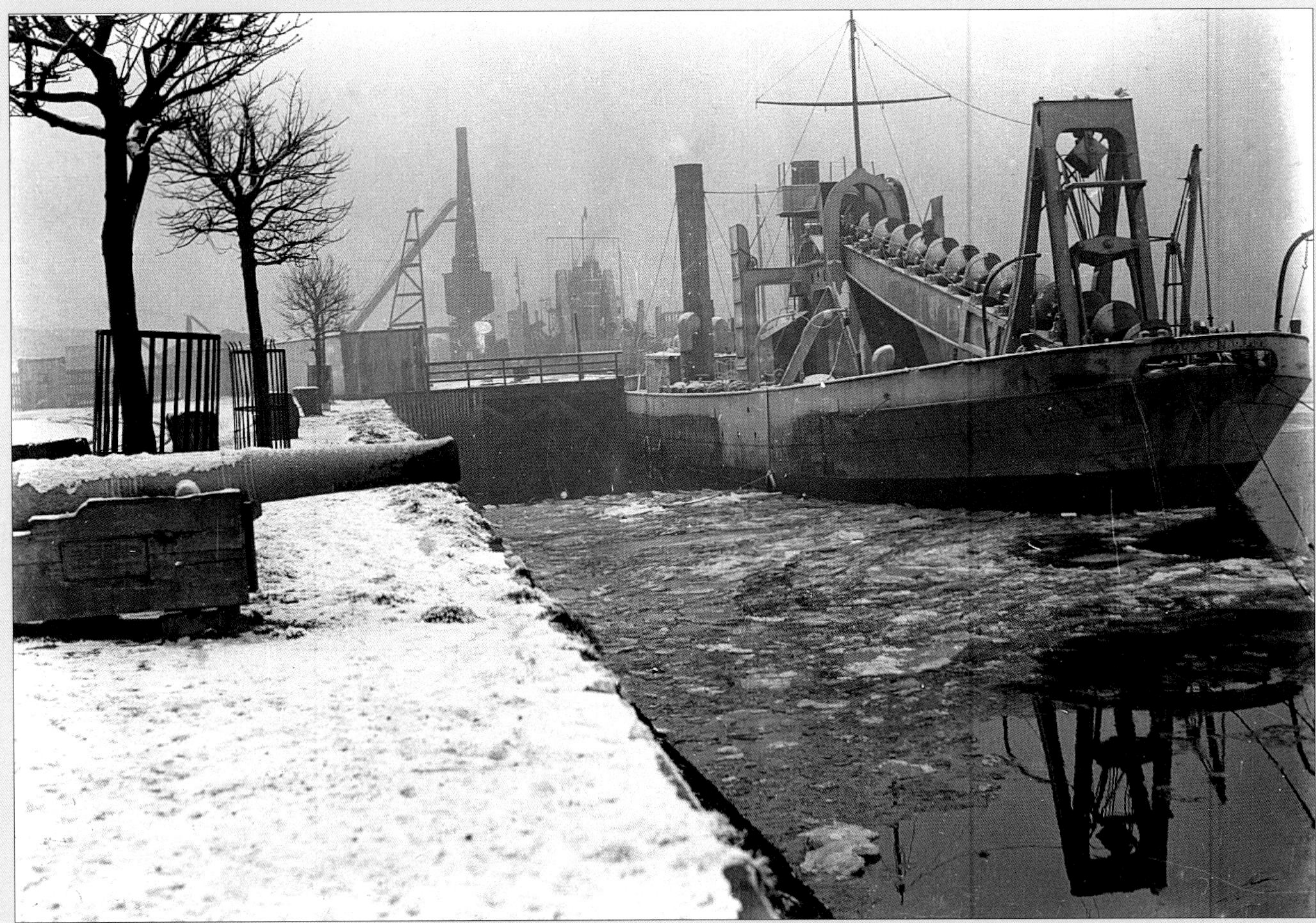

The bucket dredger *Hercules,* berthed at Rock Jetty by Rock Mills, was purchased by the Harbour Commissioners in 1887 to cut a deep-water channel through Lough Foyle and Rosses Bay. Built by Harland and Wolff, *Hercules* was one of the largest and most powerful dredging machines in the United Kingdom at the time. A crew of 13 were required to operate it. Owing to the work of this dredger, large vessels drawing up to 25 feet could come right up to Queen's Quay and discharge grain shipments of 6,000 tons. *(POR 1-14)*

## HARBOUR COMMISSIONERS: GRAVING DOCK

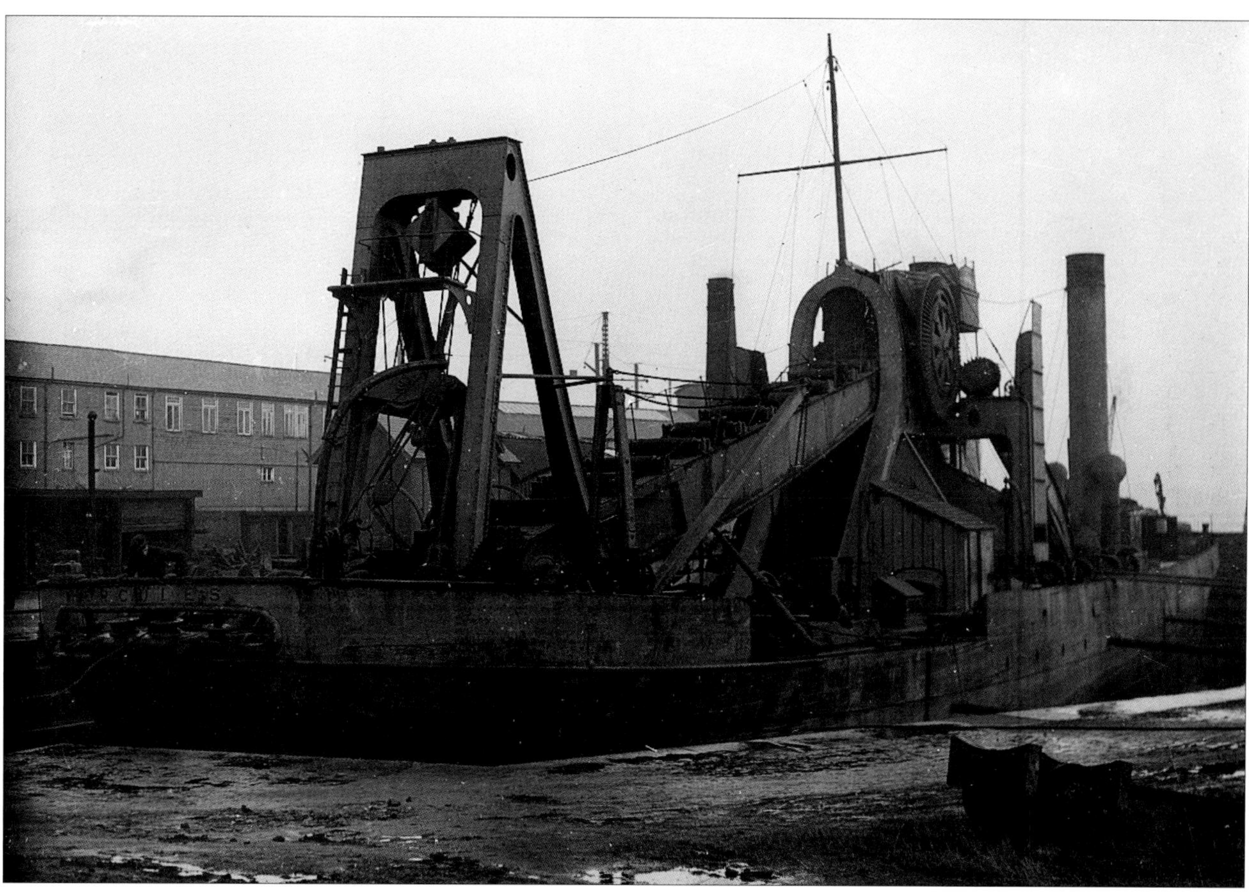

Bucket dredger *Hercules* receives repair work at the graving dock. A site at Pennyburn for a new graving dock, for the dry-docking of large vessels, was identified downstream from Gilliland's mill at the Rock. The graving dock, 345 feet long and 50 feet wide, set at an angle to the river and lined with granite walls and fitted with heavy oak gates, was built by the Harbour Commissioners at a cost of £25,000 and took its first vessel in February 1862. In 1976 the decision was made to permanently close the dry dock at Rock Quay as the demand for this facility was very slight relative to the expenditure that would be required to repair the dry dock gates, capstans and pumps. The dry dock was filled in and this area, known as Meadowbank, was developed in the 1980s by the Harbour Commissioners prior to their relocation to a deep-water port at Lisahally in 1993. *(POR 2-13)*

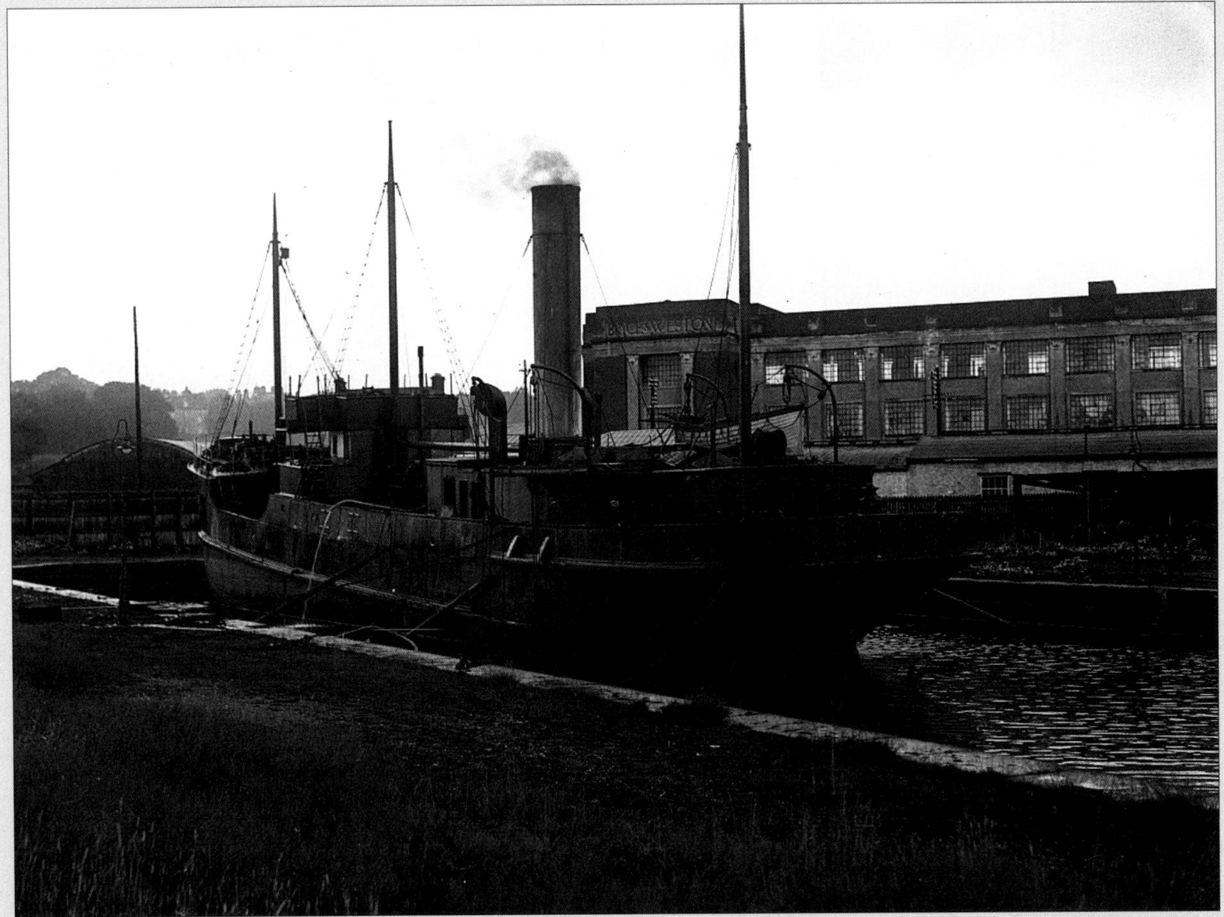

In August 1931, the SS *Carricklee* (334 tons, 141 feet long) was dry docked in Derry for repairs after going on the rocks at Tor Point in Rathlin Sound. She was owned by Derry coal merchants, Henry Lane & Co. The graving dock was adjacent to the former shipyard of North of Ireland Shipbuilding Company which opened in 1912 and closed in 1924. The shirt factory of Bryce and Weston on Strand Road (now a supermarket and apartments) can be seen in the background. *(POR 5-14, 17 August 1931)*

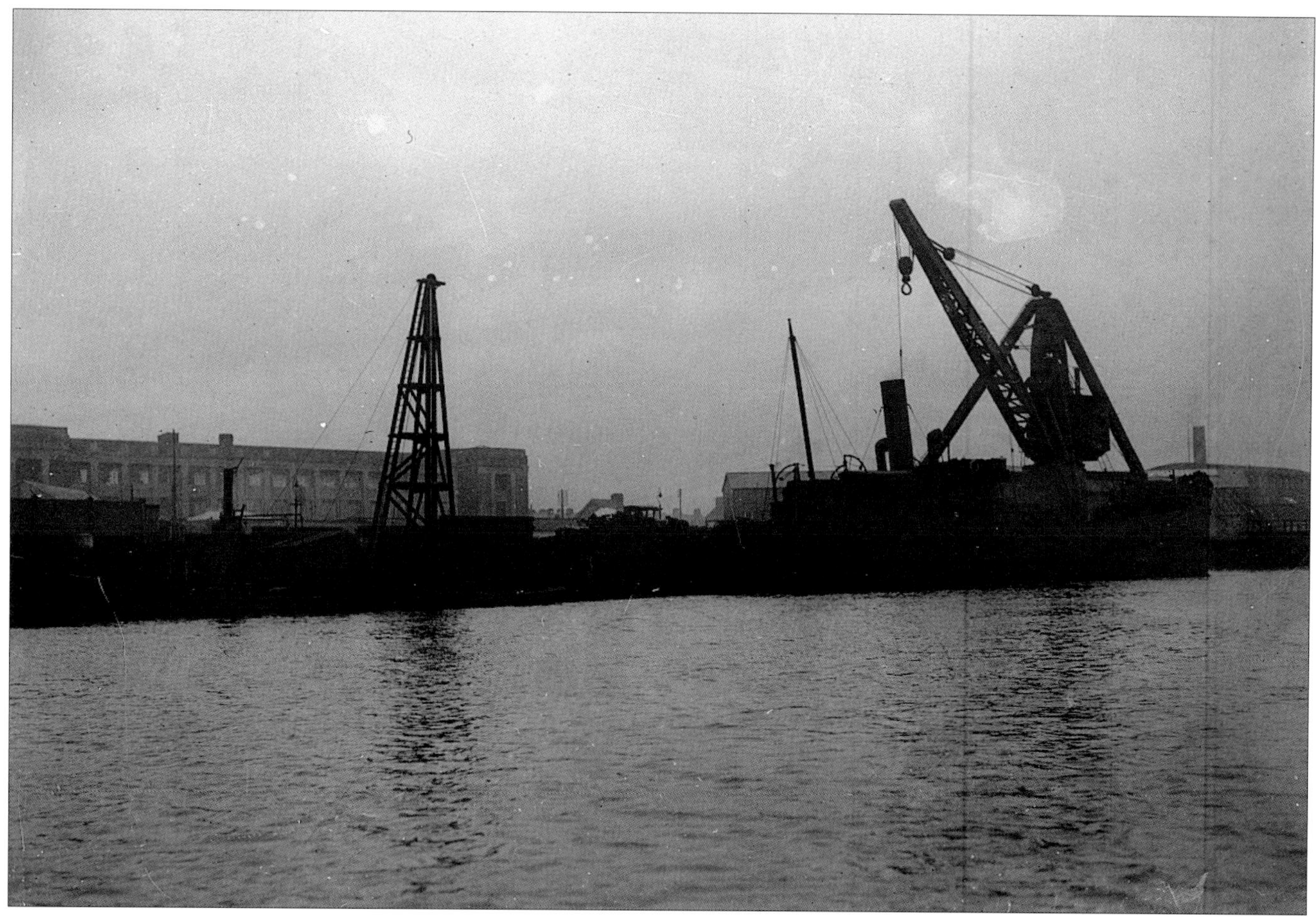

Entrance to the graving dock. The buildings in the background are (to the left) the shirt factory of Bryce and Weston on the Strand Road and (to the right) the soon-to-be-demolished sheds and furnace of the North of Ireland Shipbuilding Company, which had closed in 1924. It is now a Sainsbury's supermarket and car park. *(POR 8-4)*

# HARBOUR COMMISSIONERS: PENNYBURN SHIPYARD

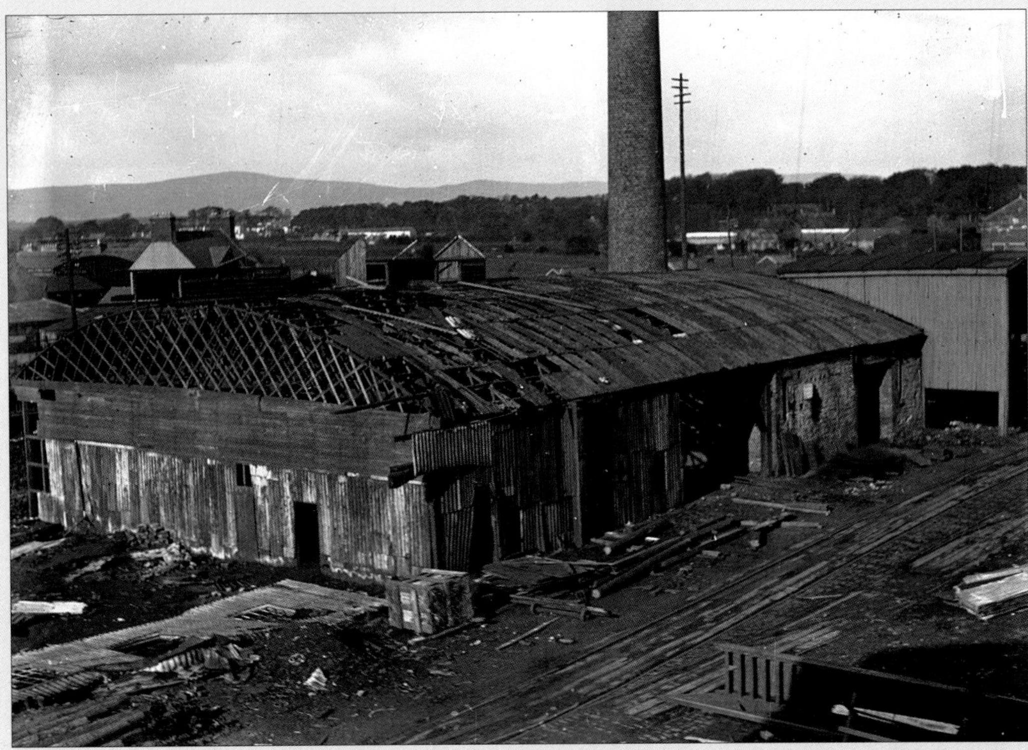

'Demolishing the Sheds in Derry Shipyard. The Furnace, upon which the work of demolition has begun' in November 1930. In the 1880s, the Harbour Commissioners invested £25,000 in turning the slobland adjacent to the graving dock into a shipyard. In October 1886 Charles J Bigger, son of William F Bigger who owned one of the largest bacon manufacturing firms in the city, applied to the Harbour Commissioners for lease of their shipyard. Although the shipbuilding industry in Derry failed to develop on a scale that became self-sustaining, it was nevertheless a very important industry. As a major male employer, the shipbuilding industry acted as a counterbalance to the predominantly female workforce of Derry's shirt industry. In addition, shipbuilding, with its need for skilled labour, employed shipwrights, platers, caulkers, boilermakers, drillers, turners, riveters, plumbers, carpenters and electricians, and acted as another balancing feature in a city with a vast number of unskilled workers. Three attempts were made to establish a shipbuilding industry in Derry in the Harbour Commissioners' shipyard at Pennyburn: Charles J Bigger's Foyle Shipyard, in operation from 1887 to 1892; Londonderry Shipbuilding & Engineering Company, from 1899 to 1904; and North of Ireland Shipbuilding Company, from 1912 to 1924. *(POR 8-5, 5 November 1930)*

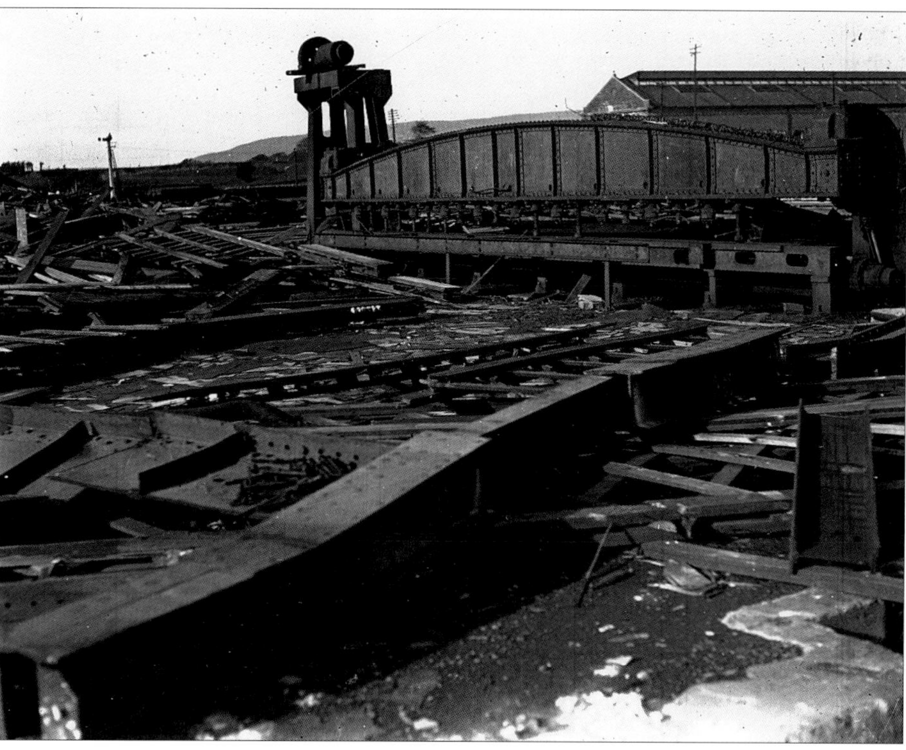

'The Plater's Shed' of former North of Ireland Shipbuilding Company at Pennyburn 'showing the girders and wood strewn over the yard after it was demolished' in November 1930. In May 1912, Trevisa Clarke arrived in Derry and within a year his company, North of Ireland Shipbuilding Company, built three ships and employed 450 men. In the spring of 1919, there were 2,200 men and apprentices employed in the shipyard, the largest ever male labour force in the city's history. Yet by 1924 the yard was closed, and it never re-opened.

*Londonderry Sentinel* of 1 January 1925 reported, 'during 1924 the North of Ireland Shipbuilding Co., Ltd, turned out three vessels – the *Chemong*, 1,902 tons, a bulk freighter, for service on the Great Lakes and Gulf of St. Lawrence; the *Drumahoe*, of similar type, for the same service; and the *Ville d'Amiens*, 7,143 tons, a passenger and cargo steamer for a French firm... After gradually reducing the number of their hands as the different orders were completed, the shipyard directors decided upon closing the yard, pending the receipt of fresh work. The machinery is being kept greased in the hope that with restored buoyancy in shipbuilding the yard will remain operational.' Rationalisation and restructuring within the UK economy and Derry's peripheral location on a contentious border, created by partition of 1921, spelt economic hardship for Derry and the North West for the remainder of the inter-war years. *(POR 8-3, 5 November 1930)*

## HARBOUR COMMISSIONERS: LAUNCH *TF COOKE*

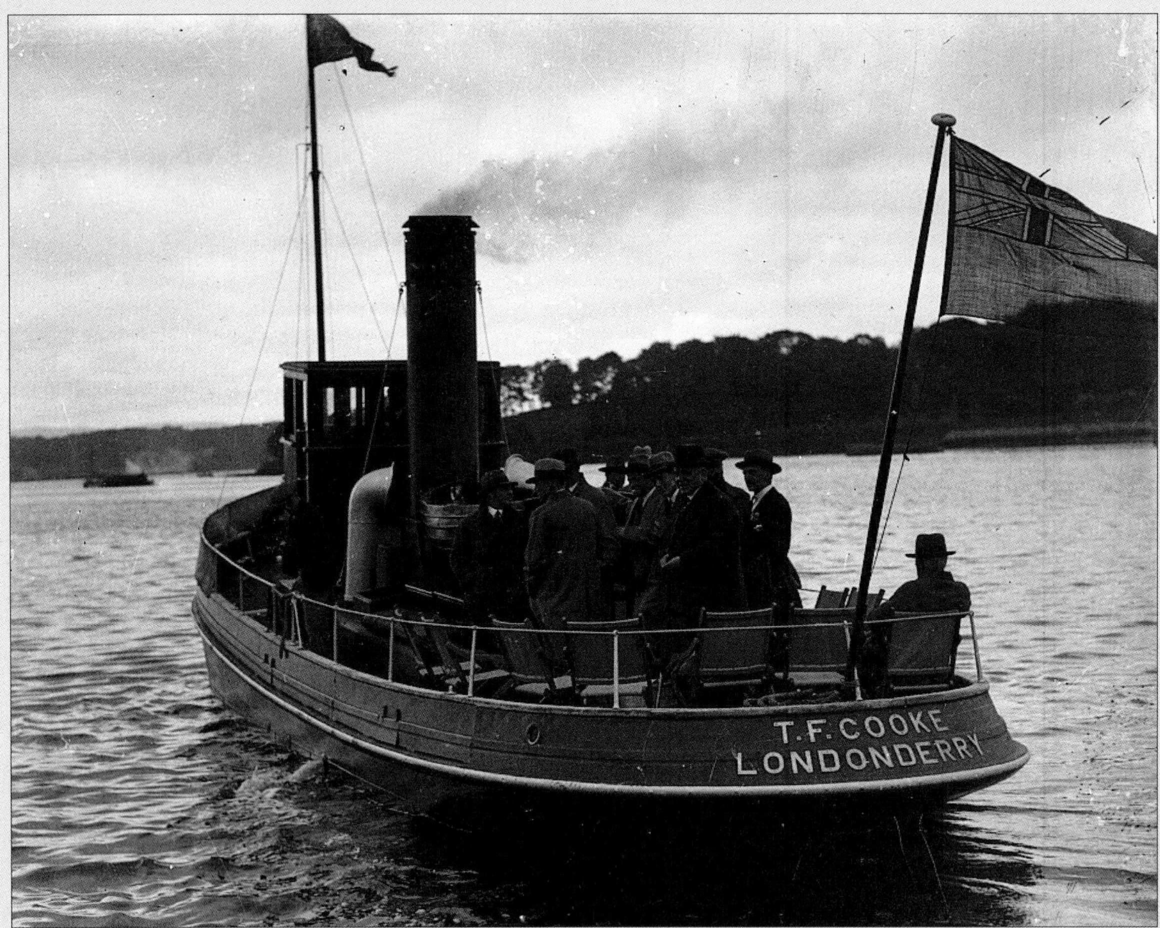


Members of The Honourable The Irish Society, on their annual visitation to the city, on board the *TF Cooke*, heading for Culmore Point on Wednesday afternoon 23 July 1930 in order to visit their school at Culmore. Later on that evening the annual banquet of the Irish Society was held in the Guildhall.

The Harbour Commissioners' launch *TF Cooke* was purchased about 1910. This small tug was used for light duties on the Foyle as it was not powerful enough to tow ships.

The Honourable The Irish Society, composed of 'six and twenty honest and discreet citizens of London', was formally constituted by Royal Charter of James I on 29 March 1613 to direct the affairs of the plantation of the City and County of Londonderry. *(POR 17-8, 25 July 1930)*

# LAURENTIC SALVAGE SHIP

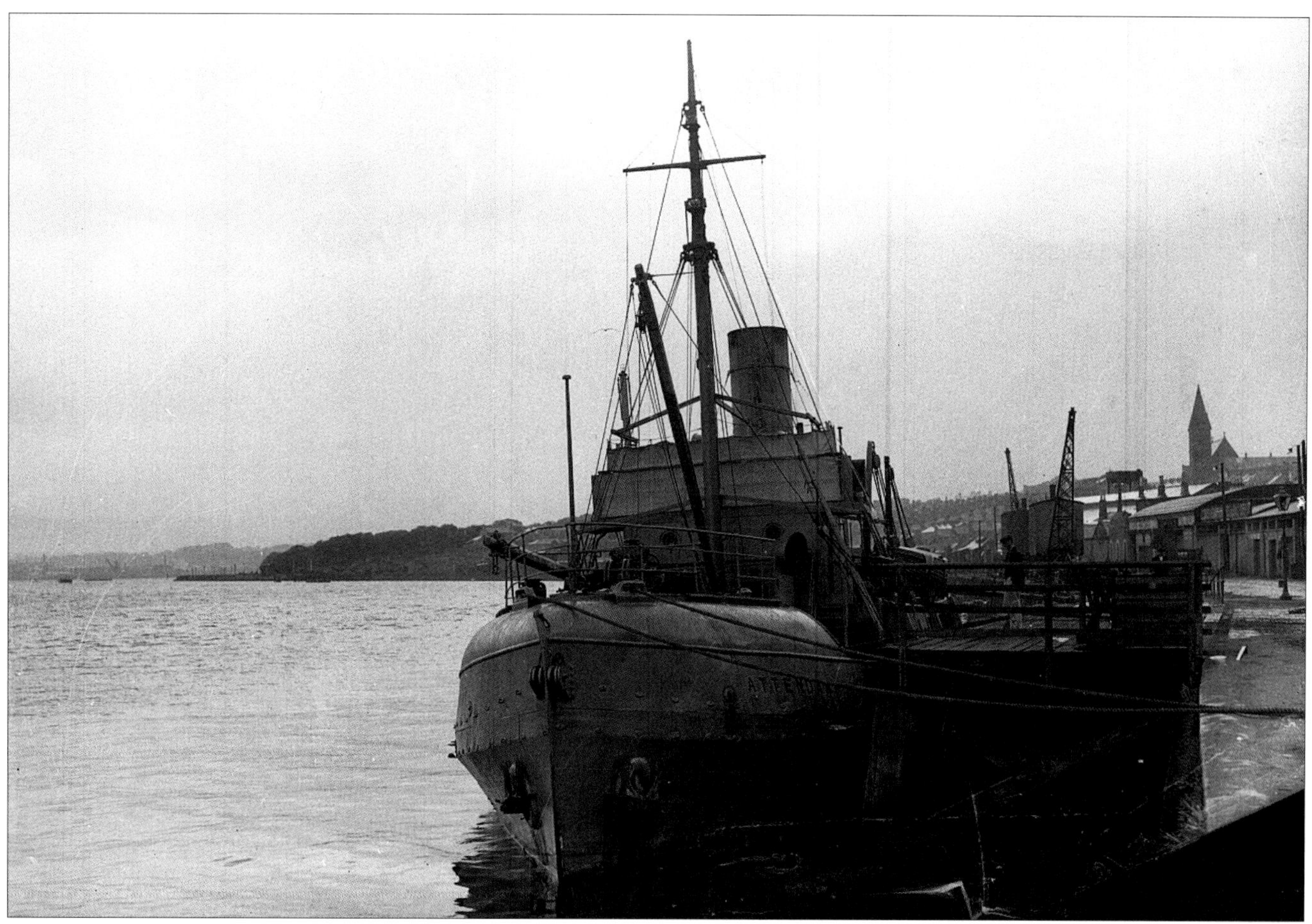

'The salvage ship *Attendant* at Derry Quay' in September 1934. 'She is at present engaged in salvage operations on the S.S. *Laurentic* that was sunk off Lough Swilly during the war.' On 25 January 1917, the *Laurentic*, on leaving Buncrana, struck two German mines off Lough Swilly and sank within an hour, 354 passengers, mostly naval personnel, lost their lives. The ship was also carrying 3,211 gold ingots (about 43 tons) to pay for war munitions. Royal Navy divers made over 5,000 dives to the wreck between 1917 and 1924 and recovered all but 25 of the ingots. In 1934, three more ingots were recovered by a private salvage company. As of 2018, 22 bars of gold remain unaccounted for. *(POR 1-1, 19 September 1934)*

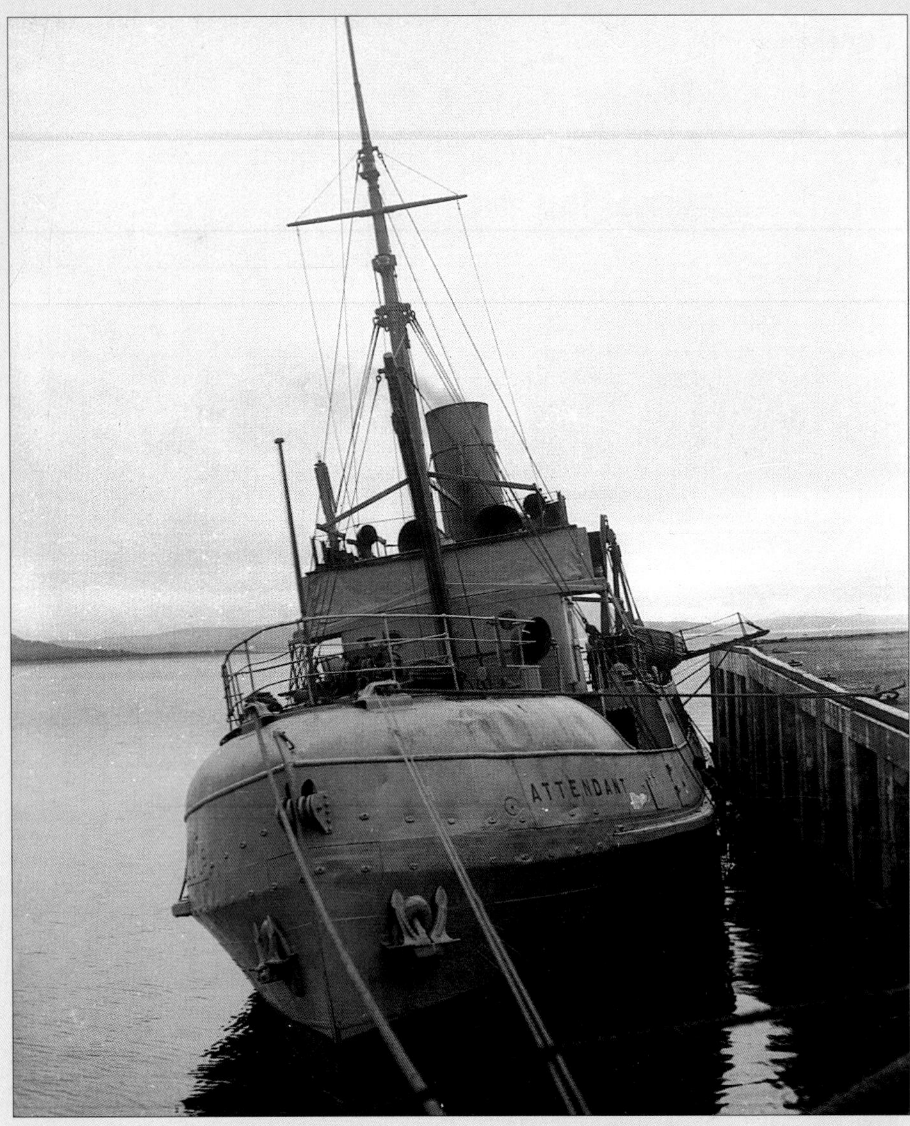


'The Salvage ship *Attendant* at Buncrana Harbour' in August 1937. 'She is engaged in recovering the remainder of the gold lost in the S.S. *Laurentic* off Lough Swilly.' This attempt also failed to find any of the remaining 22 bars of gold. *(POR 4-4, 9 August 1937)*

# DERRY REGATTA

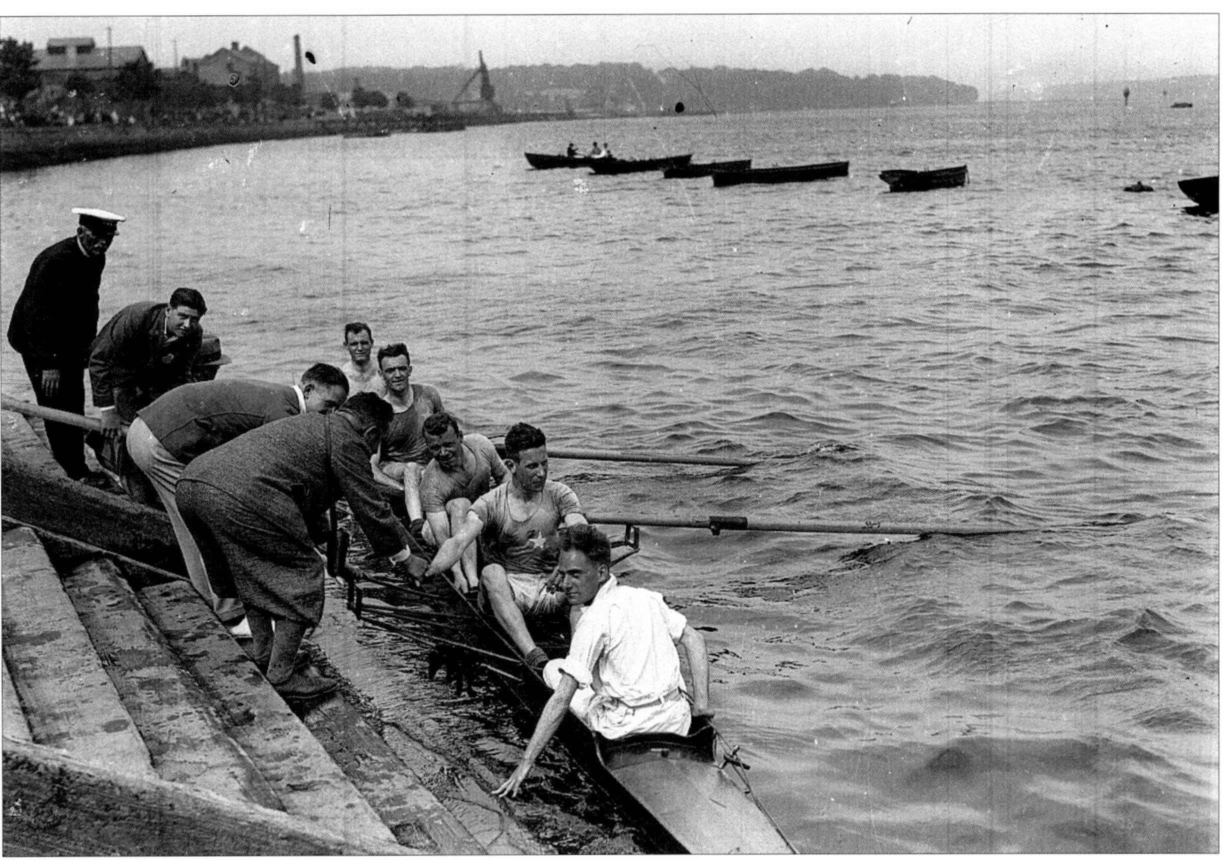

City of Derry Senior Four, with crew of TD Ward, VS Ward, JM Scott, F Buchanan (stroke) and JA Hamilton (cox), who beat Bann in the final of City of Derry Grand Challenge Cup at the City of Derry Rowing Club's Annual Regatta, held in glorious weather on Thursday 6 July 1933. The steps shown in this scene were sited almost opposite the club's headquarters (built 1869 but now a restaurant) on the quay at the foot of Boating Club Lane. *Derry Standard* of 7 July 1933 reported that 'the result of this race was a reversal of the verdict at Bann Regatta three days ago, when Bann won. The two crews raced level to halfway, when Derry gradually forged ahead and won by five lengths. Bann had shipped a quantity of water and stopped rowing.' Crews competing in this Regatta, under the patronage of the Duke of Abercorn, included City of Derry, Bann, Belfast Commercial, Portadown and University College Dublin. A large number of spectators lined the various vantage points along the river to watch nine races: Bann won five events, Derry three and UCD one. *(ROW 1-11, 7 July 1933)*

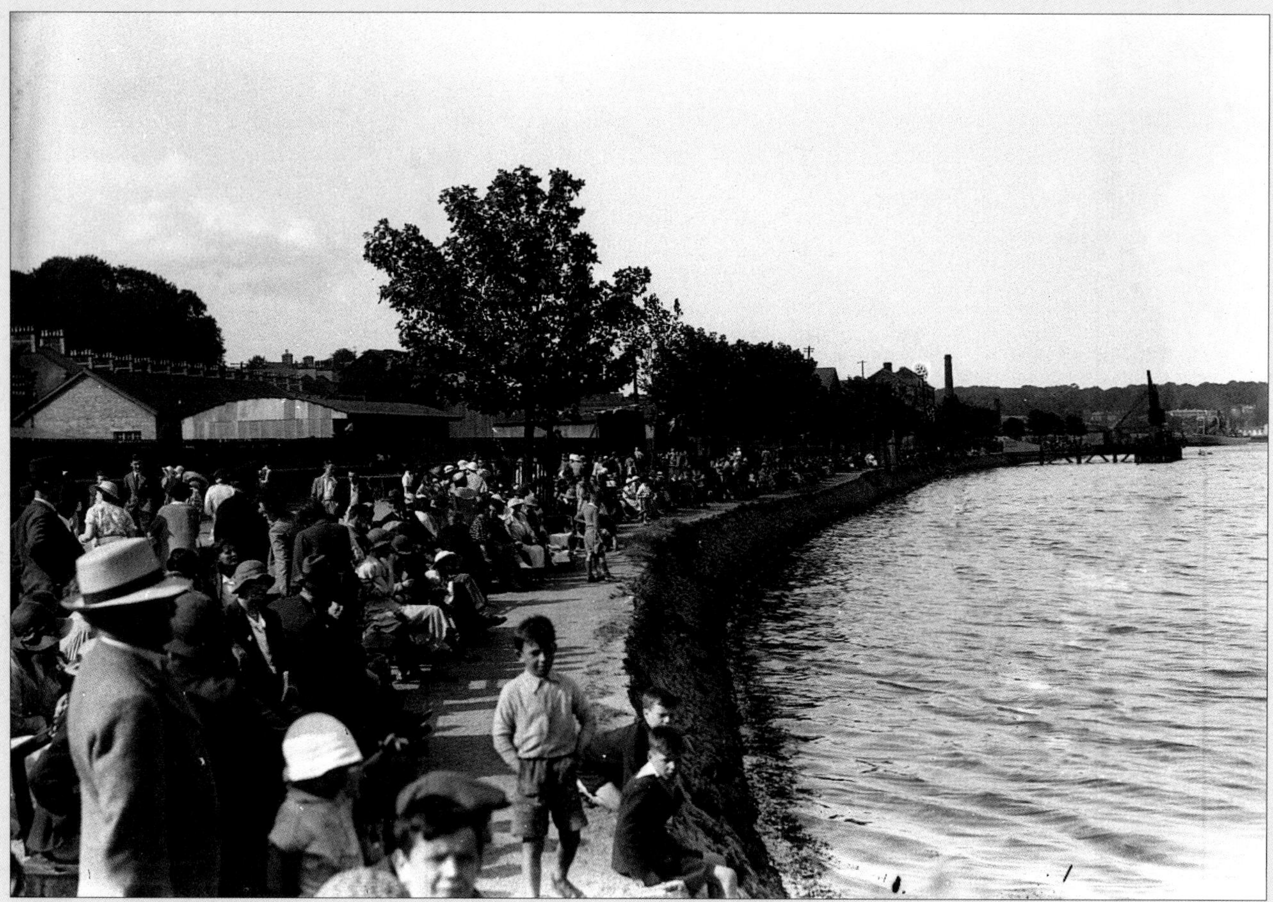

A section of the crowd in the enclosure at the annual City of Derry Regatta on the Foyle on Thursday 11 July 1935. The *Standard* of 12 July 1935 reported that 'the sun shone in a blaze of glory on a scene of animation, and the river, smooth and placid, made rowing conditions ideal.' It also remarked, 'time was when the name of City of Derry was feared on every river in Ireland, but if Derry's star has been on the wane of late years, it has not been due to a lack of enthusiasm on the part of the members of the club.' Crews competing in eight races at the Regatta included City of Derry, Bann, Belfast Commercial, Portadown and Drogheda: Bann won five events, Portadown two and Drogheda one. *(ROW 3-6, 12 July 1935)*

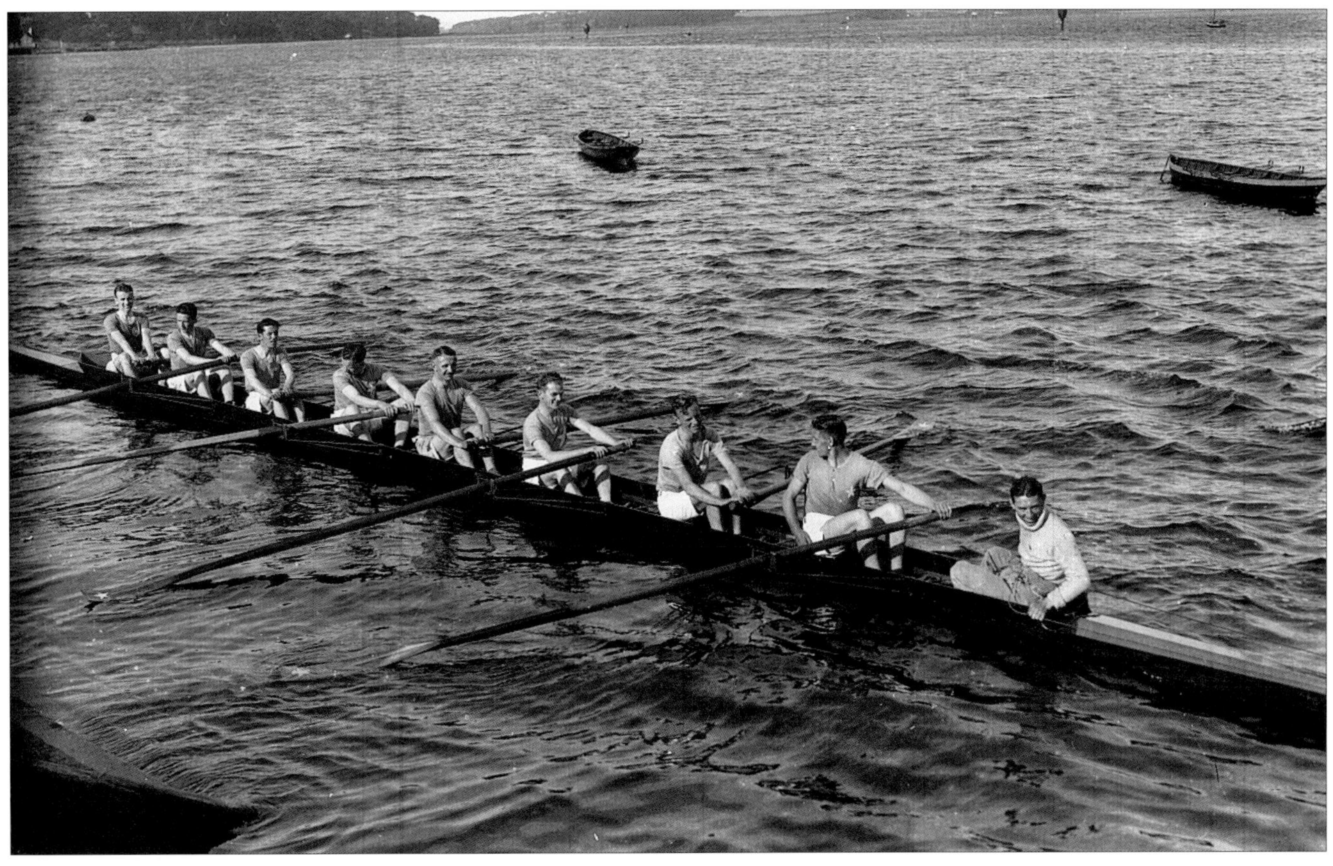

City of Derry Maiden Eights, with crew of JL Gilfillan (bow), WJ Donaghey, B Faulkner, GEC McLeer, JA Lowry, W Bell, HB Phillips, HT Lee (stroke) and H Mitchell (cox), going out from the Clubhouse steps to compete against Drogheda in Heat A of the Victory Challenge Cup at City of Derry Regatta on Thursday 11 July 1935. The *Standard* of 12 July 1935 reported that Drogheda RC and City of Derry BC 'raced neck and neck from the start… but Drogheda hung on grimly and near the finish produced a spurt which put them in front. They won by a canvas.' Bann lifted the Victory Challenge Cup in the final. *(ROW 3-13, 12 July 1935)*

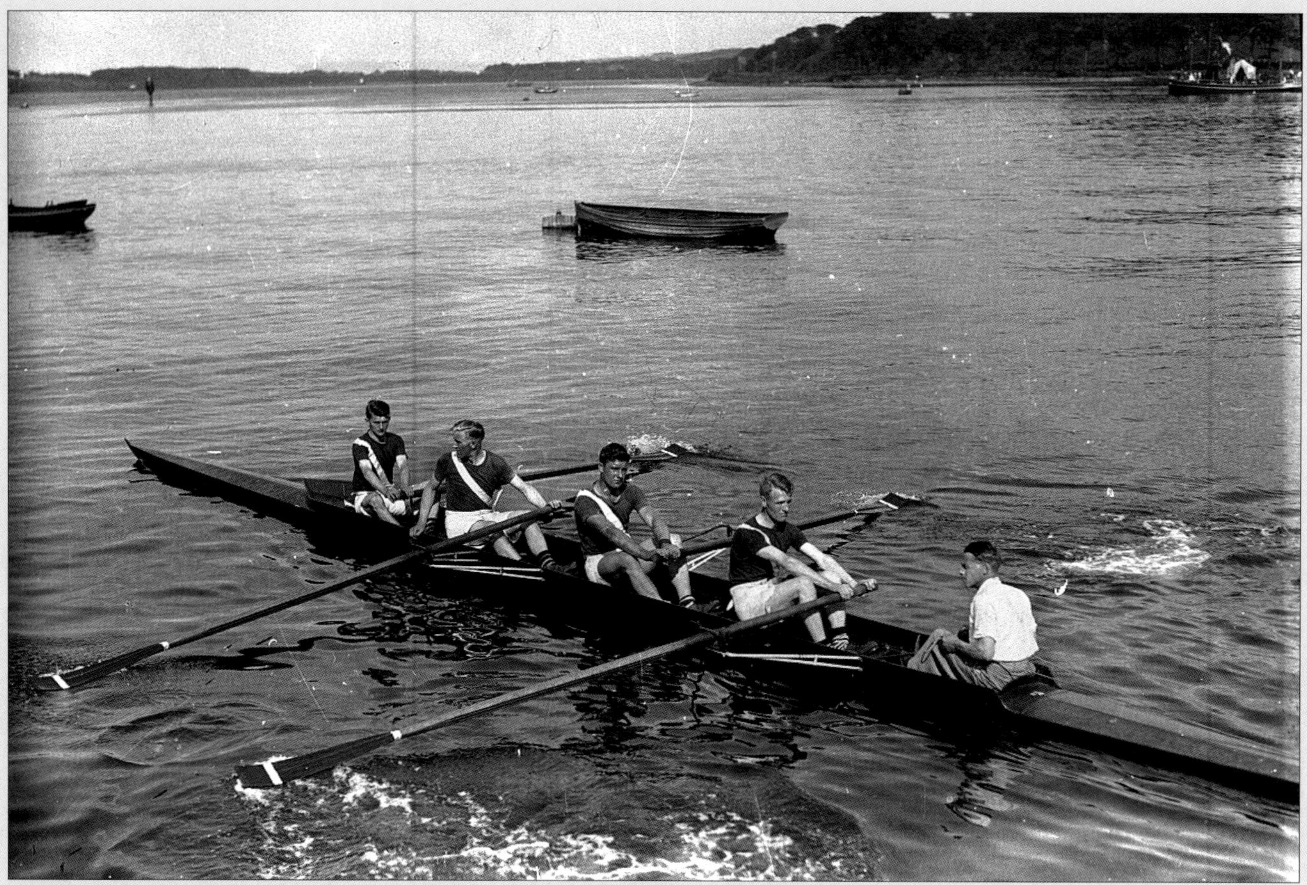

Bann Junior Fours, with crew of DJ Murdock (bow), S McQuigg, HMN Oliver, WJ Morrison (stroke) and RA Wilson (cox), who 'won a good race over Portadown by two lengths' in the final of the Ladies' Challenge Cup at City of Derry Regatta on Thursday 11 July 1935. *(ROW 3-2, 12 July 1935)*

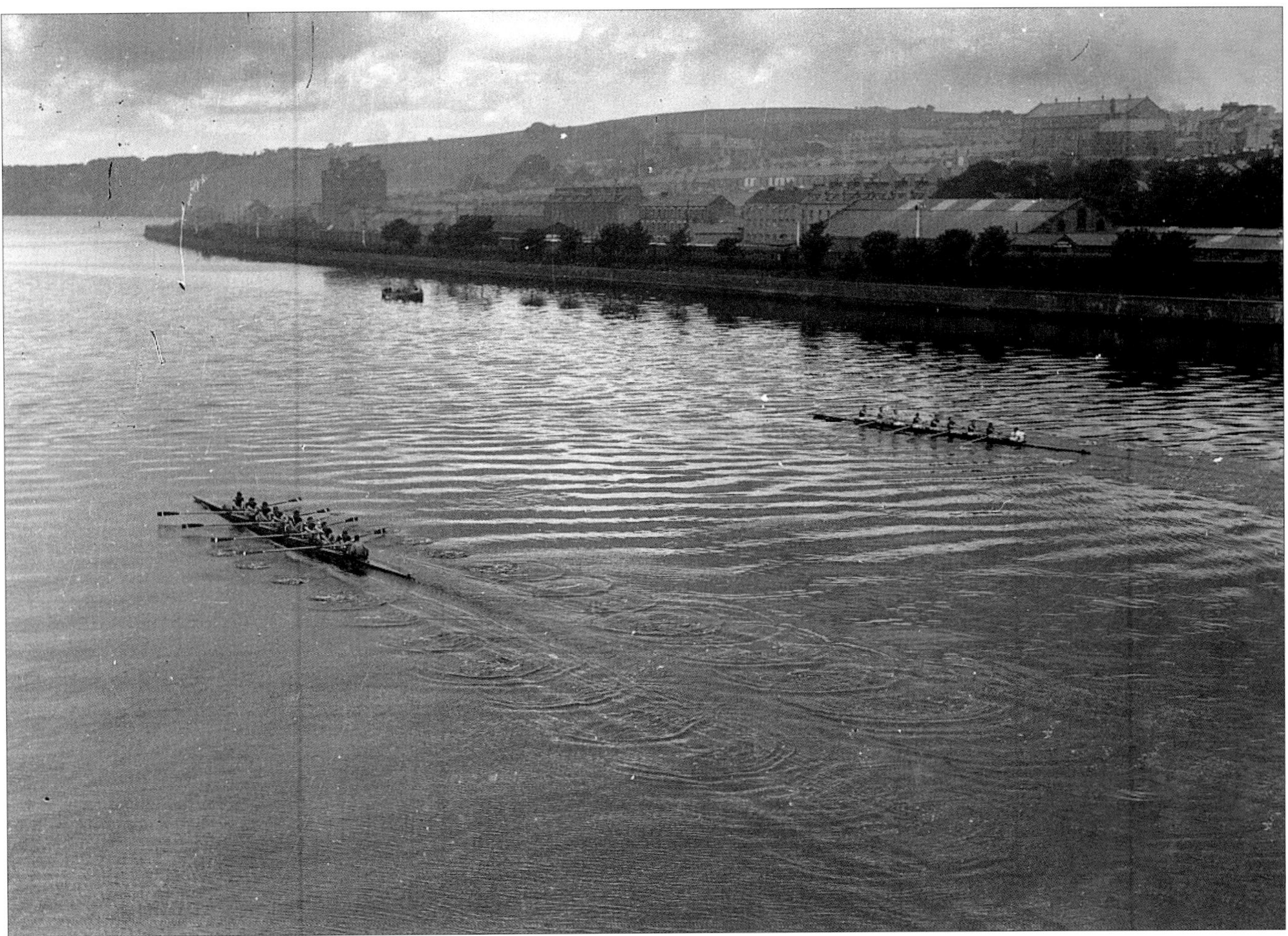

Bann (left), who beat Derry by a quarter of a length in the first heat of the Senior Eights Championship of Ireland at the City of Derry Regatta on Thursday 16 July 1936. In this photograph, taken from Craigavon Bridge, Star (shirt) Factory and Goods Shed of the Great Northern Railway on Foyle Road are visible. *Derry Standard* reported that 'Dublin University, who have proved themselves the premier oarsmen in Irish waters this year, won seven of the ten trophies competed for' at 1936 Derry Regatta. It continued 'the remaining three cups were shared by Portadown and Belfast Commercial. City of Derry and Bann each had a blank day.' *(ROW 2-8, 17 July 1936)*

## MILITARY SEAPLANES: ROYAL AIR FORCE

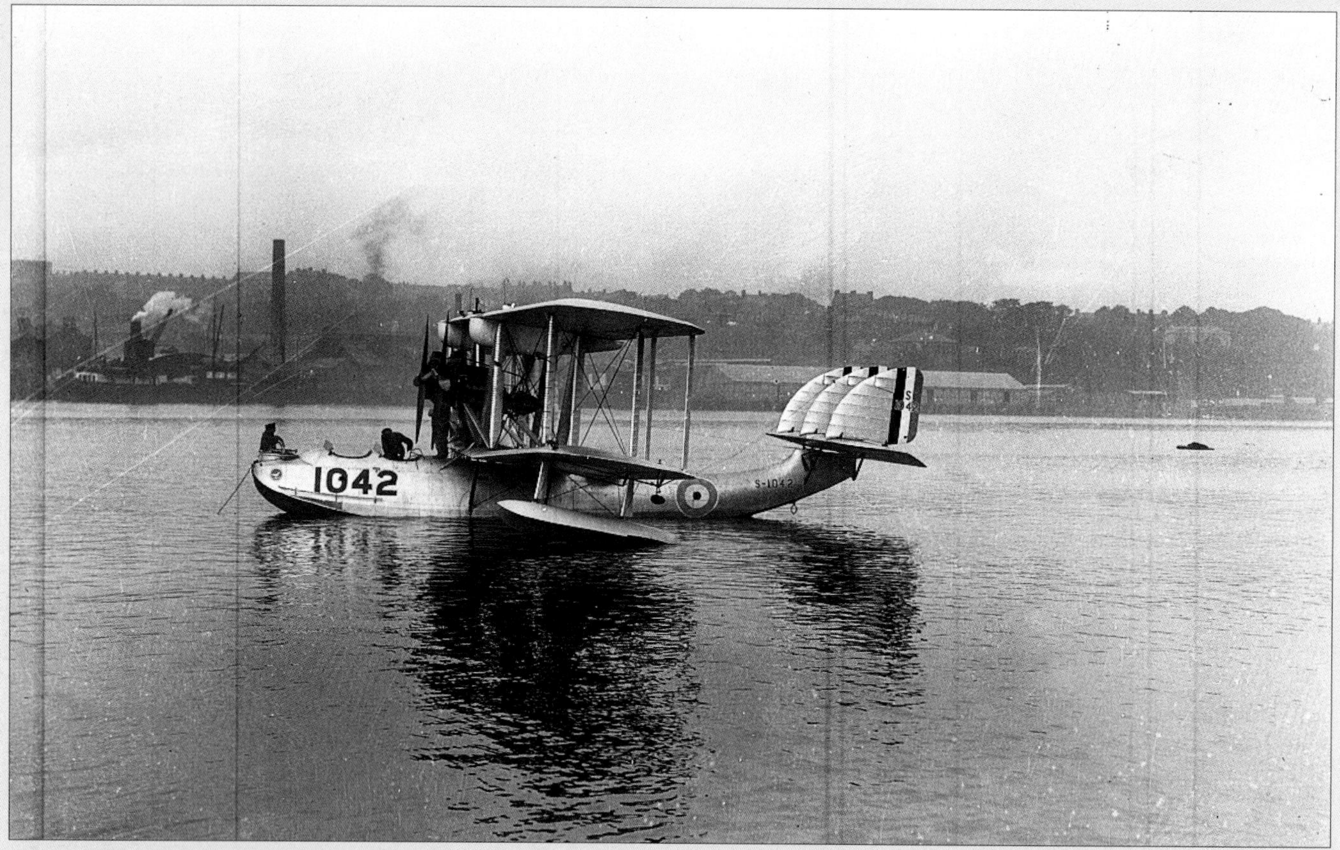


'The Seaplane, S.1042, arrived in the Foyle yesterday [15 September 1931]. Being the first seen in Derry it aroused much interest.' During the 1930s there were periodic visits for training purposes by the Royal Air Force's Supermarine Southampton Flying Boats, one of the most successful flying boats of the inter-war period. It was a twin-engine biplane flying boat, with the tractor engines mounted between the wings. Armed with three Lewis machine guns in the bows and amidships, the main purpose of the Southampton was to locate enemy shipping or submarines and then summon up the bombers and torpedo squadrons to make an attack. *(AER 1-6, 16 September 1931)*

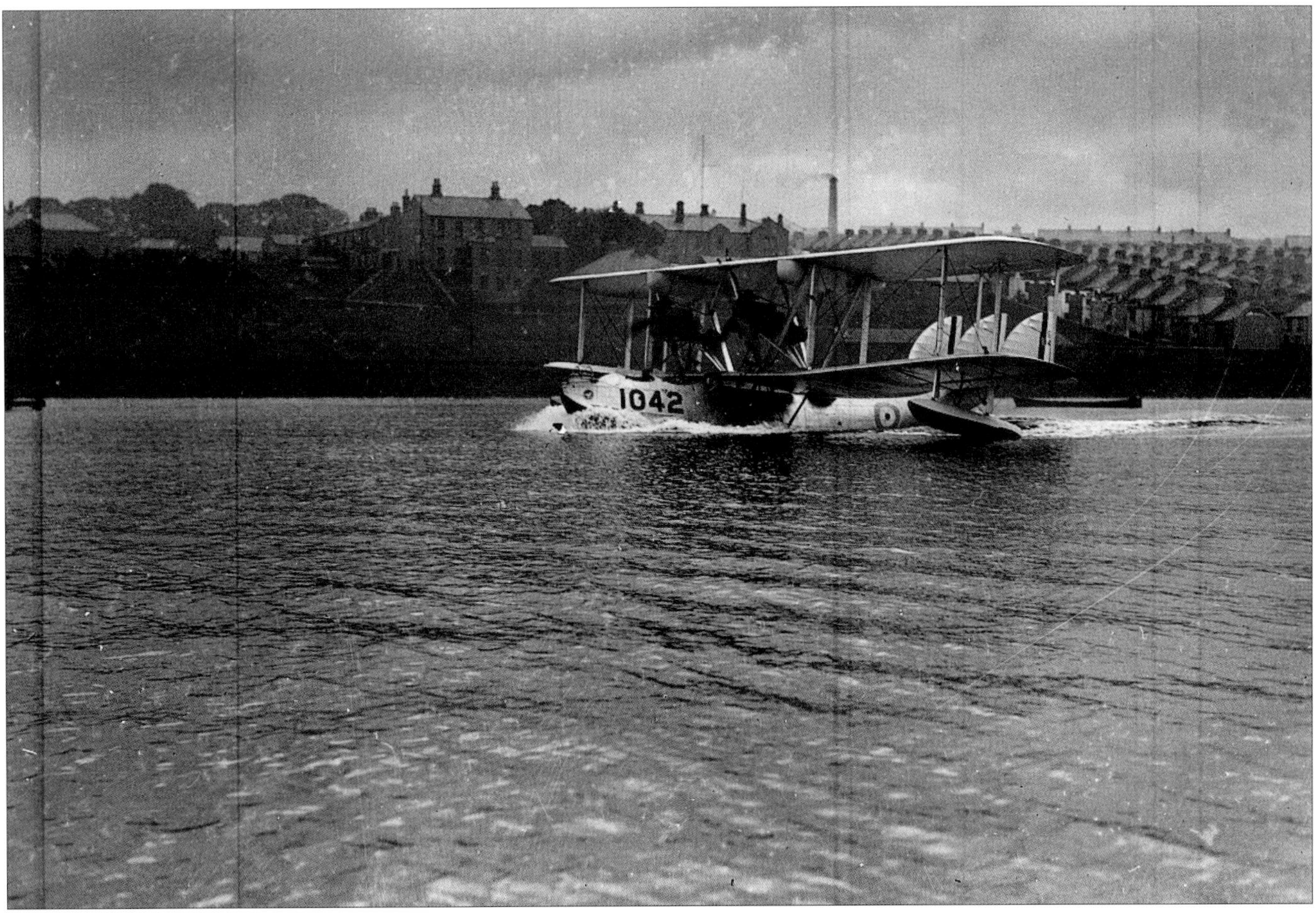


Another photograph of the RAF's Supermarine Southampton Flying Boat, S.1042, gliding along the surface of the River Foyle in front of Ebrington Barracks on 15 September 1931. Delivery of Supermarine Southampton seaplanes to the RAF started in 1925. It was designed by the team of RJ Mitchell, better known as the designer of the Spitfire, the iconic Second World War fighter, and built by Supermarine, a British aircraft manufacturer based at Woolston, Southampton. Fifty-one feet in length, wingspan of 75 feet, with cruising speed of 80 mph and a maximum range of more than 900 miles the Southampton had achieved fame for a series of long-distance flights, the most notable being 'The RAF Far East Cruise' in which a flying unit of four Southamptons flew from Felixstowe to Singapore via the Mediterranean and India in 1927 and 1928. *(AER 1-5, 16 September 1931)*

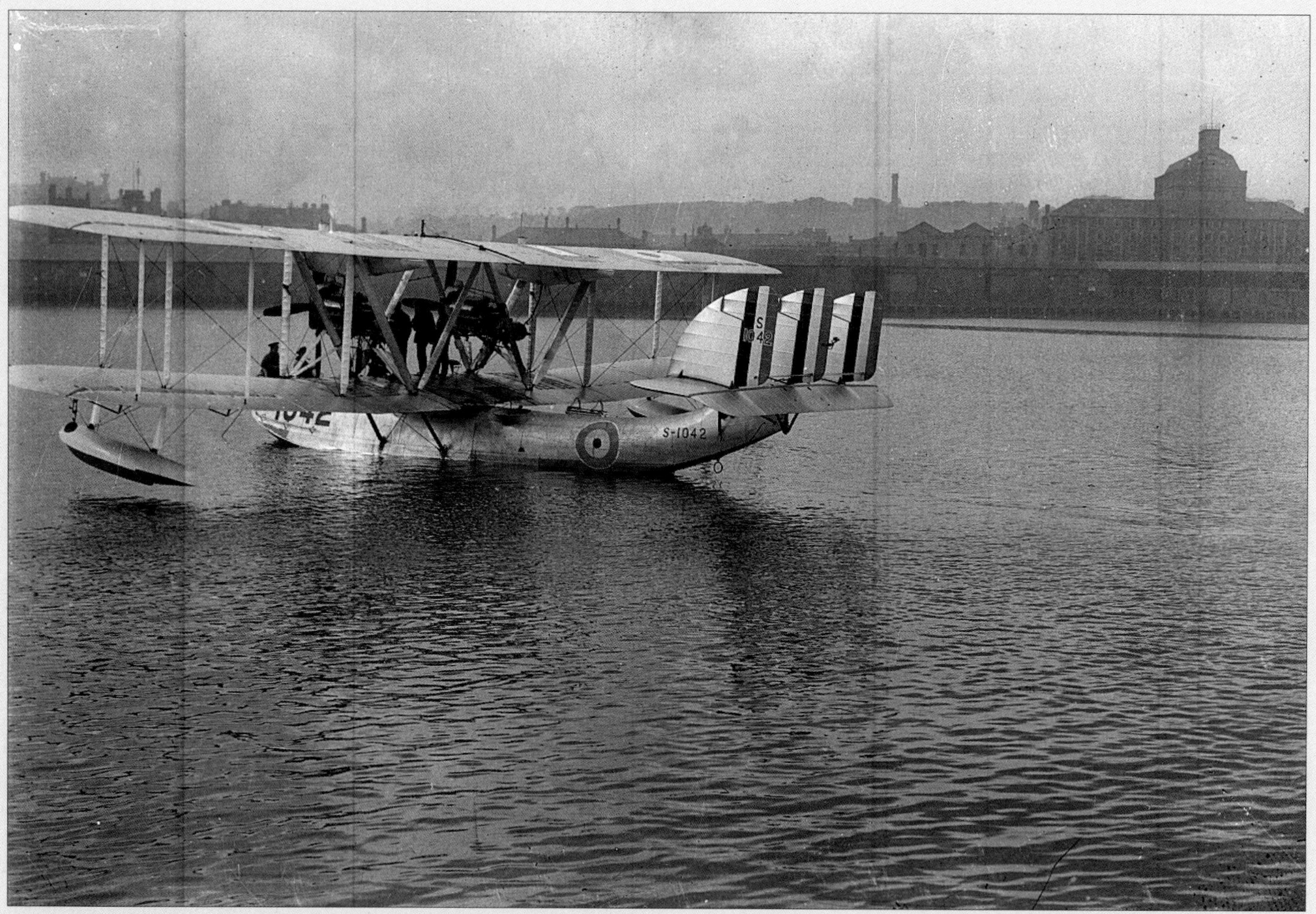


The RAF's Supermarine Southampton Flying Boat, S.1042, photographed on the Foyle at McCorkell's Mill on 15 September 1931. *(AER 1-10)*

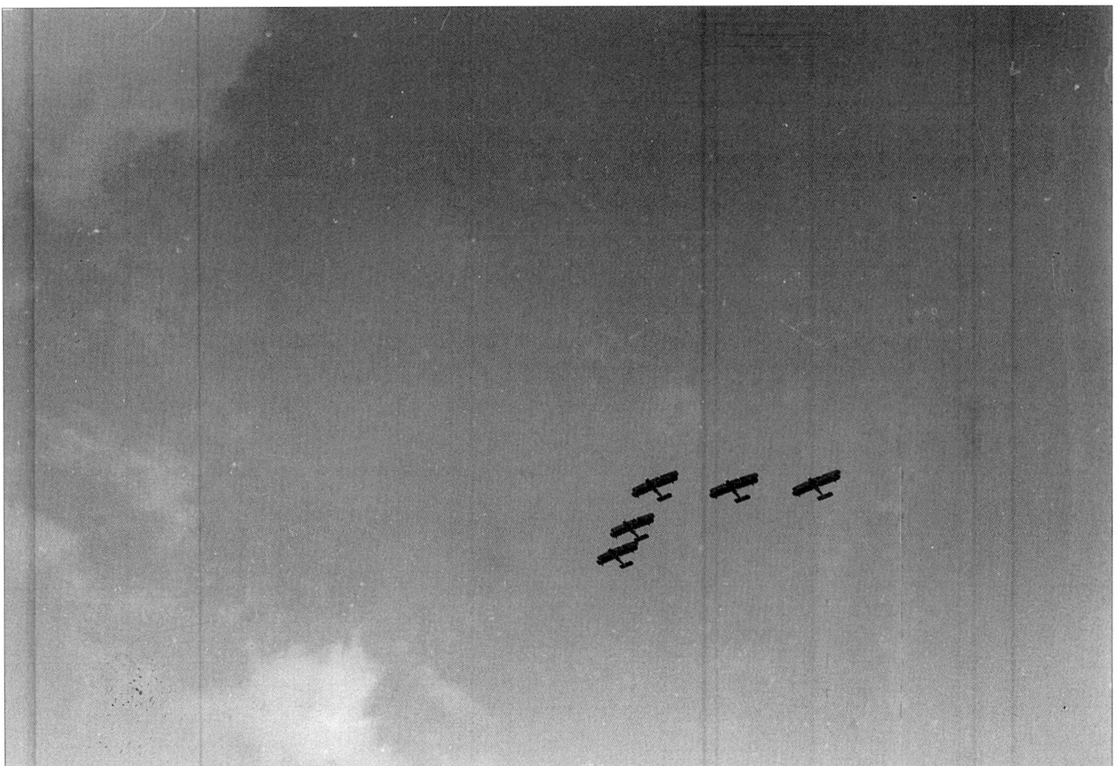

Flying in formation over the city in September 1933 are five Supermarine Southampton Flying Boats of Number 201 RAF Squadron. *Derry Standard* of 27 September 1933 reported their arrival on Lough Foyle commanded by Squadron-Leader Cecil George Wigglesworth. This Squadron had initially come to Derry on 2 July 1933 to 'welcome General Balbo and his Air Armada on the occasion of their transatlantic flight.' It is claimed that CG Wigglesworth, a First World War airship pilot, was the inspiration of Biggles. James Bigglesworth, nicknamed Biggles, was a fictional pilot and adventurer in the Biggles series of adventure books, written for young children, by WE Johns, between 1932 and 1968.

The British pilots of 201 RAF Squadron were officially welcomed to the city on Tuesday 26 September 1933 at the Harbour Office by Robert H Smyth, Chairman of the Harbour Commissioners. The *Standard* stated that 'the R.A.F. have at present two bases in Northern waters, one at Oban and one at Stranraer, and the people of Derry are still hopeful that a third will be established in the Maiden City.' During the Second World War, Castle Archdale on the banks of Lough Erne, was developed as an important base for flying boats of the RAF and the Royal Canadian Air Force due its close proximity to the Atlantic, just 30 miles away. *(AER 1-11, 27 September 1933)*

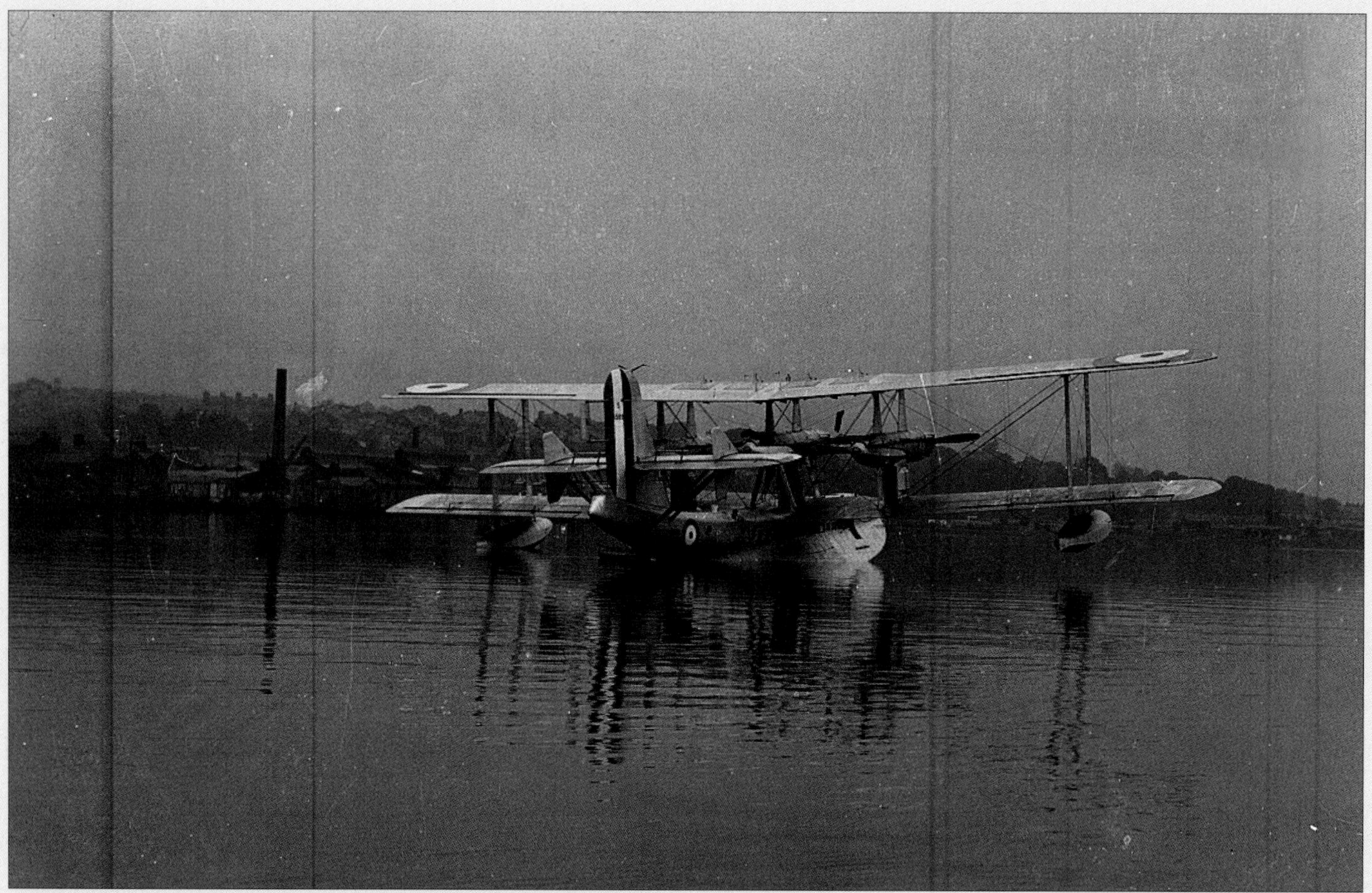

One of the five '30-ton' Supermarine Southampton Flying Boats of No 201 RAF Squadron moored in the Foyle in September 1933. *Derry Standard* of 27 September 1933 reported that the Squadron is expected to remain until Thursday 28 September, 'when it will leave for Stranraer and afterwards for Calshot.' Number 201 Squadron can claim to be one of the oldest British military flying units tracing its origins back to 1914. Disbanded on 31 December 1919, it was reformed on 1 January 1929 as a flying-boat unit and based at RAF Calshot, near Southampton. *(AER 1-9, 25 September 1933)*

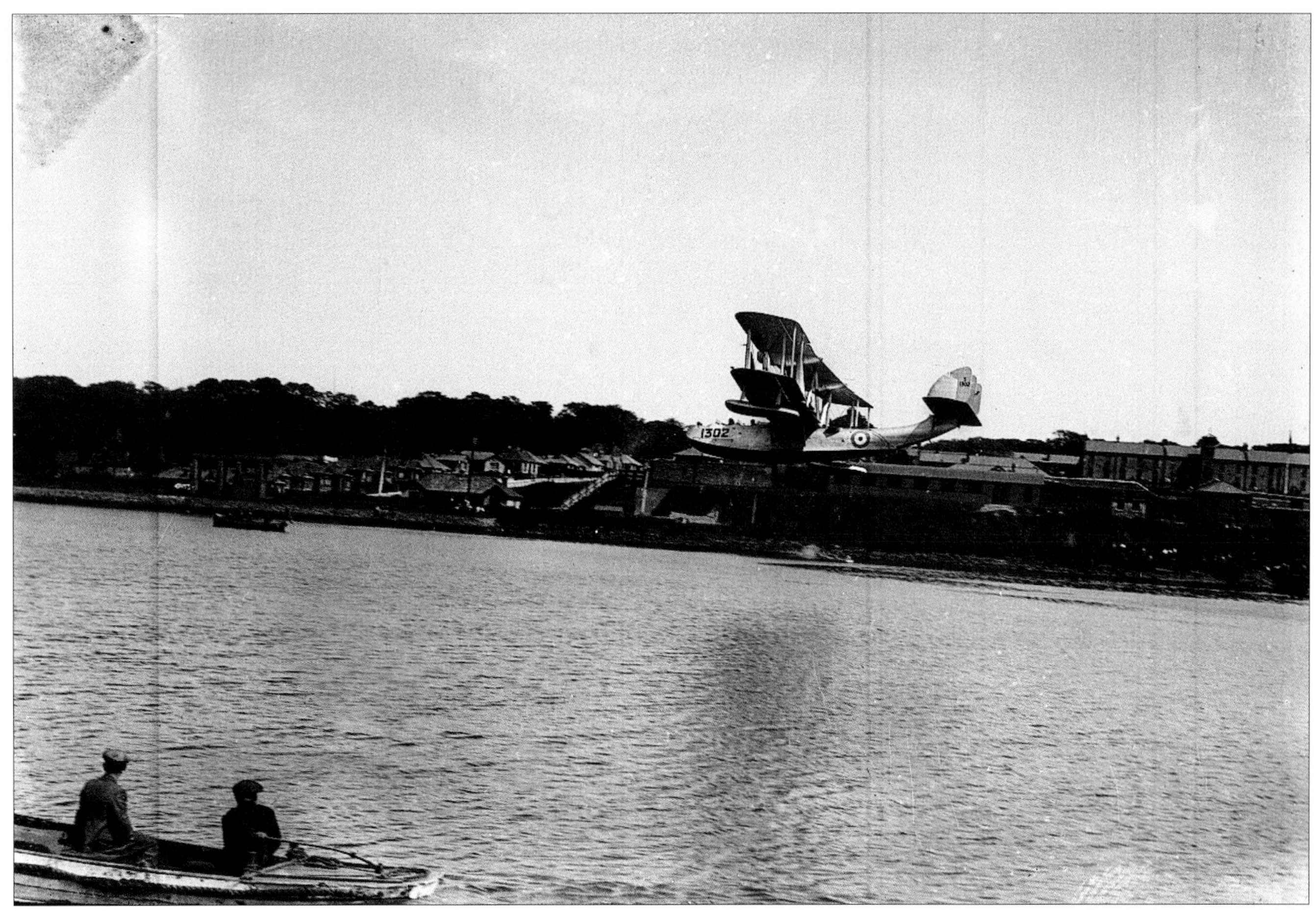


Supermarine Southampton Flying Boat, S.1302, of No 201 RAF Squadron lands on the Foyle in front of Ebrington Barracks in September 1933. *(AER 1-7)*

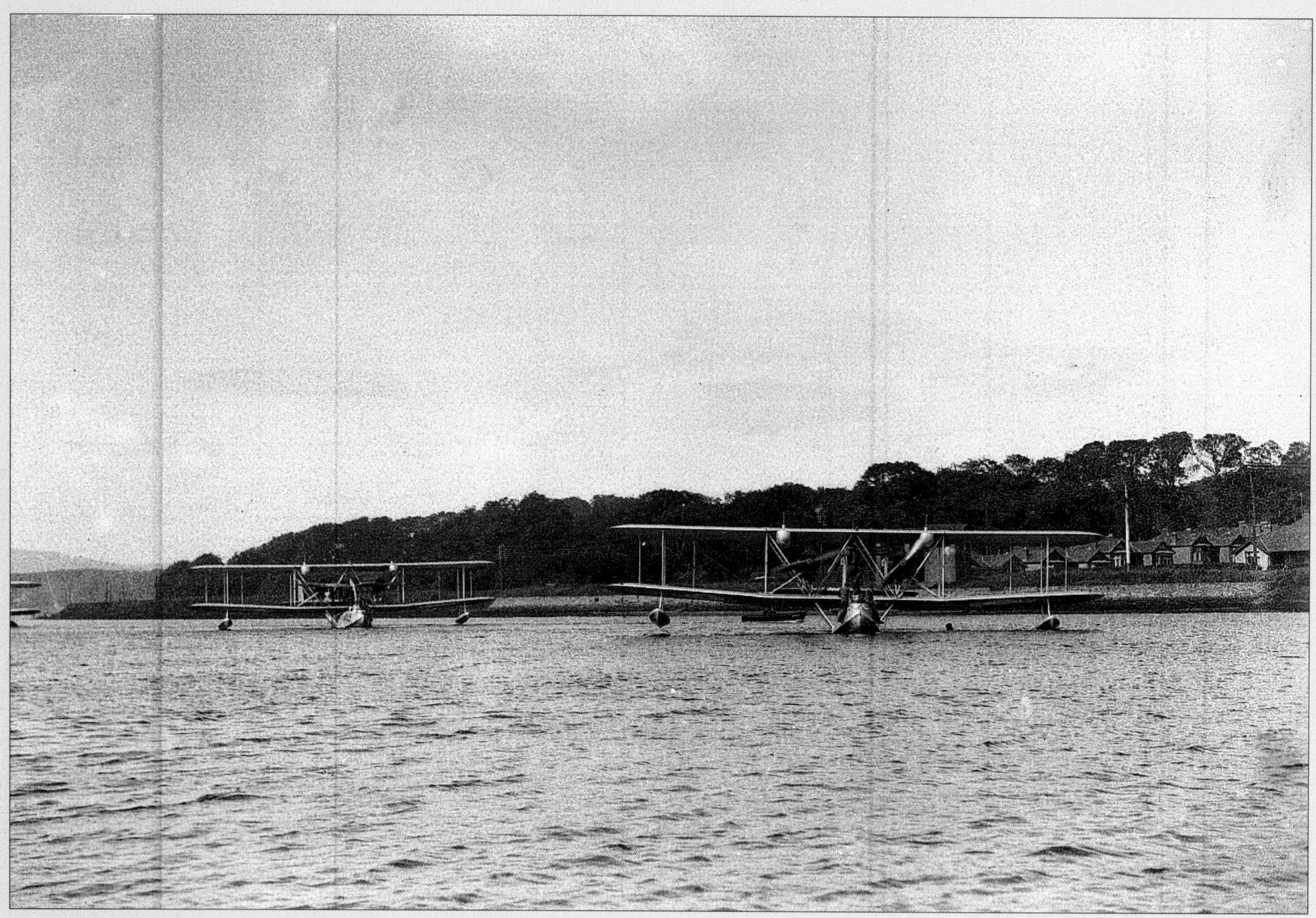

Two Supermarine Southampton Flying Boats of No 201 RAF Squadron, just recently arrived on the Foyle in September 1933, moored upstream of St Columb's Park and Browning Drive. *(AER 1-14)*

## MILITARY SEAPLANES: ITALIAN AIR MINISTRY

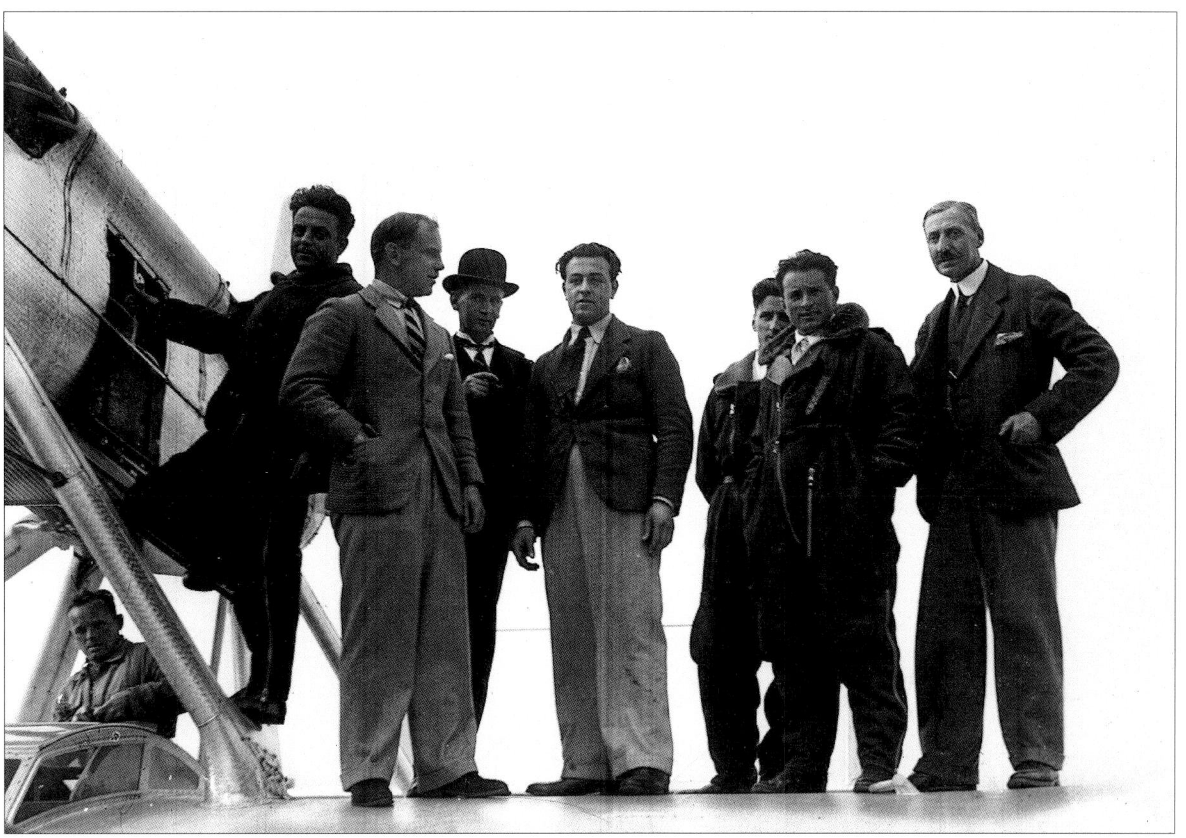

Sir Basil McFarland, second from left, welcomes the Italian crew of seaplane *I.Slan* which landed on the Foyle on Wednesday evening, 15 June 1932. *Derry Standard* of 17 June 1932 reported that the seaplane *I. Slan*, which is to take part in an international Arctic survey on behalf of the Italian Air Ministry, arrived from Amsterdam, where it made a stop on the journey from Rome, encircled the city, and dropped gracefully on the waters of the River Foyle at Rosses Bay. The newspaper reported that 'in an incredibly short time thousands of people gathered' on the quayside. The plane was afterwards taken up river to a spot near the old Shipyard where it was refuelled. *(BAL 1-9, 17 June 1932)*

# CROSSING THE ATLANTIC: ELSIE MACKAY AND CAPTAIN HINCHLIFFE

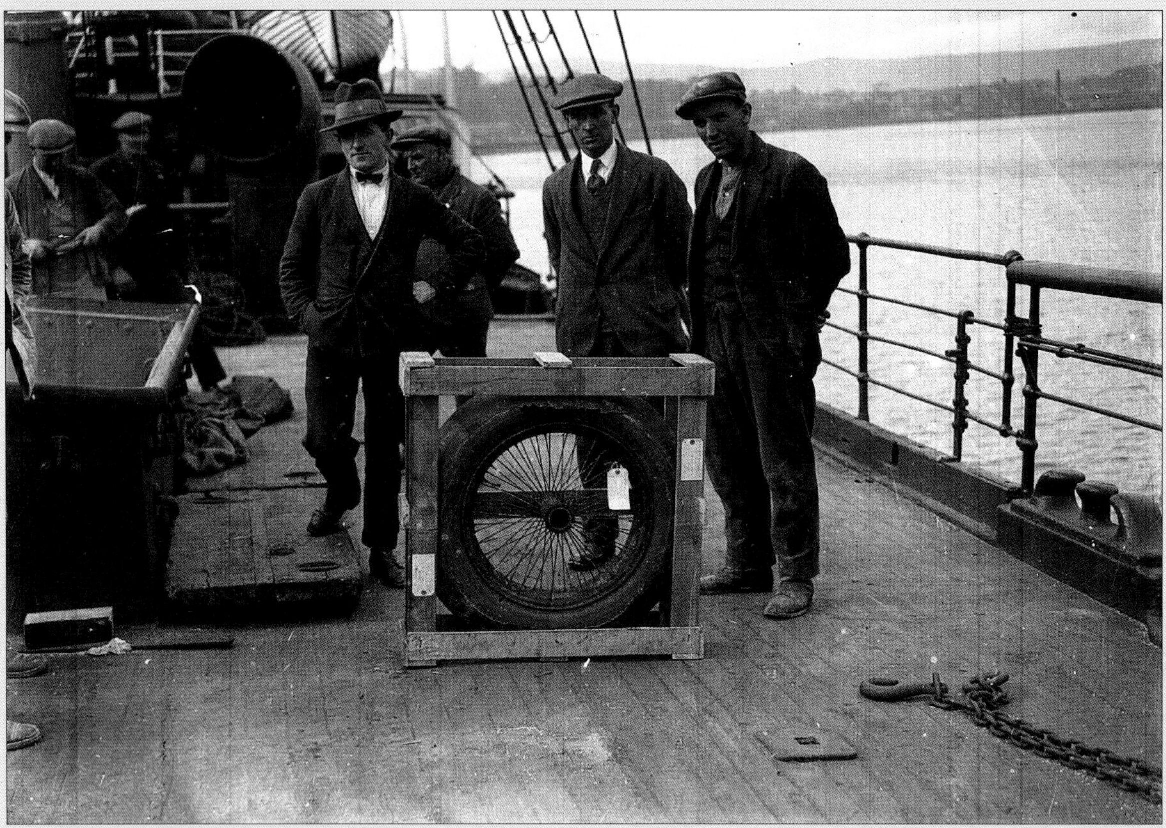

This photograph with caption – 'Wheel of aeroplane recently washed ashore on the Donegal coast, photographed on the SS *Caloric*, on which it was shipped to Mrs Hinchcliffe's home in Surrey. It is believed the wheel is part of the ill-fated aeroplane in which Captain Hinchcliffe and Miss Mackey lost their lives in an attempt to fly across the Atlantic' – was published in *Derry Standard* of 24 April 1929. Captain Walter George Raymond Hinchliffe, a distinguished First World War pilot, died on 13 March 1928 when he attempted to fly across the Atlantic with Elsie Mackay, daughter of P&O Chairman, James Mackay. She wanted to be the first woman to fly across the Atlantic Ocean. On 13 March 1928, they departed 'in secret' from RAF Cranwell, Lincolnshire; five hours later their plane was spotted over the south-west coast of Cork, on course for Newfoundland. The plane, however, never reached its destination and in December 1928, eight months later, this single piece of identifiable undercarriage was washed ashore. *(POR 18-9, 24 April 1929)*

## CROSSING THE ATLANTIC: GENERAL BALBO

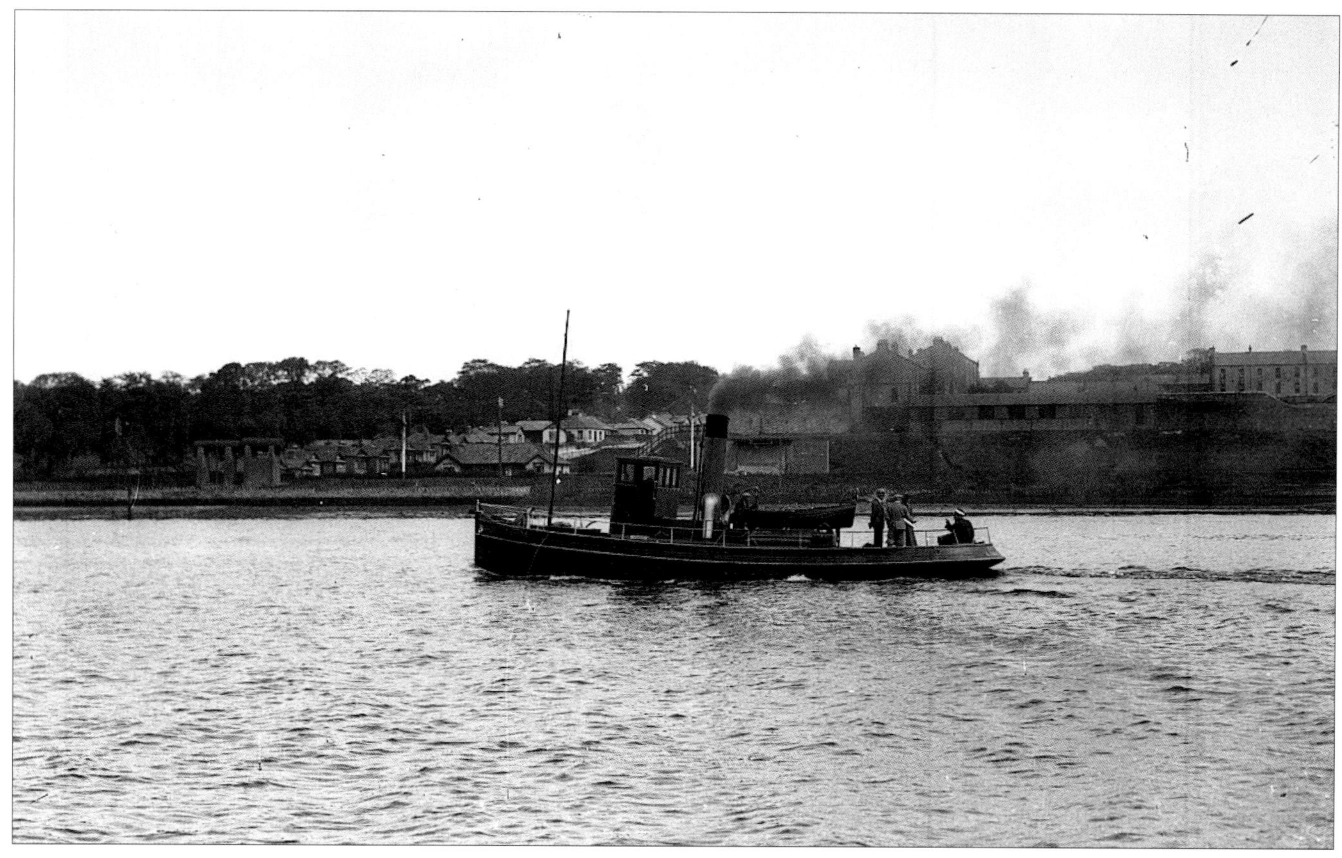

‘The Harbour launch, *T. F. Cooke*, on her way to Culmore with representatives of the Italian Air Force’ in May 1933 ‘to inspect the site in connection with the visit’ of the Italian squadron of twenty-four seaplanes, intending to cross the Atlantic to Chicago’s World Fair. *(POR 17-9, 10 May 1933)*

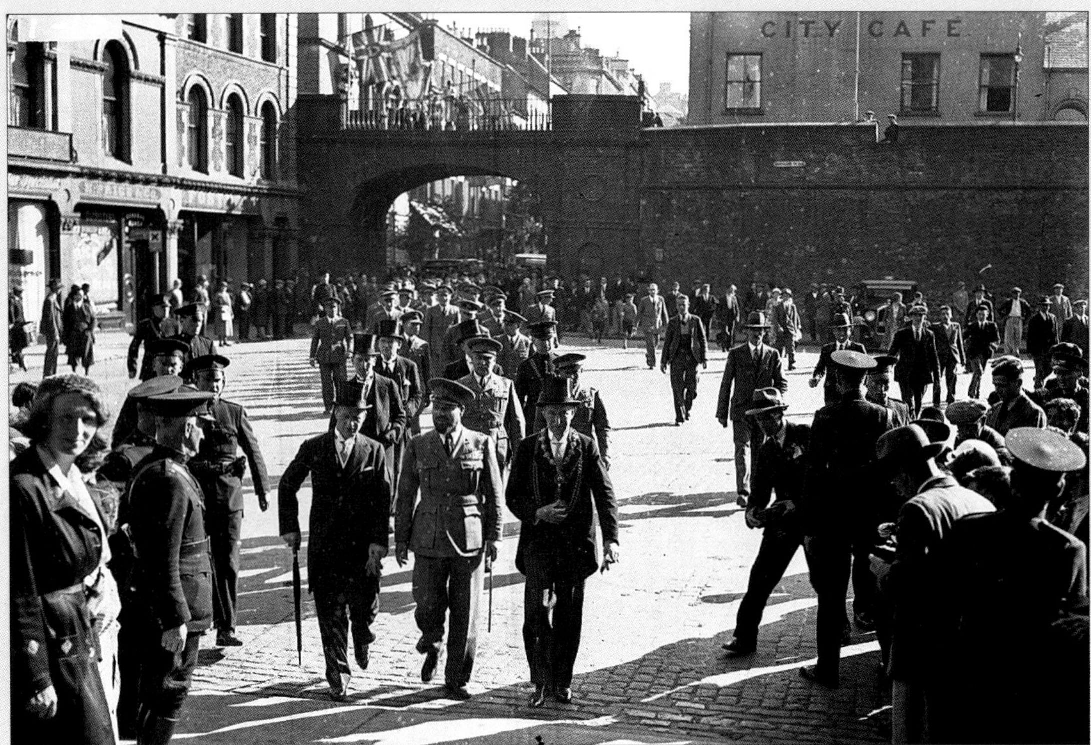


'The Italian flyers marching back to the Guildhall after the ceremony at the War Memorial, where General Balbo laid a wreath.' The *Derry Standard* of 3 July 1933 reported the arrival of the 'Italian Transatlantic Air Armada' in Derry at fifteen minutes after noon on Sunday 2 July. It continued: 'thus the patience of the people of Derry was rewarded at last, and they saw the fleet of twenty-four huge flying-boats which has undertaken one of the most romantic and courageous feats in the history of aviation… The city was agog with excitement when first there was seen three squadrons which appeared to be nothing more than so many black specks against the background of an azure sky. The airboats were first seen rising from behind the trees on the Culmore side of Browning Drive and Ebrington Military Barracks… The airmen were given a rousing reception… The banks of the river and the lough at Culmore were crowded, as were also the quays and the Guildhall Square.'

From 1 July to 12 August 1933, General Italo Balbo led a flight of twenty-four flying boats on a round-trip flight from Rome to the Century of Progress in Chicago, Illinois, USA. The flight had seven legs: Orbetello – Amsterdam – Derry – Reykjavik – Cartwright, Labrador – Shediac – Montreal ending on Lake Michigan near Burnham Park. Balbo received a warm welcome in the United States, especially by the large Italian-American populations in Chicago and New York. To a cheering mass in Madison Square Garden he said: "Be proud you are Italians. Mussolini has ended the era of humiliations." The term 'Balbo' now entered common usage to describe any large formation of aircraft. *(BAL 2-5, 7 July 1933)*

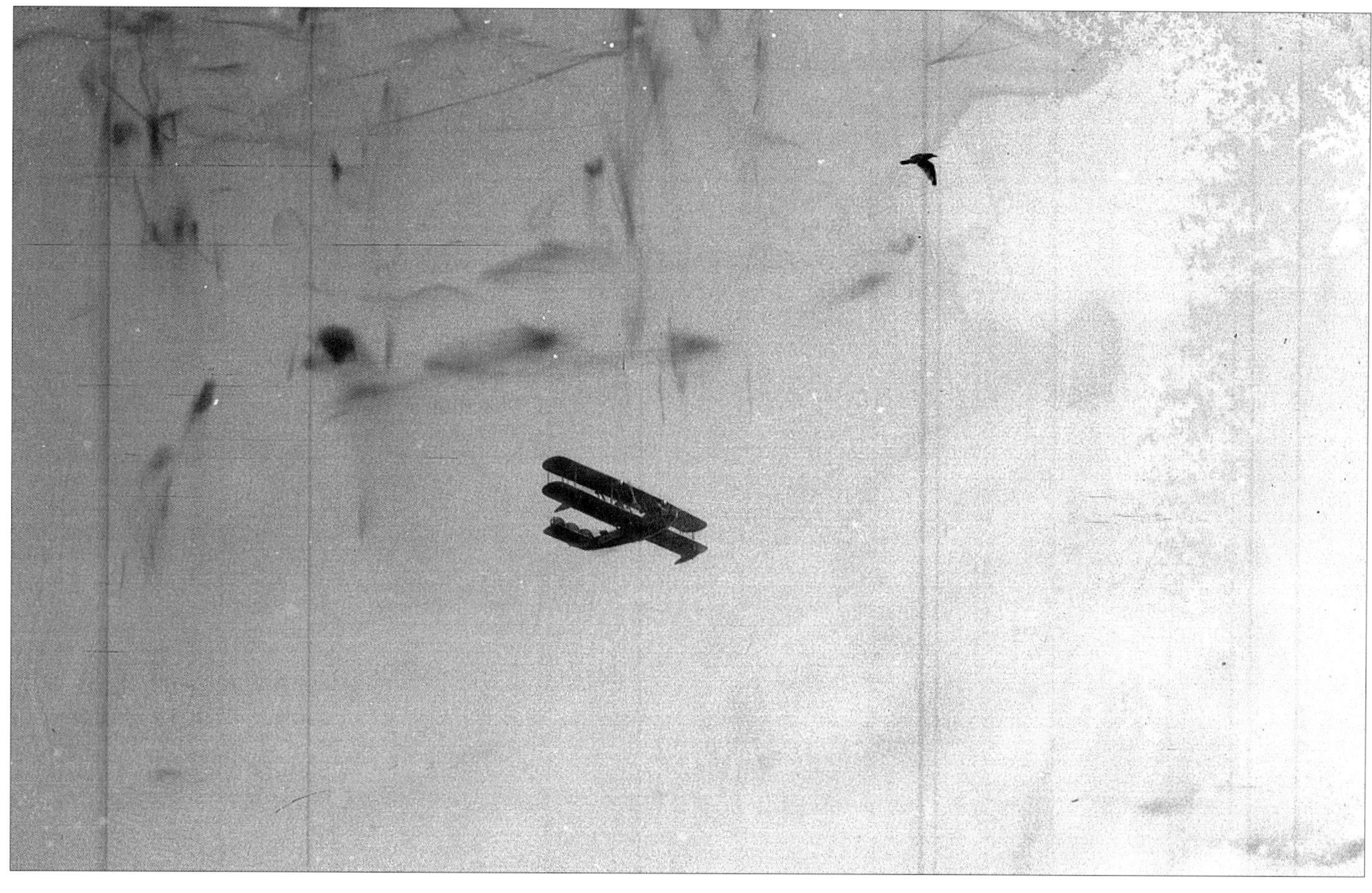

A Supermarine Southampton Flying Boat of No 201 RAF Squadron departs Derry with Signor Grandi, Italian Ambassador and Signor Junta, Italian Minister of Finance, who was heading the Italian delegation to the world economic conference. In the summer of 1933, the RAF's 201 (Flying Boat) Squadron had been in Lough Neagh for air-firing and bombing practice and 'then proceeded to Londonderry in tandem with an Italian transatlantic flight, of twenty-four seaplanes, visiting Lough Foyle.' Various senior Italian personnel were flown in squadron aircraft. *(AER 1-12, 5 July 1933)*

## CROSSING THE ATLANTIC: AMELIA EARHART

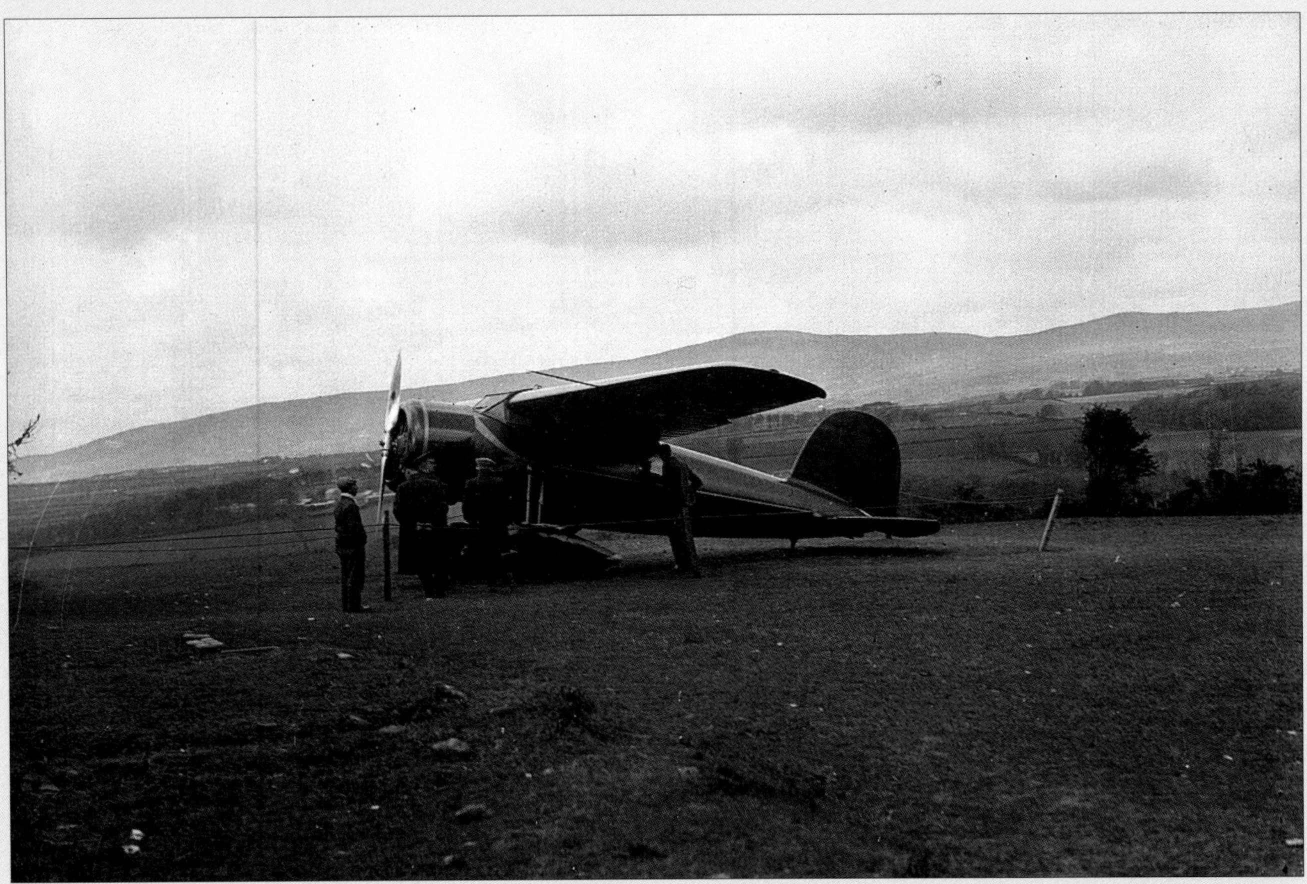

Amelia Earhart's plane *Friendship* in the field on Robert Gallagher's farm at Ballyarnet, just to the north of Derry, where it made a dramatic landing on Saturday 21 May 1932. The plane was a Lockheed Vega aircraft. Amelia Earhart had taken off from Newfoundland, hoping to land in Paris, but owing to bad weather and technical problems she altered her course and, after a flight lasting almost 15 hours, landed near Derry. *(AE 1-5)*

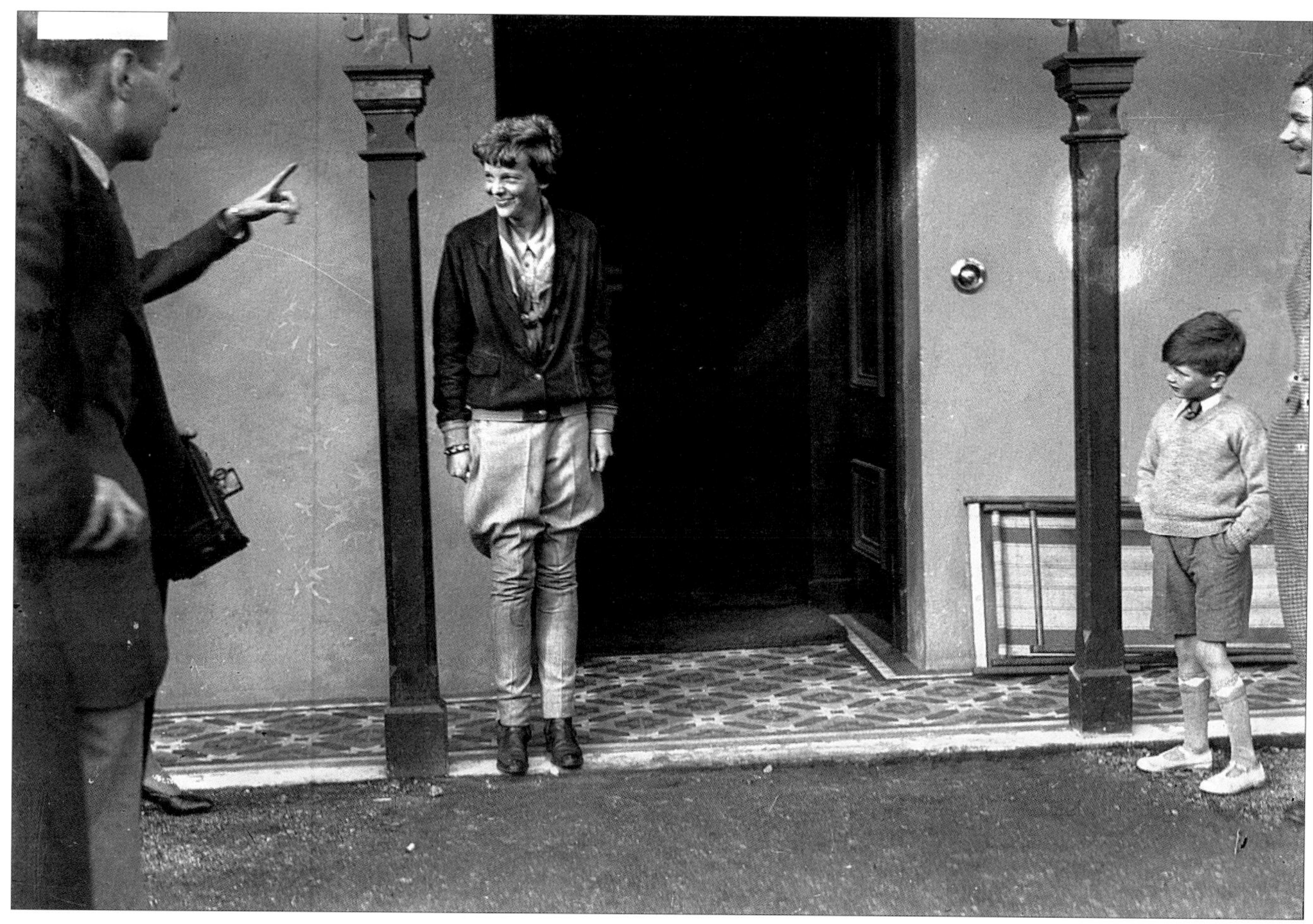

Amelia Earhart, the first female to fly the Atlantic solo, pictured in the doorway of Robert Gallagher's house, Springfield, after her eventful flight on 20/21 May 1932. The distance covered was 2026 miles. *(AE 1-6)*

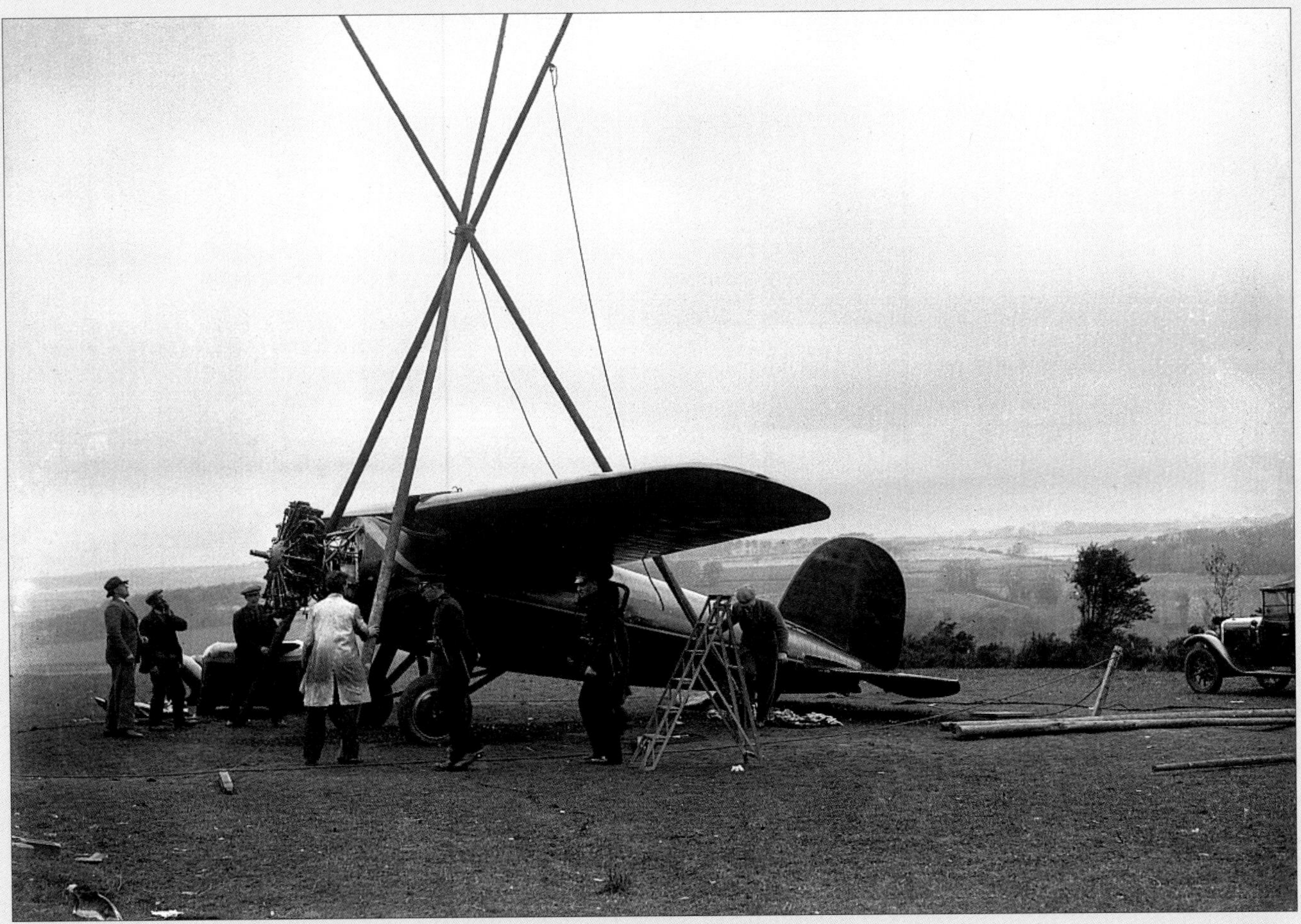

Four photographs were published in *Derry Standard* of 30 May 1932 with headline 'Dismantling Miss Earhart's aeroplane.' Here workers are 'getting into position for lifting off the wings.' *(AE 1-1, 30 May 1932)*

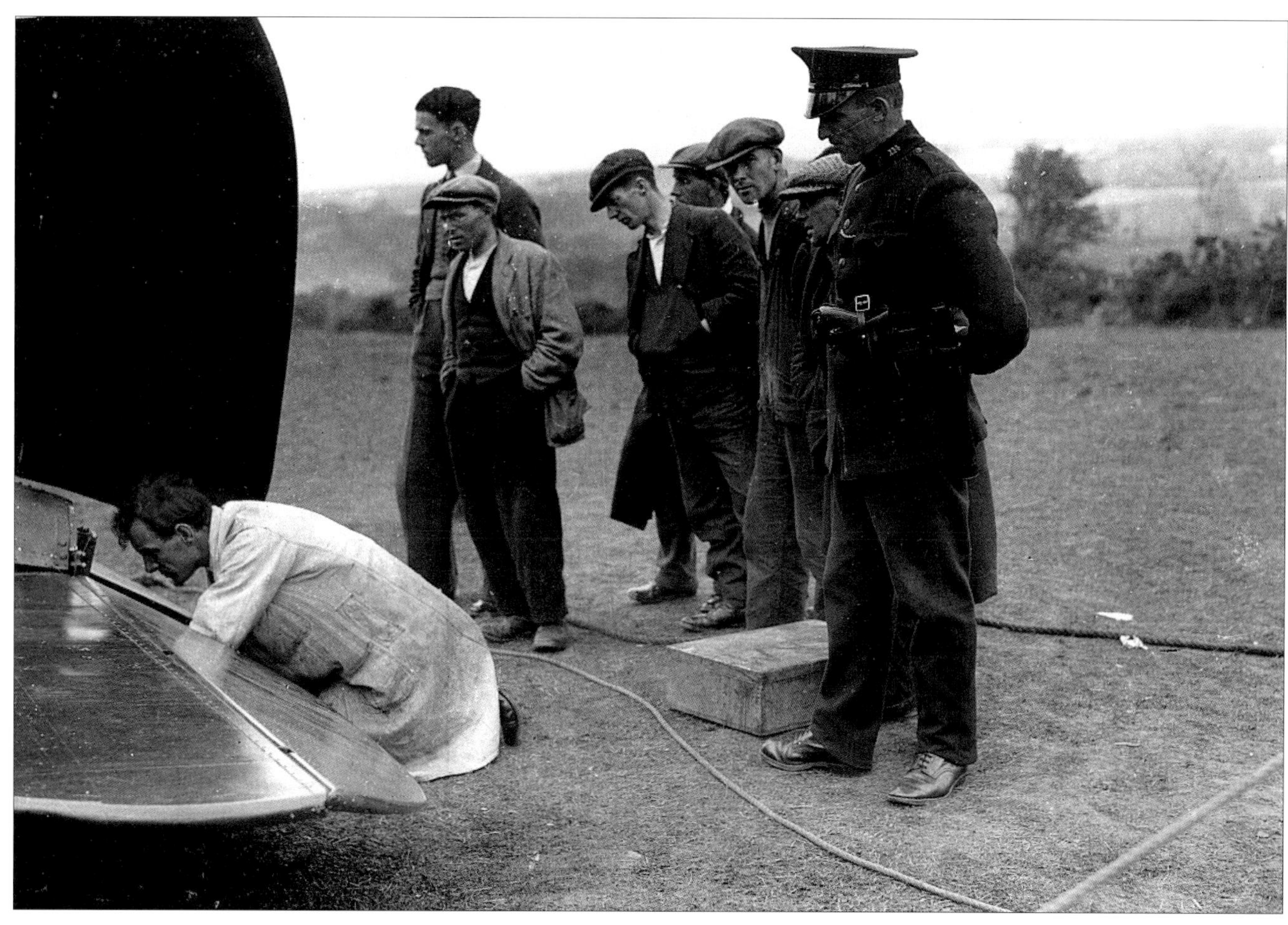

'A mechanic working at the rudder.' *(AE 1-3, 30 May 1932)*

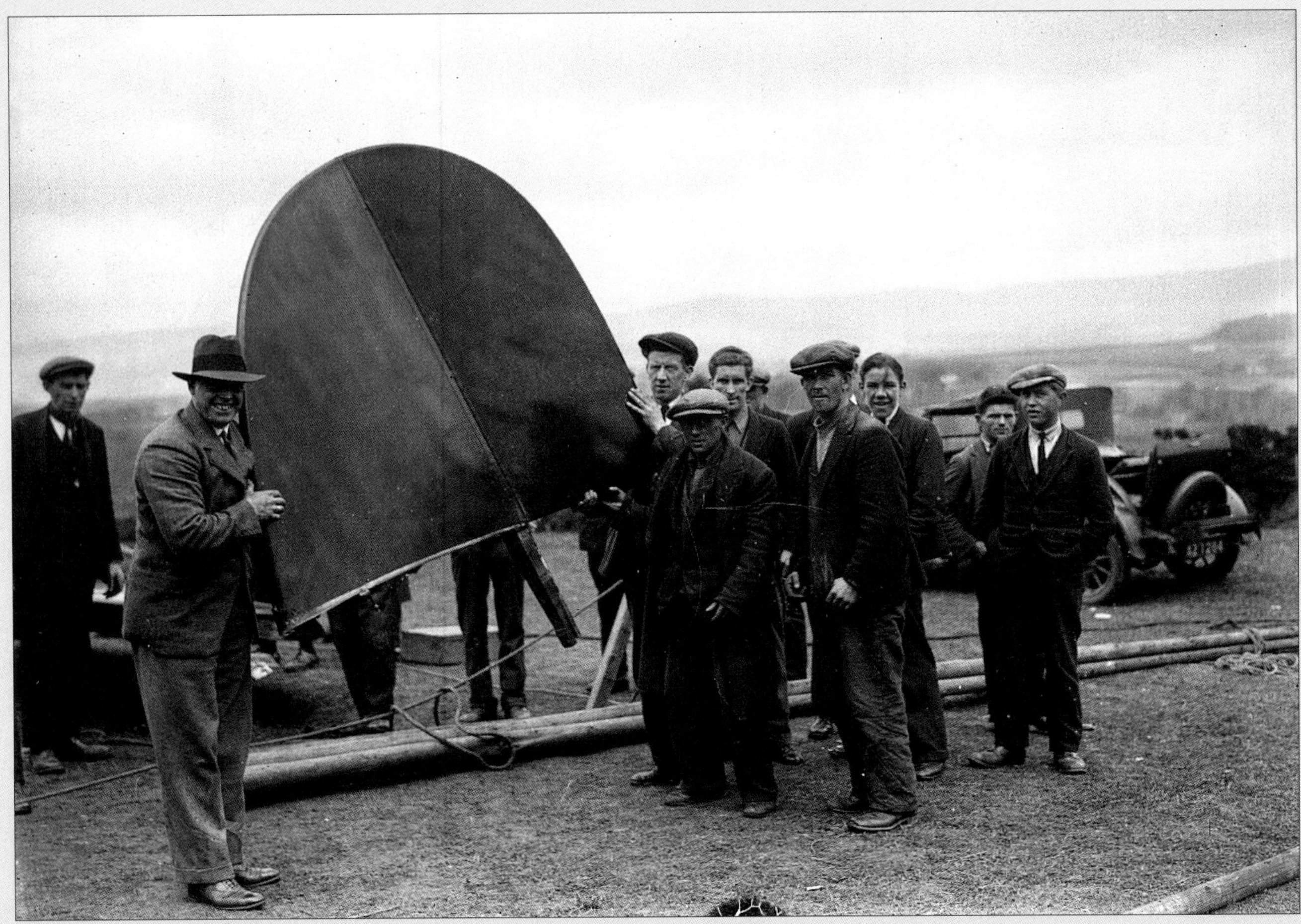

'The rudder after being safely removed.' *(AE 1-4, 30 May 1932)*

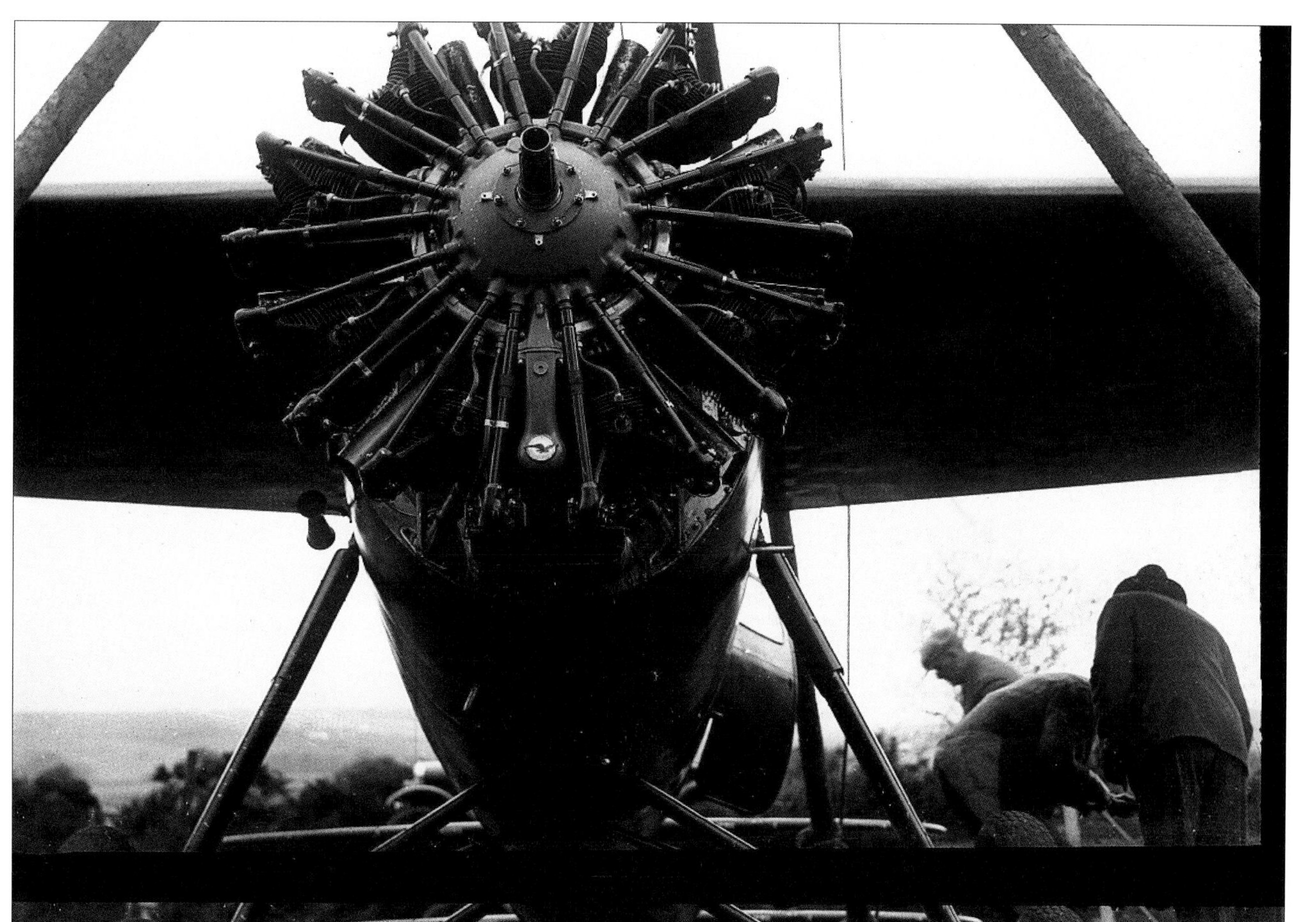

'The front of the plane stripped, showing the engine.' *(AE 1-2, 30 May 1932)*

# CURIO

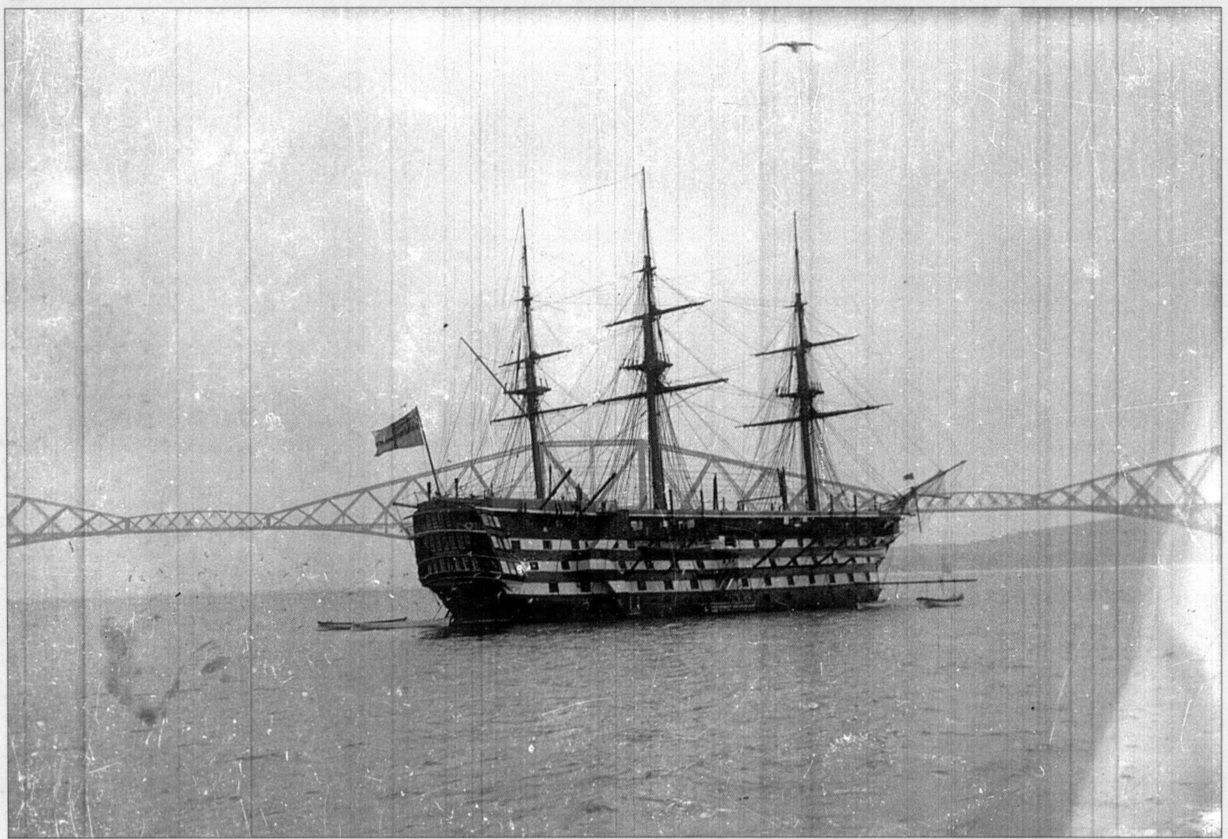

In their editorial of 15 April 1927, in which they announced their intention to publish photographs, *Derry Standard* asked for readers to send 'photographs suitable for reproduction.' This may explain the photograph with caption 'Nelson's Flagship The Victory' which was published in *Derry Standard* of 26 October 1932. HMS *Victory* was Admiral Nelson's flagship at the Battle of Trafalgar in 1805. However, what appears to be the Forth Rail Bridge in the background together with the fact that *Victory* had been moored at Portsmouth since 1812 would suggest that this man o' war is not Nelson's flagship. However, Royal Navy wooden warships continued to be used as training ships in the 20th century. Indeed, the last wooden warship to be destroyed in war was HMS *Wellesley* (built 1815), a 74 gun ship, which was destroyed in a German air raid on the Thames at Gravesend on 24 September 1940. *(POR 19-5, 26 October 1932)*